WITHDRAWN

INSIDERS' GUIDE® TO

WORN, SOILED, OBSOLETE

CIVIL WAR SITES
IN THE EASTERN THEATER

HELP US KEEP THIS GUIDE UP TO DATE

Every effort has been made by the authors and editors to make this guide as accurate and useful as possible. However, many things can change after a guide is published—phone numbers change, facilities come under new management, etc.

We would love to hear from you concerning your experiences with this guide and how you feel it could be improved and be kept up to date. While we may not be able to respond to all comments and suggestions, we'll take them to heart and we'll also make certain to share them with the author. Please send your comments and suggestions to the following address:

The Globe Pequot Press
Reader Response/Editorial Department
P.O. Box 480
Guilford, CT 06437

Or you may e-mail us at:

editorial@GlobePequot.com

Thanks for your input, and happy travels!

INSIDERS' GUIDE® SERIES

INSIDERS' GUIDE® TO
CIVIL WAR SITES IN THE EASTERN THEATER

THIRD EDITION

ERIC ETHIER AND REBECCA ALOISI

INSIDERS' GUIDE®

GUILFORD, CONNECTICUT
AN IMPRINT OF THE GLOBE PEQUOT PRESS

The prices and rates in this guidebook were confirmed at press time. We recommend, however, that you call establishments before traveling to obtain current information.

INSIDERS' GUIDE®

Copyright © 2008 by Morris Book Publishing, LLC
A previous edition of this book was published by Insiders' Publishing, Inc. in 1997.

Text design: LeAnna Weller Smith
Maps created by Melissa Baker © Morris Book Publishing, LLC

ISBN 978-0-7627-4182-3

Printed in the United States of America
10 9 8 7 6 5 4 3 2 1

CONTENTS

Directory of Maps

CIVIL WAR SITES

4 American Civil War Museum
9 Antietam National Battlefield
53 Appomattox Court House National Historic Park
28 Balls Bluff Battlefield and National Cemetery
19 Baltimore and Ohio Railroad Museum
20 Baltimore Civil War Museum at President Street Station
11 Barbara Fritchie House and Museum
40 Brandy Station Battlefield
29 Cedar Creek and Belle Grove National Historic Park
30 Cedar Creek Battlefield
44 Civil War Life: The Soldier's Museum
23 Civil War Orientation Center
47 Cold Harbor Battlefield and Visitor Center
46 Cold Harbor National Cemetery
5 Coster Avenue Mural and Amos Humiston Monument
32 Fisher's Hill Battlefield
24 Fort Collier Civil War Center
21 Fort McHenry National Monument and Historic Shrine
58 Fort Monroe's Casemate Museum
51 Fort Stevens
42 Fredericksburg and Spotsylvania National Military Park
6 Gettysburg National Military Park
16 Harper's Ferry National Historic Park
48 Hollywood Cemetery
7 Jennie Wade House Museum
18 John Brown Gallows Site
17 John Brown Wax Museum
34 John Singleton Mosby Museum and Education Center
10 Kennedy Farmhouse
25 Kernstown Battlefield
56 Lee Hall Museum
35 Liberia Plantation House
36 Manassas Museum
33 Manassas National Battlefield Park
37 Manassas Railroad Depot
57 Mariner's Museum
45 Massaponax Baptist Church
38 Mayfield Earthwork Fort
12 Monocacy National Battlefield
13 Mount Olivet Cemetery
49 Museum and White House of the Confederacy
41 Museum of Culpeper History
2 National Civil War Museum
14 National Museum of Civil War Medicine
39 New Market Battlefield State Historical Park and Hall of Valor Museum
26 Old Court House Civil War Museum
1 Old Jail Museum
55 Petersburg National Battlefield
59 Portsmouth Naval Shipyard Museum
52 Richmond National Battlefield Park
54 Sailor's Creek Battlefield Historic State Park
8 Shriver House Museum
15 South Mountain State Battlefield
31 Stonewall Jackson Museum at Hupp's Hill
27 Stonewall Jackson's Headquarters Museum
3 U.S. Army Heritage and Education Center
22 USS Constellation Museum
50 Valentine Richmond History Center
43 White Oak Museum and White Oak Church

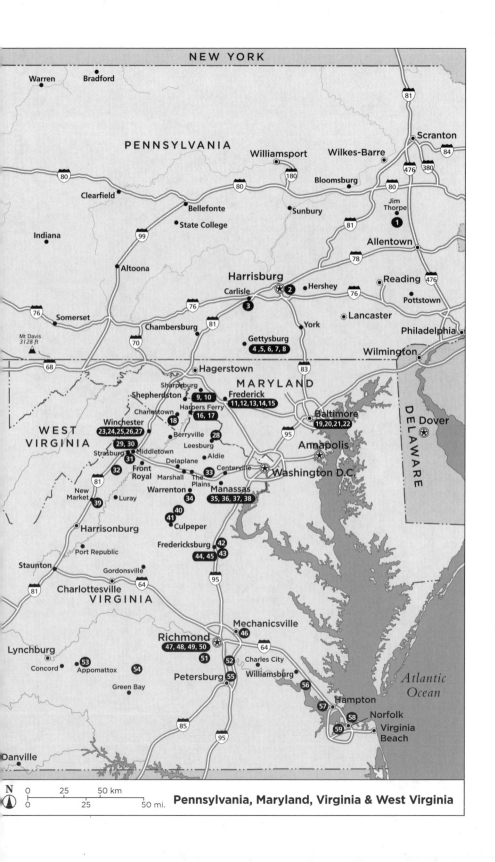

NEW YORK

Warren · Bradford ·

PENNSYLVANIA

Williamsport · · Wilkes-Barre · Scranton ·
84

80

Clearfield · · Bloomsburg · 476 380

80 180

· Bellefonte Sunbury · Jim Thorpe 1

Indiana · State College · 81

99 Allentown ·

· Altoona 78

Harrisburg Reading · 476

Carlisle · ⭐ 2 · Hershey

76 Pottstown ·

76 76 3 Lancaster ·

Somerset · 81 York · Philadelphia ·

Chambersburg ·

70 Gettysburg Wilmington ·
4, 5, 6, 7, 8

68 · Hagerstown 83 MARYLAND

Sharpsburg DELAWARE Dover ·
· Shepherdstown 9, 10 Frederick
· Charlestown 11, 12, 13, 14, 15
Harpers Ferry
Winchester 18 16, 17 Baltimore
WEST 23, 24, 25, 26, 27 · Berryville 28 19, 20, 21, 22
VIRGINIA 29, 30 Leesburg · 95
· Strasburg Middletown Aldie Annapolis
31 · Delaplane · Centerville
32 Front 33 ⭐ Washington D.C.
81 Royal Marshall The
New · Plains
Market 39 · Luray Warrenton · Manassas
· 34 35, 36, 37, 38
40
41 · Culpeper
· Harrisonburg
· Port Republic Fredericksburg 42
44, 45 43
Staunton ·
· Gordonsville 95
81 64
· Charlottesville
VIRGINIA

Mechanicsville
· 46 Atlantic
Richmond ⭐ Ocean
Lynchburg · 47, 48, 49, 50 64
Concord · 53 51 52 · Charles City
· Appomattox 54 · Williamsburg
· Green Bay Petersburg 55 56
Hampton ·
57 · Norfolk
58
85 59 · Virginia
Beach
95

· Danville

Mt Davis
3128 ft

N 0 25 50 km
0 25 50 mi. Pennsylvania, Maryland, Virginia & West Virginia

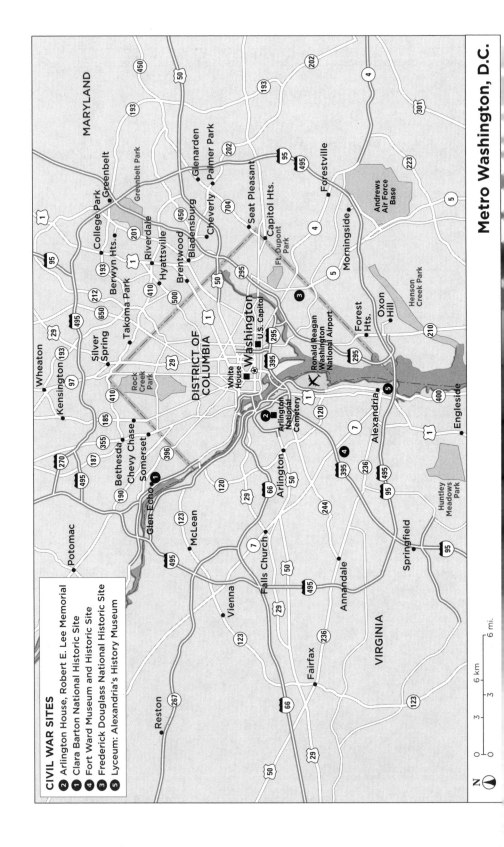

CIVIL WAR SITES
2 Arlington House, Robert E. Lee Memorial
1 Clara Barton National Historic Site
4 Fort Ward Museum and Historic Site
3 Frederick Douglass National Historic Site
5 Lyceum: Alexandria's History Museum

Metro Washington, D.C.

MARYLAND

450
50
193
202
1
193
95
Greenbelt
Greenbelt Park
Glenarden
Palmer Park
Cheverly
223
College Park
Forestville
450
201
Seat Pleasant
704
Riverdale
95
Capitol Hts.
Berwyn Hts.
Bladensburg
202
Brentwood
Ft. Dupont Park
Andrews Air Force Base
Hyattsville
410
Morningside
5
193
500
50
4
212
Takoma Park
650
295
5
Silver Spring
Forest Hts.
Oxon Hill
Henson Creek Park
29
1
U.S. Capitol
3
Washington
Rock Creek Park
210
29
DISTRICT OF COLUMBIA
295
White House
Ronald Reagan Washington National Airport
410
395
295
185
1
400
Bethesda
120
Engleside
Chevy Chase
2
Alexandria
5
355
Somerset
Arlington National Cemetery
7
Glen Echo
1
187
270
396
4
236
1
495
190
236
495
Potomac
120
95
Huntley Meadows Park
123
66
50
McLean
29
Arlington
244
395
95
Falls Church
Springfield
7
50
495
Vienna
Annandale
495
123
29
Fairfax
236
VIRGINIA
267
Reston
66
123
50
29

MARYLAND

193
97
Kensington
Wheaton
29
495

N

0   3   6 km
0   3   6 mi.

HOW TO USE THIS BOOK

According to the Civil War Preservation Trust (CWPT), one-fifth of America's Civil War battlefields have already been lost, while only 15 percent of those remaining are in any way protected.

And so the battle to acquire, preserve, and restore to historical authenticity (as much as possible) Civil War ground continues. In recent years, victories have been won. With the purchase (often with the help of the CWPT) or resculpting of a few acres of significant land at a time, some of the nation's most significant battle sites have crept closer to their original appearance than ever before.

Civil War–themed museums, such as Petersburg's Pamplin Park, have also evolved, adding fantastic and interactive new exhibits and historical collections designed to inspire greater interest and participation. Harrisburg, Pennsylvania's, impressive National Civil War Museum, meanwhile, leads the pack of new Civil War museums to open during the last few years.

The area that once comprised the Civil War's Eastern Theater is today filled with first-class museums, historical sites, and national parks, ranging from Colonial Williamsburg to the Museum of the Shenandoah Valley and countless others. The region's older towns (Annapolis, Leesburg, etc.) are rich enough in

history and architecture to provide most traveling history buffs with a full day's pleasure. Moreover, since so much Civil War campaigning took place in Virginia, practically every one of the state's towns—such as Staunton and Charlottesville—retain tangible connections (old buildings, small parks, monuments, etc.) to the war.

This guide, however, is written for the casual Civil War buff (or family of buffs)—that vacationing guy or gal with a basic knowledge of the war eager to learn a little more and have fun doing it. Rather than provide an exhaustive list of every Civil War–related building, park, or patch of lawn in the theater, we have focused on those areas with the best and most significant sites and museums, while talking up the newest facilities out there. Hard-bitten veterans of the Civil War community might gladly drive 30 miles to see a historic home (such as the Thomas L. Rosser House) that is not open to the public, but we're betting the less serious student will not. Those readers who would like to find such places, or hike along battle trails not included in this guide, might consult The Civil War Traveler (www.civilwartraveler.com), an organization that offers news and details about even the latest interpretive Civil War sites and trails.

GLOSSARY

The Civil War, and the military in general, produced such a set of specialized terminology and phrases that it almost constitutes a separate language. While we attempted to write this book in as clear and ordinary a style as possible, on many occasions there was simply no way to avoid the use of specialized terms. Here is a selection of terms used in the book.

Abatis or abattis: a defensive "wall" made of cut trees, usually arrayed in a thick, interconnected tangle, which would not completely stop a charging enemy attack but would slow one, giving the defenders additional time to bring heavy fire to bear on the points affected.

Amphibious: an attack launched from transports at sea or on a river; implies a coordinated army-navy attack, although this was not always the case.

Assault: a concentrated attack on a specific target or area; implies the maximum use of force that will fit into a given quadrant of the battlefield. It also implies an all-out attack that does not stop until the objective is taken or the attacking force is destroyed, but the term is used frequently as a synonym for any attack.

Battle flag: the flag used by each regiment on both sides for unit identification and signaling. Most battles during this period tended to break down into mass chaos and confusion unless the commander kept a firm control of his men, and the battlefield was far too noisy to hear a spoken order or even a bugle call. Soldiers were trained to recognize their regimental flag and to always follow it wherever it

went. The flag bearer was given both a high honor and a great responsibility; he had to stay right by his commander at all times, he was usually not armed, and he could not break and run no matter how bad the situation was, as his whole regiment would then follow him to the rear. The casualty rate among flag bearers was appalling.

Bayonet: a long spike or thick knife blade with mountings to attach to the muzzle end of a rifle, enabling the soldier to stab his enemy at more than an arm's length away. Both the Enfield and Springfield bayonets were 18 inches long and triangular in section, which would cause a ghastly wound that usually would not heal properly and frequently caused a fatal infection in those who lived through the initial event. The "spirit of the bayonet" is a hallowed tradition for even modern infantrymen, although its use in battle has been greatly exaggerated. Most "hand to hand" combat actually involved the use of the butt end of the rifle, swung like a club, or even just fists, rocks, and heavy sticks. The bayonet-equipped rifle is a lethal and intimidating-looking weapon, but it took great skill and discipline to effectively employ it in the heat of combat. Soldiers usually used their issued bayonets for other purposes, as skewers to cook their meat or rammed into trees or walls to serve as coat hooks. Quite often they were heated and bent into hook shapes to drag the dead bodies of their comrades off the battlefield.

Blockade: to cut off and isolate a position or area from any resupply or reinforcement. During the Civil War this almost always referred to the Union Navy's blockade of the entire

Southern Atlantic and Gulf coastlines, preventing most supplies from England and France from coming into the Confederacy.

Blockade runners: Civil War–era privateers, almost always civilians, who earned huge profits through great risk in sneaking their ships loaded with cargo through the Union Navy's coastal blockade. Although usually from the ranks of the lower classes and ordinary seamen before the war, they were the toast of Southern society as well as a major source of critical supplies for the embattled Southern armies. Northern newspapers universally decried them as the utter scourge of mankind.

Bomb-proof: a heavily reinforced, usually underground structure designed and built to protect the occupants, either civilians in an area under siege or troops in a combat area, from nearby artillery fire. Rarely would these structures protect from a direct hit by a large-caliber weapon.

Break contact: to pull back from a combat engagement, either to retreat or to shift the direction of a given assault. This is sometimes used as a polite way of saying that the men involved simply ran away.

Breastworks: a defensive barricade wall made of whatever materials were immediately available, usually logs, rocks, or fence rails. When placed in front of trenchlines, they usually were covered with the excavated earth itself, piled up, and formed into steep-faced walls. By the second year of the war, "spades is trumps" as Private Sam Watkins said, and nearly every time troops on either side stopped for more than a few minutes, their officers would put them to work constructing defensive works. On most battlefields today, these works are the only remaining evidence of the war.

Casements: refers to the lower areas in a masonry fort where the main artillery is mounted. These are usually some of the strongest parts of the fort's walls, built-up areas of stone or brick surrounding a narrow port or slit through which the cannon would fire.

Casualties: the losses for a unit, including deaths, injuries, capture or "missing" (usually from desertion), as well as losses from sickness or disease, by far the biggest killer of all during the war. On occasion the reports include losses resulting from discharge.

Chevaux-de-frise: somewhat like an early version of barbed wire, these barricades were in effect and construction very similar to abatis, with the exception of being somewhat portable. These were constructed by taking a log or (more rarely) a piece of iron post 9 to 15 feet long, drilling holes through it every 6 to 12 inches and through both angles, and inserting sharpened stakes about 4 to 6 feet long through the post. From an end view they looked like a crude cross, while from a frontal view they vaguely resembled a large version of an aerator used today on lawns. Many of these would be constructed and placed in front of other static defenses, sometimes fastened together, and always in the direct line of fire from the defenders. Although they could be moved by a squad or less of men, they slowed down infantry attacks long enough to provide an effective "kill zone" where they were placed.

Color bearer: the man assigned to carry the colors of the regiment. As the flag was usually large and unwieldy, he would most usually be unarmed, and as the rest of the regiment followed his actions to the letter (at least in theory), he must be a very brave and trustworthy man, unlikely to bolt and run from the battlefield. He would always be found standing very close to the regimental commander. Casualties were very high among color bearers.

Colors: the distinctive flag unique to each regiment. As most of the soldiers of this time were illiterate, and the smoke and noise of battle precluded effective use of shouted orders, the men were taught to recognize their own colors (in a formal ceremony, still done in today's army, called "parading the colors") and to follow them wherever they went on the battlefield.

Column: a road march formation of troops, usually in company or regimental order and as long as 3 to 9 miles. When these columns were ambushed or otherwise surprised by an enemy force, it took quite some time to get the force arrayed into a combat formation, allowing plenty of time for "hit and run" attacks to succeed in delaying the column and inflicting casualties with relatively little risk to the attacker.

Counterattack: to aggressively assault an attacking force, to try to turn the momentum from the offensive to the defensive side.

Deploy: to move into either an offensive assault formation or to man defensive positions. Occasionally used to indicate simply being sent somewhere.

Doctrine: the established way of doing a particular mission or task; doing it "by the book." Most of both the Confederate and Union general officer staffs had trained at West Point, and early in the war it was clear who had done their homework better, as tactics and strategies used were nearly identical. Later in the war the doctrine of the Confederate armies was to maintain their forces intact even at the cost of positions and territory, while Union doctrine was to bring the heaviest mass possible of men and supplies into every given situation.

Earthwork/sandwork: a fort with outer defense walls made from earth or sand rather than some sort of masonry. Ironically, although these forts were made of local materials due to supply or cost problems, they turned out to be much better at handling

incoming artillery fire than the massive, expensive masonry forts.

En barbette: guns or cannon mounted on a low platform on the top floor of a fort, able then to fire over the top of the parapet without any firing slit or cutout needed. This was a very exposed and dangerous position for the artillerymen.

Enfilade: attacking an enemy force from a sharp angle, the side, or the rear. This usually implies the direction of fire, rather than an assault or such action.

Envelopment: to attack the sides and/or rear at the same time, usually requiring a high level of command coordination. Many well-planned attacks of this nature turned into disasters when the attack went in piecemeal, allowing the defenders to concentrate their forces as needed rather than spread them out to face multiple attacks.

Flanks: the sides or rear of a formation or position, usually one of the weakest points for an attacker to hit given the "line of battle" tactics of the day. The emphasis throughout most of the war was for an attacking force to maneuver into a position where they could hit the enemy's flanks; Grant and Lee in Virginia and Sherman and Johnston in Georgia provided classic examples of this.

Fleet: a group of warships and/or transports under a single commander, usually detailed for a general mission or task. A "flotilla" is generally a smaller grouping of the same sort, used for a single specific action or task.

Garrison: the body of troops assigned to a single fixed position, usually for a prolonged length of time and normally used only for guard duty or action from that one position.

Gundeck: on a ship, the main deck where cannon or guns are mounted; in a fixed fortification, any of the positions where artillery is mounted.

Ironclads: special warships armored with iron plating, usually enough to deflect both rifle and smaller cannon fire. Early in the war these were just standard wooden naval vessels hastily outfitted with crude armor, but by the second year of the war, ships were being designed from the hull up to be steam-powered armored warships. The USS *Monitor* is the most familiar example of this genre, a low-freeboard hull mounting a single movable turret housing two large guns.

Lunette: a special type of earthwork fort consisting of an angled, L-shaped wall, with the rear completely exposed. These were used primarily as outlying artillery positions.

Militia: prewar local defense groups organized originally in colonial days for protection from Indian attacks. Later used as the core of the Continental Army and organized extensively in the South after the Revolutionary War to guard against slave insurrections. As the United States had only a tiny "professional" standing army well into the 20th century, the militias were relied upon to provide a trained cadre of fighting men that could be called up quickly in times of war (this is the "well-regulated militia" spoken of in the Second Amendment to the Constitution). By the 1840s the militias had become a sort of social culture, with many units dressing in all sorts of outlandish uniforms and drilling primarily for show in parades and such. These militias were quickly absorbed into the regular Union and Confederate Armies after the start of the war and their stylish uniforms soon packed away.

OR: a shorthand reference to the massive reference work *War of Rebellion: Official Records of the Union and Confederate Armies*. This 128-volume set began as an 1864 project to preserve all the correspondence of Union officers and other government papers pertaining to the war. Soon after the Confederate surrender, its papers were collected and work began on indexing them. The last volume was not compiled and published until 1901, with a "second series" of assorted and miscellaneous papers begun in the 1980s. These two sets, an associated (and exquisite) atlas, and a 31-volume sister compilation of naval records are the holy grail so far as Civil War research is concerned. Every significant fact in this book was checked against entries in the *OR*—helped in no small part by an excellent CD-ROM version produced by Guild Press of Indiana (available in most museum and battlefield bookstores for around $70). This is the most significant advance in Civil War research in quite some time, because, while the *OR* did have a three-volume index, it was not inclusive by any stretch of the imagination, and the "keyword search" function of electronic documents is a far more efficient and effective way of looking up references. It is also the most cost-efficient way of having your own copy of the *OR*, which costs around $3,500 for a new set (available from Broadfoot Publishing Company; www.broadfootpublishing.com) and takes up an incredible amount of shelf space.

Palisade: the steep outer walls of an earthwork or masonry fort.

Parapets: a low wall or fence along the top of a fort's ramparts, to provide some protection for the gunners manning en barbette positions. It now serves in existing forts to help keep the tourists from falling off the upper gundecks and ramparts.

Picket: a guard or sentry for either a fixed position or mobile force, these were usually placed well outside friendly lines or the head of the column, where they could best look for or hear any enemy movement. They were almost always the first to fight in any engagement and suffered appallingly high casualties. This duty would usually rotate from company to company in a regiment. During times of battle, they would work in conjunction with skirmishers and vedettes.

Quick-time: to walk in step at 120 steps per minute—the standard pace for infantry on the march. "Double quick time" is 180 steps per minute, which means you are moving at a sort of jog, but still in step with the men around you in a formation. "Charge" means to run flat-out at whatever lies ahead; obviously, calling for a faster pace or to run should only be done when nearly in contact with the enemy, as otherwise you have a bunch of worn-out infantrymen able to do little but gasp for breath.

Rampart: the top of a position's palisade, usually flattened so that artillery may be mounted and men may move about for guard and combat duties. To "take the ramparts" means the position has been breached by an enemy force that now holds the high ground and thus the tactical advantage.

Redoubt: another term for a reinforced protective shelter, usually made of logs covered with earthwork, but implies that this is a fighting position as well, as opposed to the bomb-proof, which implies simply a hideout or isolated shelter. This term is also used frequently as a reference to any defensive trenchwork or earthwork.

Refuse: a line of battle or wall of fortifications that is angled sharply back from the main enemy advance or attack. This helps prevent the enemy force from attacking the flank of a formation or position.

Reinforcements: troops brought into the battle either from an already established reserve force or from other commands moved into the area.

Reserve: troops kept back away from the main battle area to use to exploit any breach in the opponent's line, to replace casualties in the main battle force, or to use as the last line of defense. The rule of thumb is 2:1, keeping two parts of your command on the line of battle and one back as a reserve. There were some Civil War commanders who prided themselves on never using their reserves, no matter the situation, and others who would plug them in at the slightest sign of trouble.

Salient: a part of a defensive line or fortification that juts out from the rest of the line toward the enemy. Before the war this was taught to be something desirable, as it would naturally break up any enemy line of attack (and in theory allow the defender to fire straight into the flanks of an attacker on either side), but during the war most attacks focused on this feature to the distress of the defender.

Sapper or Sappier: a specially assigned soldier, charged with the construction of mines and associated structures, usually aimed at the destruction of an enemy's works.

"See the elephant": an expression used to refer to engaging in combat. A soldier who has just lived through his first battle has "seen the elephant." While it is debatable (and fiercely argued over in some circles) where this expression came from, the most plausible explanation is that it refers to the circus. During a time when the vast majority of the population were cloistered on farms, rarely going more than 20 miles from home in their entire lifetime, seeing the exotic animals in a circus was one of the highlights of their lives.

Shrapnel: listed under Artillery section.

Siege: to surround and cut off an enemy position from resupply or reinforcement and then "starve them out." The earliest known military histories (Homer's *The Iliad,* for one) mention this kind of warfare, which is brutally effective if one is facing an enemy position without hope of a strong relief effort and if one is very patient. During the Civil War a siege was usually accompanied by bombardment from heavy artillery manufactured and brought in for this specific situation.

Skirmishers: troops, usually of company strength or less, assigned to protect the head and flanks of a main battle formation. These infantrymen fought very much as modern infantrymen do, using cover, concealment, and individual maneuvers to "pick away" as much as possible from the main enemy force before withdrawing into their own lines. During times of battle, they would work in conjunction with pickets.

Squadron: a naval formation, usually consisting mostly of gunboats and other armed vessels and usually assigned to a given geographic area. Sometimes used as an alternative term for fleets or flotillas.

Staging bases: main bases usually well removed from the battle areas where men and supplies are funneled out to the necessary commands. This is where the main supply depots would be located, as well as training camps for the men.

Strategy: the overall plan for conducting the war or even just a single battle. A good example is the "Anaconda Plan," the grand overall plan for conducting the war against the Confederacy. Army commands and above would deal with plans on this level, leaving the specifics of exactly how to carry out these objectives to the lower commands.

Tactics: the specifics of how a particular strategy will be carried out on the battlefield. There are some sources in military science and theory circles that claim a distinction between strategy and tactics is ridiculous, as both talk about more or less the same thing, but we believe it is a useful distinction to mean you are talking about the grand strategies of politicians and top generals versus the battle tactics of field commanders and soldiers.

Theater: the general area of combat or a large area covered by a single command. For example, "theater armies" means all the combatant forces in a given major geographic area. The "theater armies" referred to at Resaca (during the Atlanta campaign) meant all four armies commanded by Sherman as well as the three corps commanded by Johnston—all the troops they had immediately available to them. A "theater" can also mean something

such as the "Western Theater," which included everything in the South from the Carolinas to the Mississippi. This book concentrates on the Eastern theater of the war.

Transports: unarmed ships attached to fleets or flotillas, carrying army troops to use in assaults or amphibious invasions.

Trench work: a line of dug-out ditches, providing both cover and concealment for infantrymen who fought from inside them. Depending on how long the troops had been in their position before being attacked, these could be as crude as a shallow, scratched-out series of "foxholes" or a deep and elaborate series of interconnected ditches, bombproofs, and redoubts.

Vanguard: the forwardmost elements of a command or column. In modern military parlance, this is the "point element," the troops most vulnerable to a sudden ambush or attack.

Vedette or vidette: a mounted guard or sentry, who otherwise did the same duty as a picket. During times of battle, vedettes would work in conjunction with pickets and skirmishers.

Volley fire: a line of infantry all firing at the same time on command. A central element of the Napoleonic tactics used throughout the war, massed infantry firing volleys was the only way that smoothbore muskets of limited range could gain a real advantage on a fluid battlefield; the infantrymen would form three lines slightly offset one behind another, and each would fire in turn on the order of their officer. By the time the third line fired the first would be reloaded, so a near continuous volume of outgoing fire could be maintained so long as the ammunition held out. As Civil War–era rifles had ranges 3 to 10 times longer than Revolutionary War–era muskets, could be reloaded a bit faster, and had a much more lethal ammunition load, the same close-in volley fire tactics resulted in appalling casualties.

ARTILLERY

Artillery had its own specialized language; the following list is a sampling of the most commonly used terms.

Barrage: to use multiple guns firing on a single target or to saturate an area with as heavy a rate of fire as possible.

Battery: the basic organization of artillery units, which contained four, five, or six guns of single or multiple type, which usually worked together in a combat action. Occasionally batteries were broken up into two-gun sections for use in special circumstances.

Bombardment: the use of artillery to reduce either a military or civilian target to rubble.

Caisson: the ammunition wagon and container for an artillery piece. Usually the piece and the caisson were hauled together by a single team of horses, called the caisson team. As these wagons were very sturdily built and had flat tops, they were often used as ambulances and even as hearses. The U.S. Army still uses caissons in formal military funerals; the 3rd Infantry, the "Old Guard" at Arlington National Cemetery, is often seen using caissons to haul the coffins of the honored dead to their final rest.

Canister/grapeshot: a tin can similar to a coffee can filled with either 27 or 48 iron balls, designed to burst open right after it left the muzzle and spray the area in front of the piece like a giant shotgun. Grapeshot is a slight variation that uses nine larger iron balls either sewn together in a cloth sleeve or held together in a light iron frame. The size of these balls varied with the caliber of the gun they were used in. This round was useful out to about 300 yards but was more usually employed at much closer range, including at literally point-blank range. When things were really bleak for the artillery crews, they would load up with "double canister," knocking the powder bag off the rear of the second round and ramming it in on top of the first. This cut the range roughly in half, but doubled the effectiveness up close. This was a deadly weapon to use against closely packed infantry charges and would result in the lines being literally blown apart, creating huge gaps.

Cannon: a generic term for a piece of artillery, not specific as to the type or size.

Columbiad: a very heavy-barreled, smoothbore weapon originally introduced in 1811, which could fire either shot or shell from either flat or high trajectories, giving it the combined characteristics of guns, howitzers, and mortars. For many years these were the backbone weapon of coastline defense, and nearly every coastal fort featured them at the outbreak of war. Early Columbiads could fire a 50-pound solid round shot about 1,800 feet. A variation of this gun, known as a Rodman, was manufactured in a way that created an exceptionally strong barrel, giving the improved guns the ability to fire shells that weighed up to 320 pounds out to nearly 3 miles away.

Counter-battery: to use artillery fire against an enemy artillery position to try to knock their guns out of the fight.

Dahlgren: a very heavy-barreled weapon, very similar in look to a Columbiad. These were used primarily on board naval vessels and came in both smoothbore and rifled varieties. They were built in sizes ranging from 12-pounders to 150-pounders, as well as 9-inch to 20-inch calibers, with the 15-inch smoothbores being the most popular.

Friction primer: the "match" that was used to set off a cannon. It consisted of two short pieces of copper tubing soldered together at right angles, with one tube filled with mercury fulminate and the other, slightly longer tube filled with gunpowder. After the charge had been loaded and the gunpowder-filled charge bag torn open by a vent prick, the friction primer was inserted into the vent hole, directly over the now-opened charge bag, and attached to a lanyard. The mercury-filled tube had a short, twisted wire inserted that, when pulled out rapidly, created a friction spark with the mercury fulminate. This caused the gunpowder in the other tube to flash and, in turn, caused the pricked charge bag inside the tube to deflammate, expelling the round from the tube.

Fuse: a length of flammable cording inside a plug that burned at a known rate and that was used to cause an explosive shell to go off at a given time after firing. A gun crewman cut the fuse to the length (time) desired and then inserted the fuse and plug assembly into a shell before handing it off to be loaded into the piece. The firing of the piece ignited the fuse, and artillery officers were well trained in the mathematics of figuring out exactly when a shell would arrive over a given target at a given range. The advantage of this was the ability to do "air bursts," which spread the lethal shrapnel over a much wider arc than if the shell had hit the ground before bursting.

Gun: a generic term for any artillery piece, although, to be precise, it really refers only to rifled cannon.

Hot-shot: solid shot heated to red-hot in special ovens and then quickly loaded and fired at flammable targets: ships and their rigging, wagons and caissons, wooden palisades, abatis, etc.

Lanyard: a 12-foot-long rope with a wooden handle on one end and a hook on the other that was attached to a small loop in the wire of a friction primer. Used to fire the artillery piece.

Mortar: a short, very heavy-barreled artillery piece that used exceptionally heavy powder charges in order to loft solid shot or shell nearly vertically. These were extremely useful in lobbing charges over a walled enemy position or trenchwork that was resistant to direct fire.

Parrott rifle: a rifled, muzzle-loading cannon, ranging in size from a 3-inch (or 10-pounder) to a 10-inch (300-pounder). These are some of the easiest cannons to identify, having a thick band attached around the rear of the barrel, used to help withstand the tremendous pressures rifled cannons build up during firing. These rifled guns fired oblong "bolts," cucumber-shaped solid shot and explosive shells, that had brass rings attached to the base that "grabbed" the rifling during firing. Many accounts of soldiers on the wrong end of Parrott rifles firing talk about the particular "whiffling" shrill noise these bolts made when flying overhead. A deadly accurate weapon found in both armies in every theater of the war.

Piece: another generic term for a cannon, although usually used to indicate a specific or singular gun.

Shell: a hollow round filled with gunpowder, which would burst either from striking a target or by the action of a timed fuse.

Shot: solid round balls or oblong "bolts," usually used against masonry structures or other such heavy, solid objects. However, cannoneers had absolutely no qualms about using solid shot against infantry formations.

Shrapnel: red-hot, jagged bits of metal flying about at high rates of speed, produced by the exploding casing of a bursting shell. A shell bursting in the air above an infantry formation could produce many times the casualties of a solid shot blasting through the line.

Spike: to render a cannon unable to fire, usually by driving a soft iron nail through the vent hole and cutting off the protruding end. This would be done, if possible, when an enemy force was about to overrun an artillery position and the guns could not be withdrawn. There were frequent occasions, especially late in the war, when Union gunners simply shot all their caisson horses when on the verge of being overrun and left the guns intact, knowing that the Confederates would lack the horses needed to take the guns when they retreated. Then the Union gunners could simply move back in and resume their firing with little fuss.

Trails: the rear "legs" of the gun carriage, which had a short pole (called a trail handspike) attached for ease of aiming by moving the gun left and right. This is also where the cannon was attached to the rear of the caisson, being hauled tube pointed backward.

Tube: sometimes used as a generic term for cannon, it is the heavy iron or bronze casting that is the barrel of the gun. It is attached to the gun carriage by means of two trunnions cast on either side, near the barrel's center of gravity, and raised up and down by means of various attachments to the knob and neck cast on the rear of the barrel.

ON THE EVE OF WAR

The Civil War was a long time coming. Negotiation—resulting in the Missouri Compromise and Compromise of 1850—over the future of slavery had failed to settle the issue. Other events—the 1854 Kansas-Nebraska Act, the Supreme Court's 1857 Dred Scott Decision, and John Brown's 1859 raid on Harpers Ferry—only drew the nation closer to conflict. By 1860, in fact, pro- and antislavery forces had been fighting on the plains of Kansas Territory for a good five years.

And yet, when P. G. T. Beauregard's Confederate gunners opened fire on Fort Sumter on April 14, 1861, neither side was prepared for war. A merchant power, the United States nevertheless had just a small navy, and an army of less than 17,000 officers and soldiers—most of whom were scattered across the frontier—with which to suppress a rebellion supported by eleven states. But the Northern states had the resources with which to build ships (more than 600 by war's end) and produce cannon, uniforms, and rifles.

In Richmond, the new Confederate capitol, the military situation was a little more worrisome. The fledgling nation had no army or navy whatsoever, and it had little time in which to create them. While he could never scrap together a force as large as the Union navy—which grew big enough to blockade the South's entire seacoast—Confederate Secretary of the Navy Stephen Mallory did manage to threaten it with a single vessel, the ironclad *Virginia* (along with several other ironclad ships and rams).

One thing each side had—at least initially—was recruits, and in terms of training her men, the Confederacy was in good shape. Many of the U.S. Army's best officers were leaving to join the Confederacy's army, including Colonel Robert E. Lee, who turned down President Abraham Lincoln's offer of command of all United States armies to take charge of Virginia's state troops. (Lee later served as military advisor to President Jefferson Davis before taking command of the Army of Northern Virginia.) Confederate President Jefferson Davis was a also a West Point graduate, as were James Longstreet, James Ewell Brown "Jeb" Stuart, A.P. Hill, and more than 250 other officers who gave the Confederate army immediate legitimacy and, at least in the beginning, a decided battlefield edge. (Lee's best lieutenant, Thomas J. "Stonewall" Jackson was a graduate of the Virginia Military Institute.)

More than 600 other U.S. Military Academy graduates—including George McClellan, Ulysses S. Grant, George Gordon Meade, Phillip Sheridan, and George Armstrong Custer—stayed to fight for their flag. Only three years of battle would shake loose the worst material—the political generals and glory hunters—after they'd cost thousands of young men their lives, allowing West Point's best to decide the outcome of the war.

WAR IN THE EASTERN THEATER

As we drove through the Chickamauga and Chattanooga National Battlefield recently, a friend asked why people seem to study the Civil War's eastern campaigns more than those conducted out west. After all, historians say, out west is where the war was really won. (To most Americans during the 1860s, the west roughly meant the land between the Appalachian Mountains and the Mississippi River area.) Robert E. Lee clearly foresaw this possibility in the wake of the Union victory at Chattanooga. He is reported to have warned Confederate President Jefferson Davis that the defense of the country greatly depended on the safety of the land being held by the Confederacy along the Atlantic. By then Ulysses S. Grant's capture of Forts Henry and Donelson had given Yankee armies access to Kentucky and Tennessee, while Union victories at New Orleans and Vicksburg had secured the mighty Mississippi, divided the Confederacy, and added teeth to the constricting Federal blockade of the South.

And yet, for most students of the war, the Eastern Theater has always held greater appeal. One of three main areas of military operations during the Civil War, the Eastern Theater ranged from the Atlantic Coast to the Appalachian Mountains, and included the mid-Atlantic states of Pennsylvania, Maryland, and Virginia, and the coast of North Carolina. (The Western Theater extended from the Appalachians to the Mississippi River, and included Mississippi, Tennessee, Georgia, and most of the Carolinas. The Trans-Mississippi Theater covered lands west of the Mississippi, including Arkansas, Texas, Louisiana, Missouri, and the Indian Territory [now Oklahoma]. These theaters were further broken down into military departments.)

In the east, raw recruits eager to "see the elephant" and the enemy "skedaddle" first met in great numbers on the plains of Manassas, Virginia. The war (practically speaking) also ended here, at Appomattox Court House, Virginia. Here, too, just 100 miles apart, sat the nations' capitals—Washington, D.C., and Richmond. The defense of these cities sparked many of the war's biggest battles, at Gettysburg, Manassas (twice), Antietam, and Brandy Station—the site of the largest cavalry battle ever fought on the continent. Compared to key Western Theater battles—which often featured siege warfare or combined land and river operations—these were wide-open affairs featuring massive armies, crushing flank movements, and (especially after mid-1863) clashes of horsemen. It may be, then, that historians simply find the Eastern Theater more exciting.

As much as anything else, geography dictated how and where battles—even entire campaigns—were fought. Overflowing rivers blocked routes of advance or retreat; ridges offered terrific defensive positions; mountains screened army movements; and thick forests and rocky terrain rendered cavalry and artillery all but useless. Terrain had to be conquered if victories were to be won. So if marching soldiers could occasionally enjoy new and strange lands as they passed through them, army planners had no such luxury. As unique and fertile as Virginia's sandy soil might be, for instance, to logisticians it was just another nagging enemy that might affect the movement of an army. Dry weather transformed that soil into a choking dust that incapacitated soldiers; heavy rain turned it into a thick, malevolent glue that shredded shoes, swallowed up wagon trains, and bedeviled thousands of footsore infantrymen, engineers, and teamsters.

Today, Civil War buffs traveling through the rolling countryside of the Eastern Theater should, of course, enjoy its considerable beauty and natural resources. To truly understand how the Civil War was fought, however, they might ask themselves a few questions as they take in the sites and sights: Why was a battle fought here? How did this landscape affect the battle's outcome? And how on earth did these gargantuan armies—with their thousands of men, miles-long wagon trains, and heavy artillery batteries—manage to get here in the first place?

MAJOR PERSONALITIES

While it would take a massive chapter to list every important name from the Civil War here, for easy reference, we list the full names and ranks of the most prominent figures mentioned in this book.

CONFEDERATE

Alexander, Major Edward Porter
Armistead, General Lewis
Beauregard, General Pierre Gustave Toutant (P.G.T.)
Breckinridge, General John C.
Early, General Jubal
Echols, Brigadier General John
Evans, Brigadier General Shanks
Ewell, Lieutenant General Richard S.
Gordon, Major General John
Heth, Major General Henry
Hill, Major General A.P.
Hill, Major General Daniel Harvey
Jackson, General Thomas J. "Stonewall"
Johnson, Major General Edward
Johnston, General Albert Sidney
Johnston General Joseph Eggleston
Lee, General Robert Edward
Longstreet, Lieutenant General James
Magruder, Major General John
Marshall, Colonel Charles
McGowan, General Samuel
McLaws, General Lafayette
Mosby, Colonel John Singleton
Pemberton, Lieutenant General John Clifford
Pettigrew, Johnston
Pickett, Major General George Edward
Pleasanton, Major General Alfred
Stuart, Lieutenant J. E. B. "Jeb"
Sullivan, Brigadier General Jeremiah
Trimble, Isaac
Walker, General John
Wharton, Brigadier General Gabriel

UNION

Banks, General Nathaniel Prentiss
Buford, John
Burnside, Major General Ambrose Everett
Butler, General Benjamin Franklin "Spoons"
Chamberlain, Colonel Joshua Lawrence
Custer, Major General George Armstrong
Davis, Brigadier General Jefferson C.
DuPont, Captain Henry
Fremont, General John Charles
Ford, Colonel Thomas
Franklin, Major General William
French, Brigadier General William H.
Grant, Lieutenant General Ulysses S.
Greene, Brigadier General George Sears
Gregg, Major General David
Hancock, Major General Scott
Hooker, Major General Joseph
Howard, Major General Oliver Otis
Hunt, Major General Henry
Hunter, General David
Jones, Lieutenant Roger
McClellan, General George Brinton
McDowell, Brigadier General Irvin
Meade, George Gordon
Meagher, Brigadier General Thomas
Merritt, Wesley
Miles, Colonel Dixon
Milroy, General Robert H.
Patterson, Major General Robert
Pope, Major General John
Porter, Major General Fitz John
Reynolds, General John
Ricketts, General James B.
Scott, General-in-Chief Winfield "Fuss and Feathers"
Sedgwick, Major General John
Sheridan, Major General Phillip H.
Sherman, Major General William Tecumseh
Sickles, Major General Daniel
Sigel, General Franz

MAJOR PERSONALITIES

Slocum, Major General Henry Warner
Stahel, Major General Julius
Stone, Brigadier General Charles P.
Stoneman, Major General George
Sumner, General Edwin
Sykes, Major General George
Wallace, General Lew
Wright, Brigadier General Horatio

ORGANIZATION OF THE ARMIES

Both Union and Confederate armies were organized along the same lines as a result of practices in the prewar U.S. Army. The following lists the smallest usual organization of troops up to the largest field command, but remember that these are just the "way it was supposed to be" numbers and that very few field units came anywhere close to these strengths. Confederate forces toward the end of the war were especially decimated—with no replacements available, desertion widespread, and each battle taking a heavier and heavier toll; many regiments or brigades were represented by a mere handful of men when they surrendered.

Ranks of officers who commanded at each level were as irregular as the number of men they commanded. Listed below are the "book" numbers, those that at least on paper were the authorized commander's rank and number of men, but these also tended to vary wildly, especially toward the beginning and end of the war. Battlefield casualties among the upper ranks were very high when compared with other conflicts; this was a war where, by and large, the officers took seriously their charge to lead their men into battle.

COMPANY

A company was the basic unit to which a soldier belonged and was usually raised in a single county, often having a great percentage of its men related by birth or marriage. It was supposed to have 100 (sometimes 101) men and officers and was usually commanded by a captain. In the postwar South, it became habitual to refer to a distinguished veteran as "Captain John Smith"; some sources suggest this was a title given to the last survivor of a company, and thus the de facto company "commander," but this seems highly speculative. Depending

heavily on which theater and which army, companies also had one to three lieutenants, one to six sergeants, and assorted numbers of corporals. A first sergeant usually ran the nuts and bolts of the company and stood behind them in battle to help keep the lines properly formed and to make sure no one ran away.

BATTALION

More usual in today's army than during the Civil War, a battalion consisted of three to five companies, usually commanded by a major. Most independent battalions were assimilated into regiments by the second year of the war, but a few stayed on as organizations of sappers, snipers, engineers, or other such special-duty troops.

REGIMENT

The central and often most important element of both sides' armies, a regiment consisted of 10 companies with 1,000 men, commanded by a lieutenant colonel or sometimes a full colonel. Regiments usually had a strength of 200 to 500 on the battlefield. Almost always raised from the same geographic area, the men identified with their regiment both on and off the battlefield and always looked to the "colors," the unique regimental battle flag, for where they should stand, fight, and advance during battle.

Most regiments, particularly Union regiments, had a small command staff consisting of a major as adjunct (doing the same duties today's executive officer does); a surgeon and one or more of his assistants to treat the wounded and sick; a quartermaster, who looked after their supplies; a commissary, who controlled the kitchens and food supplies; and one or more senior sergeants.

BRIGADE

Brigades were composed of two to seven (or even more on occasion) regiments and usually commanded by a brigadier general. Some brigades had artillery or cavalry commands attached to them, particularly early in the war, and would almost always have a brigade staff very similar in size and positions to the regimental staffs. Brigades at full strength would, at least in theory, have somewhere between 3,000 and 6,000 men, but most often had in the neighborhood of 1,500 to 2,000 effective troops.

DIVISION

A division was composed of two to six brigades and was almost always commanded by a major general, accompanied by a larger staff than on the brigade level, but again performing almost the same tasks. Divisions were the usual maneuver organization, meaning that when the highest headquarters involved in a battle planned an attack, divisional level organizations were usually sent in to perform a specific task. In theory a division commanded some 6,000 to 15,000 troops but only rarely had more than 10,000 available at any given time.

CORPS

A corps was the largest usual maneuver organization on either side, commanded by Union major generals or Confederate lieutenant generals and composed of two to six divisions. Again, in theory, they could field about 20,000 to 60,000 troops but most often had in the neighborhood of 35,000 men. A very large staff was the norm for corps, with a large and ungainly staff encampment that was difficult to move swiftly.

ARMY

Armies were generally associated with an entire theater of action in the Confederacy, while the Union generally used them as their largest maneuver organizations. An army might consist of only one corps, while other examples had as many as four corps. Union major generals and Confederate (full) generals commanded this organizational force that included widely varying numbers of men—from as few as 30,000 to as many as 120,000.

Cavalry and artillery units were organized under the same basic structure, with a few levels known by different terms.

CAVALRY

The basic unit was the troop, which was otherwise the same as an infantry company. Some Union cavalry formations were called squadrons, which consisted of two or three troops. Both sides removed their cavalry from troops supporting infantry formations and collected them together in all-cavalry battalions, divisions, and corps.

ARTILLERY

The basic formation of artillery was a battery, which almost always had four or six guns, usually of the same type or just two different types (this made ammunition supply easier). Initially these batteries were deployed as semi-independent units loosely attached to an infantry brigade or division, but later in the war they tended to be grouped under one specified division or corps level artillery commander, usually a major or lieutenant colonel.

CAVALRY, ARTILLERY, AND INFANTRY

Early in the war the Confederacy organized several legions, which were combined infantry, artillery, and cavalry formations of between 1,000 and 2,000 men. Few, if any, actually saw any combat; most were broken up when they were assigned to an army and reorganized into their respective branches. Other "special" formations were marines, heavy artillery, engineers, sappers, sharpshooters, prison garrisons, and dedicated skirmishers, all of which tended to be organized similarly to infantry companies.

Cavalry

The simplest definition of "cavalry" is the use of armed soldiers mounted on horseback. Starting at about the time of Darius I of Persia's invasion of western Asia and the Greek city-states (circa 500 B.C.E.), mounted soldiers began developing into the preeminent force on the battlefield. While infantry was certainly still used and was an important element of military tactical deployment, the cavalry became the fighting element that all military planning revolved around. This situation continued into the early medieval period in Europe, finally fading out in favor of concentration on infantry combat around the period bookmarked by the battles of Stirling Bridge, Scotland (1198 C.E.), and Agincourt, France (1415 C.E.), both of which demonstrated the complete failure of heavy cavalry formations to break up an infantry position.

By the time of the American Civil War, cavalry had been relegated to the tasks of scouting and forward patrolling, guarding railroads, and providing keen-looking escorts to politicians and generals. During combat actions, they were primarily used as "first strike" attackers, charging at full tilt toward the enemy line, firing pistols and screaming as loudly as possible, the tactic designed to try to either scare off the enemy or at least blow a hole in his lines that follow-up infantry attacks could exploit. At the beginning of the war, cavalrymen bore the brunt of sometimes mean-spirited ridicule from the infantry, who regarded them as dandies at best and shirking cowards at worst. A frequent jibe, admittedly hard to translate into today's culture, was an infantryman's cry when he saw a line of cavalry approaching: "Mister! Here's your mule!" That was a real knee-slapper back in 1862.

By 1863 things had started to change across the board in military thought, including the role and use of cavalry in combat. Still maintaining their primary role as advance scouts and vedettes (mounted sentries), the cavalry on both sides began being used for dedicated attacks on enemy flanks and marching columns, even when unsupported by infantry. That same year, cavalry-on-cavalry battles became more common, peaking with the cavalry-only battle at Brandy Station, Virginia, which was the opening fight of the Gettysburg campaign. This rapidly escalated into the use of regular army cavalry in roles—raids into enemy camps, supply depots, and even cities—that had been reserved for the disdained "guerrilla" and "partisan ranger" units (thought to be roughly on the same level as murderous mercenaries). The end result of all this expansion in the use of cavalry was that garrison units had to be expanded and changed from those staffed by the sick, lame, and lazy into combat-ready units that had to be able to respond to a lightning-fast attack by a raiding cavalry unit.

The relatively small cavalry units, especially the Confederate regiments led by Lieutenant General Nathan Bedford Forrest and Major General Joseph Wheeler, had an impact on grand campaigns far beyond what their size would suggest. During the 1863 approach to Vicksburg, Major General Ulysses S. Grant of the Union Army was forced to abandon his initial overland movement across Mississippi after Forrest's raids on his supply lines in southern and western Tennessee threatened to leave his men cut off without ammunition and food deep inside the Confederacy. Later that same year, Wheeler led a raid through central Tennessee that cut off the besieged Union garrison at Chattanooga from desperately needed supplies, routed Union supply columns, caused havoc with the central Union command structure in the area, and could have resulted in a collapse of the entire Union control of the area if General Braxton Bragg, the local area commander, could have bothered to follow up on the advantages Wheeler had handed him.

War means fightin', and fightin' means killin'.

Lieutenant General Nathan
Bedford Forrest,
Confederacy, 1864

The last act of the war in the Western Theater was a cavalry raid, led by Brigadier General James Harrison Wilson of the North. After
routing what was left of General John Bell
Hood's decimated Army of Tennessee after the
battle of Nashville, in 1864 Wilson rebuilt his
force into a 13,500-man command, all
mounted, based out of Gravelly Springs in
northern Alabama. In late March 1865 he led
his command south to Selma, taking and
destroying the essential Confederate arsenal
there, routing most of Forrest's command in
the process, and then turned toward Georgia.
For the next three weeks, his command ranged
all through central Alabama and central and
southern Georgia, destroying warehouses and
manufacturing facilities and capturing scores
of local militias and independent commands,
almost without opposition. Finally, on May 10,
near Irwinville, Georgia, an element of his command captured the fleeing Confederate president himself, Jefferson Davis.

Despite the enmity of the infantry, the life
of a cavalryman was far from glamorous or
safe. As the fastest moving military force in
the field at the time, a cavalryman could be in
the midst of battle literally at a moment's
notice, and the swift movement of combat
meant that near-instantaneous decisions and
lightning-quick reflexes were an absolute
necessity in order to live to tell about it. The
individual weapons that the cavalrymen used
changed as rapidly as their tactics, with the
early-war drawn-saber charges changing into
the near-abandonment of edged weapons in
favor of pistols and eventually rapid-fire,
breechloading carbines.

One similarity to the infantry, however,
was the grossly overloaded manner in which
they left home. One Texas cavalryman with
the W. P. Lane Rangers, described by eminent
historian Bell Irvin Wiley in his monumental
work *The Life of Johnny Reb*, carried a typical
load with him when he first marched off:

*. . . saddle, bridle, saddle-blanket,
curry comb, horse brush, coffee pot,
tin cup, 20 lbs. ham, 200 biscuit, 5
lbs. ground coffee, 5 lbs. sugar, one
large pound cake presented to me by
Mrs. C. E. Talley, 6 shirts, 6 prs. socks,
3 prs. drawers, 2 prs. pants, 2 jackets,
1 pr. heavy mud boots, one Colt's
revolver, one small dirk, four blankets,
sixty feet of rope with a twelve inch
iron pin attached . . . and divers and
sundry little momentoes from friends.*

Again, similar to their infantry counterparts, carried equipment rapidly downgraded
until the typical load consisted of a light steel
saber, one or two .36 or .44 caliber six-shot
pistols, a short-barreled carbine, a saddle and
other horse-related necessities, a shelter half,
blanket, poncho, sometimes a change of
clothes and socks, and a saddle bag holding
coffee, food, and other absolute necessities.

One element of the cavalry that never
completely died out during the war was their
dash and elan, perceived or real as it was.
Largely promoted by the dashing personality
of Major General James Ewell Brown Stuart of
Lee's Army of Northern Virginia, the image of
the cavalryman developed into one of the gal-
lant cavalier, forever prancing about the battlefield in a rather hyperactive sort of way or
swooping down into an unprotected Northern
town, where the women would be romanced,
the men respectably placed out of the line of
danger, and some random supplies would be
gathered up to take back to the unglamorous,
starving infantry. Dressed in a rather fancy
yellow-trimmed uniform (the color associated
with the cavalry), tall polished boots, a gleam-
ing saber buckled over a yellow silk sash,
topped with a slouch hat trimmed with a large
ostrich feather, and his own personal band in
tow (literally), the rather weak-chinned and
somewhat homely Stuart somehow proved
irresistible to Southern (and some Northern)
women, particularly after he hid his shortcom-
ings behind a thick and usually immaculately
groomed beard. The popular perception of

his cavalry, promoted in newspapers both North and South, was that his war was a sort of grand adventure, fought in a gentlemanly manner and treated by friend and foe alike as some sort of great lark, in which both sides could not wipe their grins off their faces from the pure joy of it all. This was helped in no small part by a popular song of the day, said to be Stuart's favorite:

JINE THE CAVALRY
(by Sam Sweeney, one of Stuart's musicians)

CHORUS:
If you want to have a good time, jine the cavalry!
Jine the cavalry! Jine the cavalry!
If you want to catch the Devil, if you want to have fun,
If you want to smell Hell, jine the cavalry!

We're the boys who went around McClellian,
Went around McClellian, went around around McClellian!
We're the boys who went around McClellian,
Bully boys, hey! Bully boys, ho! (Chorus)

We're the boys who crossed the Potomicum,
Crossed the Potomicum, crossed the Potomicum!
We're the boys who crossed the Potomicum,
Bully boys, hey! Bully boys, ho! (Chorus)

Then we went into Pennsylvania,
Into Pennsylvania, into Pennsylvania!
Then we went into Pennsylvania,
Bully boys, hey! Bully boys, ho! (Chorus)

The big fat Dutch gals hand around the breadium,
Hand around the breadium, hand around the breadium!
The big fat Dutch gals hand around the breadium,
Bully boys, hey! Bully boys, ho! (Chorus)

Ol' Joe Hooker, won't you come out of The Wilderness?
Come out of The Wilderness, come out of The Wilderness?
Ol' Joe Hooker, won't you come out of The Wilderness?
Bully boys, hey! Bully boys, ho! (Chorus)

The truth, of course, is not anywhere close to this romantic fantasy, but as in so many other situations, image won out over substance. The sight of a dirty, nasty cavalry trooper mounted on top of an unbathed, rather fragrant horse could set the heart of a Southern belle all aflutter, while the sight of an equally dirty, unkempt infantryman would usually make her wonder if she had adequately hidden all the silverware. The media of the day, and many latter days, kept up this romantic hogwash, with images of saber-drawn cavalry at the gallop toward lines of faceless enemy remaining popular well into the 20th century. On a related note, the last-known charge by horse cavalry into the face of the enemy was during the 1939 German invasion of Poland—the attack by saber- and lance-equipped Polish cavalry against the armored tank formations was not successful.

Artillery

The subject of Civil War artillery could encompass (and has done so) whole books in and of itself. From an ancient tradition of a branch of military service used primarily for harassment and minor support of the more dashing infantry and cavalry branches, the science of artillery underwent a renaissance in the post-Napoleonic antebellum years. Along with the field of military engineering, artillery became the branch of choice for some of the brightest minds emerging from West Point in the 1830s and 1840s (including Confederate general Pierre Gustave Toutant Beauregard and his old friend, West Point instructor and opponent at Fort Sumter, Major Robert Anderson of the Union Army) and had evolved into a central part of planning for both defense and offense. During the war, the use of artillery further evolved in the disparate directions of "flying" batteries (horse-drawn, relatively light, and very mobile), used to support rapidly moving cavalry operations, and in the deployment of heavy siege guns, used as the primary offensive weapon in a static situation.

Basically put, artillery was the use of heavy cannons designed to toss a solid or explosive round for distances varying from point-blank to more than 10,000 yards (just under 6 miles). Artillery weapons came in three basic types: rifled guns, long-barreled heavy cannons designed to fire heavy solid shot great distances at very high velocities and with very flat trajectories in order to hit distant targets or batter down masonry structures; smoothbore guns, relatively short-barreled howitzers originally designed to shoot explosive shells with less of a powder charge needed and used for more rapid and direct fire, which also had the advantage of having a shorter and lighter tube than the rifled guns, making them easier to transport and set up; and mortars, very short, very thick, and heavy barreled weapons used to shoot large explosive shells at very high trajectories, able to drop their charges in almost vertically.

Each of these three basic types came in several varieties and a wide range of sizes, measured by their "caliber," the internal diameter of the tube, or the weight of the ammunition itself. However, to make this subject as confusing as humanly possible, there never was a universally agreed upon standard of how to name cannons. In antebellum days, it was more or less standard to designate cannons based on the weight of the solid shot ammunition, e.g., a cannon that fired a solid round shot that weighed six pounds would have an inside barrel diameter (or "caliber") of a bit over 3.5 inches (3.67 inches, to be precise) and would be designated a "six-pounder." The advent of rifled cannons caused this system to collapse, as they fired oblong rather than round shot and therefore had no standard weight: The longer the round, the heavier it could be, depending on

whether it was solid shot or explosive shell. One of the most common (and notorious) artillery pieces, the 10-pounder Parrott rifle, fired a range of ammunition that weighed between the 9-pound shell to an 11.5-pound case shot, and the tube itself had a caliber of 2.9 inches (1861 model) to 3.0 inches (1863 model). Larger models of the Parrott rifle, the so-called 200-pounder and 300-pounder, actually fired shells weighing 175 and 250 pounds apiece, respectively. Confused? Don't feel lonely, even experts in the field of Civil War–era artillery sometimes have a hard time keeping up with the whole mess.

Just like their infantry counterparts, artillery weapons were almost all muzzleloaders, requiring a team of six to eight men to set up, load, aim, and fire the weapon. A well-drilled team could fire two shots per minute "by the book," but in the heat of combat shortcuts were sometimes undertaken that increased this rate to an average of three or even four shots a minute. A battery could keep up a sustained fire of one shot every 5 to 10 seconds, and larger assemblies of cannon could put out amazing rates of fire.

Union batteries usually had four or six guns, almost always of the same type and size. Confederate batteries were almost invariably four guns and very frequently had two or sometimes even three different types and sizes of weapons within them, making supply and logistics a nightmare. As per the usual in artillery, even this basic setup was not universally standard. A battery was usually commanded by a captain, called the "battery commander." Early in the war batteries were usually assigned to infantry brigades, and the captain would answer directly to the general commanding the brigade. Later in the war both sides gradually moved away from this system into one where the artillery was organized into independent artillery battalions (Confederates) or brigades (Union), headed by divisional "chiefs of artillery," usually of the rank of colonel, and having three to five individual batteries.

Obviously, with all this variation in command structure, it is impossible to set a precise figure on how many men each battery contained, but on average, a four-gun battery would have about 70 men and 45 horses, while the largest batteries might have more than 170 men and 100 horses. Organization structure within the battery itself was remarkably similar on both sides; a lieutenant "section chief" would command two guns, each individual gun was commanded by a sergeant "chief of the piece," two corporals were the "gunner," in charge of the firing operation, and the "chief of caisson," in charge of supply and reloading operations. Six privates rounded out the individual gun crew, all with very specialized and specific tasks to perform during a firing operation. Other assigned personnel were the first sergeant (sometimes known as the orderly sergeant), who assisted the captain in administrative matters and served as a second-in-command of the battery; a quartermaster sergeant, responsible for the logistics and supply of the battery; drivers, teamsters, and wagoneers of the horse teams, usually privates; an artificer (blacksmith) and farrier (who kept the horses and mules shod); musicians, usually just one or two buglers; a guidon, who carried the battery's colors and was usually the most trusted and reliable man. In the smoke and noise of battle, verbal orders were impossible to properly relay, so the guidon stayed with the commander or at a place of his choosing. The men were trained to always keep an eye on the colors and to go where they went. If they suddenly went flying toward the rear, the prudent thing to do was to follow them, as chances were the commander had called for a sudden retreat. Obviously, if you had a skittish or untrustworthy man carrying the colors, his option to run away could take an entire unit off the field with him.

Because hauling the heavy cannons across rough roads and open fields wore out horses at an alarming rate, the cannoneers usually walked alongside their rig, riding on the horses or caisson only when very rapid movement was necessary. The "flying batter-

ies" attached to the cavalry doubled the number of horses assigned to the battery and tended to use the lighter howitzers so that everyone could habitually ride and keep up with the fast pace.

Infantry

The very heart, soul, and backbone of any army, at least since early medieval times, is the infantry. These are the so-called foot soldiers who carry the battle literally on their shoulders into the face of the enemy. In all periods of history, these men have been unappreciated by the unlearned; suffering under the burden of whatever wacky uniforms their generals had decided were in fashion at the moment; carrying food, shelter, and other comforts in packs or slings as they trudged down one dusty road after another; forever in movement but always at the snail's pace of the route march; sometimes walking down one endless road after another, sometimes even back and forth along the same road for days on end. At other times the lowly infantryman might sit in camp for weeks or even months at a time, only to be hastily summoned by the bugle's insistent call to pack up and move out, sometimes into battle, other times only to sit in yet another camp for days, weeks, or even months.

Whenever you see something blue, shoot at it, and do all you can to keep up the scare.

Lieutenant General Nathan Bedford Forrest, Confederacy, 1864

Most histories of the Civil War ignore these men—and almost all were men, even though there are at least 200 documented cases of women posing as men in order to fight (and at least 400 documented cases of men posing as women so they wouldn't have to)—reserving the prose for those whose names ring with the brassy tone of importance: Lee, Johnston, Grant, Sherman, and so on. However, as essential as the direction of these great generals might have been (and as disastrous as it was in certain other cases—Bragg and Rosecrans spring to mind here), it was the lowly infantryman who did the actual fighting and dying. Sam Watkins, the self-described "high private" from Columbia, Tennessee, wrote after the war about his personal experiences, stating that "the histories are all correct" when they speak only of the high and mighty, but that infantrymen had a different view of the war and that their story needed telling as well.

In the following pages I propose to tell of the fellows who did the shooting and killing, the fortifying and ditching, the sweeping of the streets, the drilling, the standing guard, picket and videt, and who drew (or were to draw) eleven dollars per month and rations, and also drew the ramrod and tore the cartridge.

from *Co. Aytch,* or
A Sideshow of the Big Show

The average infantryman of the war was between 19 and 21 years old (although there are both much younger and much, much older examples), single, and a farmer by trade and had never been as much as 20 miles from his home in his entire life. He was more than likely illiterate or nearly so and deeply religious, yet given to drink and playing cards when the opportunity arose—most would get rid of their cards and "dirty pictures" before battle so that if they were killed, it would not pain their mothers to see such things if and when their personal effects made it back home. The Confederate infantryman was, for the most part, reasonably comfortable living in the field and acceptably accurate with firearms and almost always a volunteer. His Union counterparts tended toward these same desirable traits but had much more of a sprinkling of city boys, foreigners, and draftees among their ranks, along with a higher literacy rate. Despite all the eloquent

speeches and patriotic rhetoric, both most likely joined for the adventure and stayed because they could not desert their friends.

The commonly heard nicknames of the two opponents, Johnny Reb and Billy Yank, seem to have arisen from the common appellations that pickets would holler across the lines to one another, usually in a friendly way in order to set up a trade of some sort. Coffee, the universal infantryman's fuel, was almost completely absent in the South by the third year of the war, as was good Virginia tobacco, that other grunt's vice, in the North, so both sides were eager to trade whenever possible, including during battle.

When the two armies left their home bases in 1861, both were burdened heavily by three things—inexperienced officers; gaudy, impracticable uniforms; and far too much baggage. While many officers on both sides had trained at West Point, the majority had either no military training whatsoever or just a smattering that they had picked up while drilling with their local militias. This did not necessarily mean they were bad officers or poor combat leaders—one prime example is the well-known commander of the 20th Maine Infantry, Colonel Joshua Lawrence Chamberlain. Although completely unschooled in military sciences (he was a professor of "real and found religion" in civilian life), he turned into one of the most outstanding tactical leaders in the Union Army, primarily by reading every book on tactics he could lay his hands on. The real weakness in the officer corps was that, by prewar militia tradition, most field officers (company and regimental commanders) were elected into office by the men they were to lead. While the thought was nice, that men would more likely follow those they trusted well enough to vote for, this, like all other political processes, soon turned into a beauty contest. Some turned into capable leaders, some destroyed their own commands though sheer incompetence, and others muddled along until the forge of combat produced the real leaders.

Uniforms were another early-war burden

on the infantrymen, whose commanders were mightily impressed with the European, and specifically French, methods of making their armies look just divine. One telling example was the adoption by both sides of so-called Zouave units, inspired by a troop of the French Algerian soldiers who had traveled the prewar United States giving displays of their precision marching to standing-room-only crowds. The Zouave uniform consisted of white leggings or gaiters, usually bright red or brilliant blue pantaloons (very baggy, knicker-length pants), white shirts under red or blue Arab-style velvet or wool vests, darker colored shell jackets, usually decorated with brass or gold trim and buttons, sometimes a short blue or red cape, and the whole affair topped off with a fez or turban. These units were noted for their esprit de corps and their drilling abilities, but the gaudy uniforms made them minié-ball magnets on the battlefield (when faced with an indistinct mass of infantry, the tendency is to pick a target out of whatever stands out—a different sounding weapon, a poorly camouflaged position, or a brilliantly dressed Arab in the woods of Tennessee). Most of these units soon abandoned these outfits in favor of more standard uniforms, but a handful wore them throughout the war, most notably Wheat's Tigers out of New Orleans.

In the collection of the Atlanta History Center in Georgia, is a splendid display of the junk sold to soldiers by equally unenlightened (or uncaring) sutlers, including Spanish conquistador–style "armor" breastplates (which could not stop or deflect rifled musket fire), backpacks containing a sort of sling chair that might fit the smallest of all imaginable infantrymen, early sorts of tin helmets, heavy iron pots, and all sorts of smaller ephemera—daguerreotypes of loved ones, fancy stationery sets, elaborate grooming and mustache-trimming sets, and even folding tables and chairs. By the end of the first year of the war, these excesses had, for the most part, been ejected by the side of some dusty road or another or sent home for safekeeping.

The standard infantry uniform in both armies (after all the prewar glamour had faded) was a wool shell or sack coat worn over a three-button white or natural-colored cotton shirt, with wool trousers held up by cotton or leather suspenders, usually with the pants stuffed into the top of tall wool socks, and topped off by either a cowboy-style "slouch" hat or short-brimmed kepi. Shoes were usually pegged-soled "Jefferson" bootees—high-topped brogans made on a straight last, meaning that there was not a distinct right or left shoe. A waist belt fastened with a lead-filled buckle held a cap box on the right front and a bayonet scabbard on the left hip. A cartridge box filled with a standard load of 60 rounds was slung over the left shoulder, resting on the right hip. A canteen and a canvas haversack (sometimes tarred for waterproofing—it contained rations and small personal items) were slung over the right shoulder (resting on the left hip).

The difference in the two armies was reflected in two things—the color of their uniforms and equipment and the way they carried their bedrolls and personal supplies. The Union Army almost universally wore dark blue coats and jackets over sky-blue pants, usually trimmed with brass buttons bearing letters designating their branch of service—"I" for infantry, "A" for artillery, and so on. Their belts and other leather gear were usually black, and most infantrymen carried black-colored canvas or leather knapsacks, with their bedroll tied on top. Their Confederate counterparts wore uniforms that were by regulation "Richmond gray" but that ranged in hue from a gray so dark it was almost black all the way to barely dyed examples that soon turned white in the sun. The late-war usual Confederate (especially in the west) color, "butternut," came from the use of plant dyes that could not truly replicate the designated gray colors and soon turned into shades of light to medium brown. As an unintended consequence, this provided a sort of camouflage for outlying pickets and vedettes. Buttons ranged from brightly polished, state-seal decorated brass, to stolen Union buttons, down to ones made of wood or bone.

Confederate leather gear was by regulation brown in color, although equipment shortages followed by the use of captured Union equipment meant that many men had mixtures of black and brown leather gear. Unlike their Union counterparts, Confederate cartridge boxes rarely had lead-filled plates attached (used both for decoration and to help keep the unfastened flap down while running), almost never had polished brass cartridge breast strap plates attached (again, used mostly for decoration), and the fancy lead-filled, brass waist-belt buckles were replaced in the Western Theater by "Georgia frame" buckles—very similar to today's minimalist belt buckles. Toward the end of the war, shortages in obtaining leather led to the use of painted canvas for belts and straps. Confederate-issue canteens tended toward the thick, round, heavier wooden type, but the Union tin "bullseye" pattern canteens were very popular and were scavenged from the dead on battlefields whenever possible.

Rather than use uncomfortable knapsacks, most Confederate infantrymen placed what little they carried—an extra pair of socks, a "wiper" to clean their weapon, a "housewife" containing sewing supplies, tobacco tin, occasionally a wallet, maybe a small Bible, and a photograph of their loved ones or a letter—inside their single blanket, rolled it up, fastened the ends together with a thick rubber band or piece of rope, and slung it cross-chest over their right shoulder.

Once again, after the noise and fuss of the early war wackiness had settled, weapons on both sides became more-or-less standardized and remarkably similar. The Union adopted the 1861 Springfield rifled musket, .58 caliber, weighing a bit over 9 pounds, with a 39-inch-long barrel, about 56 inches in length overall, and capable of hitting targets well over 500 yards distant. The Confederacy used a wide variety of weapons and calibers throughout the war, but the most prevalent was the imported British 1853 model Enfield

3-band rifled musket, .577 caliber, weighing about 9½ pounds, 55 inches long with a 38-inch barrel, and even more accurate than the Springfield in the right hands. The paper cartridge ammunition used in both weapons was interchangeable, making resupply from captured enemy ammo chests easier. Both weapons used an "angular" bayonet that was triangular in cross-section and 18 inches long—a fearsome-appearing weapon indeed. However, it took a high degree of expertise and discipline to properly use a bayonet in combat. Imagine trying to hold a poorly balanced, 11-pound, 6-foot-long stick with an off-center pointed end (the bayonet attached to the muzzle end of the weapon and was offset from the center of mass about 2 inches so that the weapon could be fired with it attached) and trying to stick it in a moving, similarly equipped, and very highly motivated (to move out of the way) target, while your hands are slick with sweat and shaking with fear and adrenaline. For these reasons, the bayonet was either "lost" by the roadside, along with the equally useless-in-combat huge Bowie and other such knives also carried along on the early fights, or put to use as candleholders, rammed into trees as coathooks, used as spits to roast the evening meal, or heated and bent into hook shapes to drag the dead bodies of their compatriots off the battlefield.

Much has been made of the incredibly high casualty rate during the war—more were killed in the single-day battle of Antietam than in all previous American wars combined (26,134 dead, wounded, and missing, total). Not only had the majority of senior officers on both sides trained together at West Point but they had learned a set of battlefield tactics that were based on the use of smoothbore, relatively inaccurate, and slow-to-reload weapons. In the 1850s a new class of weapon emerged, the rifled-barrel muzzleloader. A series of lands and grooves cut in a spiral fashion down the inside of the barrel "grabbed" the bullet as it was fired and gave it a spinning motion that helped stabilize its flight, much like a football quarterback giving a spin to the ball as he releases it. This simple change not only helped stabilize the round, increasing its accuracy, but also dramatically increased its effective range (again using the football analogy, imagine throwing a football by grabbing one end and pushing it forward—which will most likely result in the ball tumbling wildly and not going very far—just like a ball leaving a smoothbore weapon). On top of this new rifle technology, a new bullet was designed in the 1840s by a French army captain, Claude Minié, that was elongated, with a hollow base, and slightly smaller than the rifle's bore diameter. Thus the bullet could be rammed down the barrel much faster, and the gases from discharge would expand the base, engaging the rifling and giving the bullet a very stable flight. The soft lead bullet (called a minié "ball," in the parlance of the day), weighing 500 grains (about the same as 11 modern copper pennies), tended to "mushroom" when it struck anything solid, depleting the entire kinetic energy of the shot onto the target. For example, this meant that if an infantryman was struck in the shoulder, his arm would most likely be ripped off, or a hit in the leg would shatter the bone into so many irreparable fragments that amputation was the only option.

Through the first months and years of the war, nicely dressed massed lines of battle drawn up 50 to 75 yards from the enemy were the desired formations, as the earlier smoothbore weapons only had an effective range of about 100 yards maximum, and massed firepower was the only reliable way to break up an enemy's line. Using this formation with the modern weapons, with their effective range of six times that of smoothbores, the ability to fire about three times as fast (up to three shots a minute), and the incredible damage the minié ball would do to the human body resulted in an incredibly high casualty count, including large numbers of combat-ineffective wounded. It took far too many casualties from good infantry before the powers that be woke up to the realization that a

new day in combat technology had arisen. Most grunt infantrymen realized this about the time the first shots were fired in the first battle, but officers throughout history have always been about three steps behind the ones they theoretically lead. It was not long before "spades is trumps" was the order of the day, meaning the men dug out trenches and created well-protected firing positions whenever they stopped marching for more than a few minutes.

With all of these tactical changes, battlefield casualties were impressive, even at extreme ranges. Common infantrymen were able to pick off individual targets at ranges of 500 to 600 yards, using just their ordinary issued weapons. Special "sniper" rifles were acquired in both armies and issued either to special riflemen units, mostly in the Union Army, or to one or two of the best shots in a regiment, as was the fashion in the Confederate Army. The most common of these special weapons, the British-made Whitworth, had a heavy barrel and a full-length scope, weighed about 35 pounds, and, in the hands of a trained sharpshooter, could pick off even moving targets at ranges over 1,000 yards. One of the better-known examples of long-range sniping occurred at Spotsylvania, in Virginia, on May 9, 1864. Major General John Sedgewick was walking the ramparts of his redoubts, fully exposed, looking over at the Confederate lines a good 800 yards away, nearly one-half mile. When his men pleaded for their beloved "Uncle John" to get under cover after Confederate sharpshooters had sent several rounds their way, he merely laughed at them, "What? Men dodging this way for single bullets? What will you do when they open fire along the whole line? I am ashamed of you. They couldn't hit an elephant at this distance." About two minutes later came the crack of a Whitworth rifle fired by Sergeant Grace of the 4th Georgia from the distant Confederate trenchline. Sedgewick stiffened and then fell dead, a neat hole about one-half inch under his left eye.

JUMP OFF TO THE NORTH

SHARPSBURG/MONOCACY

With minor exceptions, this tour focuses on Robert E. Lee's 1862 Maryland Campaign and 1863 invasion of the North.

THE BATTLE OF ANTIETAM (SHARPSBURG)

Fought between Major General George B. McClellan's Army of the Potomac and General Robert E. Lee's Army of Northern Virginia on September 17, 1862, the Battle of Antietam was the single bloodiest day of the Civil War. Combined casualties approached 25,000—including some 3,700 dead. The battle was a tactical draw but a strategic victory for the Federals, who forced Lee to abandon his first invasion of the North. By bringing the war to the enemy, Lee had hoped to inspire peace sentiment in the North, rally recruits to his army, and—with luck—crush the Federals in a decisive battle.

Meanwhile, the world watched. A number of European nations, particularly England, relied heavily on Southern cotton, and therefore were following the American Civil War with great interest. Confederate President Jefferson Davis hoped that a convincing Southern victory on Northern soil would bring recognition and support from the South's trading partners overseas. Hoping to take advantage of disorganized Federal leadership in the wake of his victory in the Second Battle of Bull Run (August 29–30, 1862), Lee launched his offensive on September 4. Meanwhile, Lincoln reluctantly replaced Major General John Pope with Major General George B. McClellan—who had been removed from command of the Army of the Potomac earlier

that summer. As meek as ever, McClellan told his wife that he had again been called upon to save the nation. "I only consent to take it for my country's sake and with the humble hope that God has called me to it," the "Young Napoleon" wrote.

Lee advanced to Frederick, Maryland, and dispatched General Thomas J. Jackson west to capture Harpers Ferry. But when the Southern commander discovered that a copy of his plans for the campaign (the famed "Special Orders No. 191") had disappeared (a Union soldier found it, wrapped around three cigars and dropped in a vacated Confederate camp), however, he was suddenly forced to contemplate retreat. Instead, word of Jackson's imminent return (after capturing Harpers Ferry and its entire 12,000-man Federal garrison) convinced him to fight. While Confederate units stalled Federal pursuit in the gaps of South Mountain, the balance of Lee's infantry dug in between Antietam Creek and the town of Sharpsburg.

With a huge advantage in numbers (roughly 75,000 versus 40,000), McClellan should have—with proper coordination and judicious use of his manpower—been able to overwhelm his foe. Instead, he fought with caution and withheld support troops when they were most needed. The battle opened in the early morning fog of September 17, when elements of Union Major General Joseph Hooker's I Corps attacked Lee's left flank, kicking off a morning of inconclusive, bloody back-and-forth struggle through a cornfield and heavy woods. Heavy musketry mowed down soldiers and cornstalks alike—to no apparent end.

Meanwhile, Union General Edwin Sumner launched a poorly coordinated, two-division strike at the Confederate center, taking horri-

Antietam Cemetery Visitor Center NATIONAL PARK SERVICE

ble casualties in the process. As a by-product of that misguided assault, Brigadier General William H. French found himself with some 5,700 Federals opposite a sunken road filled with a bristling line of Southerners under Brigadier General D. H. Hill. Eager to break through and divide Lee's army, French attacked. For some three hours, Hill's division held its ground, as the field before them filled with dead Federals and their own cart-path turned into "Bloody Lane." Lee sent a division to support Hill. Finally, a mix-up in the Rebel line presented the Yankees with an opening: "We pressed on," a New York infantryman later wrote, "until we reached a ditch dug in the road in which the enemy lay in line, and the few who did not surrender did not live to tell the tale of their defeat." Shooting down the exposed Confederates "like sheep in a pen,"[1] the New Yorkers finally opened a gap in the Rebel lines. But neither Sumner nor McClellan chose to follow up, and the hole quickly closed.

On the Union left, meanwhile, Ninth Corps Yankees under Major General Ambrose Burnside—the round-faced Rhode Islander whose side-whiskers would inspire the term "sideburns"—had been fighting since 10:00 a.m. to get across a narrow stone bridge to assail the Confederate right. Shortly after noon, McClellan—looking to break the stalemate on his right—passed word through Burnside that the bridge had to be carried at all costs. Brigadier General Samuel Sturgis assigned the job to a regiment of Pennsylvanians and one of New Yorkers, and later described the action that followed:

They started on their mission of death full of enthusiasm, and, taking a route less exposed than the regiments (Second Maryland and Sixth New Hamp-

---

[1] Thomas B. Buell, *The Warrior Generals: Combat Leadership in the Civil War* (New York: Three Rivers Press, 1997), 119–120.

shire) which had made the effort before them, rushed at a double-quick over the slope leading to the bridge and over the bridge itself, with an impetuosity which the enemy could not resist; and the Stars and Stripes were planted on the opposite bank at 1 o'clock P. M., amid the most enthusiastic cheering from every part of the field from where they could be seen.[2]

Having finally reached enemy ground, Burnside's offensive lost its momentum as the Federals waited for ammunition to come up. By the time the blue lines reached the outskirts of Sharpsburg at around 3:30 p.m., Major General A. P. Hill's 3,300 Confederates—arriving from Harpers Ferry—had reached the field to slow them. Here McClellan might have supported Burnside with reinforcements and won the day. But he did not, and the Federals paid the price. Burnside withdrew his corps back across the creek; exhaustion and the approach of dusk prevented further fighting.

Few Civil War battles matched the fight at Sharpsburg for sheer viciousness. Even Clara Barton, who would later found the American Red Cross and who had seen her share of casualties, spoke with horror as she tended to the battle's wounded: "War is a dreadful thing. Oh, my God, can't this civil strife be brought to an end."

What might have—and should have— been a smashing Union victory ended instead in stalemate. While sickened Sharpsburg residents and soldiers began burying the dead, George McClellan sent only a small force in pursuit of General Lee's retreating army. The Federals reached Blackford's (or Boteler's) Ford—east of Shepherdstown—on the morning of the 19th, hours after Lee's tired troops had crossed. After a day of skirmishing, Union Major General Fitz John Porter's Bluecoats

drove off General William Pendleton's small covering force. This inconsequential Federal pursuit ended, however, when A. P. Hill's Rebel division counterattacked the next day. McClellan's fate as an army commander was sealed; he hung on to his command until November, when President Lincoln relieved him in favor of Ambrose Burnside.

While Lincoln was unsatisfied with the battle's result, Lee had been forced to retreat south and yield the battlefield to the Union— just enough positive news to compel the president to issue his Emancipation Proclamation. Scheduled to take effect on January 1, 1863, the proclamation added a moral impetus to the political struggle and spurred the recruitment of black soldiers for the first time. The roughly 180,000 black fighting men that subsequently joined Union forces gave Lincoln—and his generals—a powerful boost against Confederate armies shrinking by the day. Lincoln would later call the Emancipation Proclamation "the central act of my administration, and the greatest event of the nineteenth century."

THE BATTLE OF MONOCACY

Little known or understood, the July 9, 1864, Battle of Monocacy bought precious time for the defenders of Washington, D.C., who were squarely in the sights of Confederate General Jubal Early.

On June 18, Early bested Union General David Hunter's Federals at Lynchburg, ending Hunter's scorching drive through the upper Shenandoah Valley and sending him scampering into West Virginia. Jumping at the chance for an offensive, Early gathered some 14,000 Confederate troops and marched north, reaching Winchester on July 2. By now, Early had gotten the belated attention of the War Department and the eye of General Lew Wallace. Another of the Union's political generals, Wallace had shown flashes of potential early in the war before slipping up while commanding a division at Shiloh. Banished to the Union's little-known Middle Department, Wal-

[2] Robert U. Johnson, *Battles and Leaders of the Civil War Vol. 2: Struggle Intensifies* (Book Sales, reprinted 2000), 652.

lace was operating out of Baltimore when Early approached. Hoping to at least slow Early's advance, Wallace raced west and deployed his tiny force of some 2,300 men in a strong position behind the Monocacy River, southeast of Frederick. The timely arrival of James Ricketts' division of the VI Corps—which Ulysses S. Grant had sent north from Petersburg—still left Wallace with, at most, 5,800 troops, and outnumbered three-to-one.

On the morning of July 9, Early's small army pushed through Frederick to find Wallace's thin line of Federals. Early launched a total of five assaults at the Union position before Wallace pulled his men back toward Baltimore. Early's quick victory, however, cost him a full day—a precious twenty-four hours that brought Grant's XIX Corps reinforcements closer to the capital. He reached the northern outskirts of Washington's defensive ring on July 11, just ahead of the returning Federal VI Corps, which began filling the all-but-empty trenches around Fort Stevens.

In hindsight it seems unlikely that Early could have fought his way into Washington, even without the presence of Grant's reinforcements. But Wallace—and many others—believed his men had saved the capital. Even Grant, whose criticism of Wallace's performance at Shiloh had all but ruined his subordinate's career, tossed Wallace a few accolades in his *Memoirs*, which were published shortly after his July 1885 death. Regarding Early's withdrawal from Washington's doorstep, Grant offered:

There is no telling how much this result was contributed to by General Lew Wallace's leading what might well be considered a forlorn hope. If Early had been but one day earlier he might have entered the capital before the arrival of the reinforcements I had sent. Whether the delay caused by the battle amounted to a day or not, General Wallace contributed on this occasion, by the defeat of the troops under him a greater bene-

fit to the cause than often falls to the lot of a commander of an equal force to render by means of a victory.[3]

For Wallace—who in the years following the Civil War would write the best-selling novel *Ben Hur,* negotiate with an outlaw named Billy the Kid (both while Governor of New Mexico Territory), and serve as U.S. consul to Turkey—such praise must have been highly satisfying.

BALL'S BLUFF BATTLEFIELD AND NATIONAL CEMETERY

The Battle of Ball's Bluff might have been dismissed as just one more of the Union's early-war beatings if it had not claimed the life of U.S. Senator—and longtime friend of President Abraham Lincoln—Edward D. Baker.

For the men in blue, the battle was especially ugly. Since the Confederate victory at Bull Run on July 21, there had been little movement in the east. Small bodies of Union and Confederate troops watched each other from their posts on either side of the Potomac River. In October, General George B. McClellan—then hard at work assembling the Army of the Potomac—suggested that Brigadier General Charles P. Stone undertake to dislodge Confederates posted at Leesburg, just west of the river. In the early-morning darkness of October 21, Stone sent three brigades (one under the command of Oregon Senator Edward Baker) across the Potomac and up a muddy rise at a roughly equal force of Rebels under Brigadier General Shanks Evans.

Supporting units entered the fray after sporadic opening shots, and the two sides exchanged fire into the afternoon. At about 4:00 p.m. a sharpshooter's bullet ended Baker's life; soon after, the Federal lines bent then broke, and panicked soldiers stumbled and slid back down Ball's Bluff. Rebel pursuers

---

[3] Ulysses S. Grant, *Personal Memoirs of U.S. Grant,* Volume 2 (Northridge, CA: Aegypan, 2006), 160.

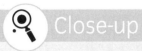

Oliver Wendell Holmes Jr.

After the September 1862 Battle of Antietam, two Hagerstown residents—Mrs. Howard Kennedy and her daughter Annie—came across a Union officer bleeding from a neck wound and in search of the train station. The young captain was Oliver Wendell Holmes of the 20th Massachusetts, the son of the Boston poet. While the women cared for the man at their home, the senior Mr. Holmes set out to find him; his search later inspired "My Hunt After the Captain," an account of his journey written for *Atlantic Monthly*. The younger Holmes eventually healed enough to take a train to Harrisburg, where he found his anxious father waiting.

Captain Holmes survived the war, graduated from Harvard Law School, and served on the United States Supreme Court from 1902–1932. In an 1895 address at his alma mater, Holmes spoke for thousands of Civil War veterans when he said: "War, when you are at it, is horrible and dull."[4] The Kennedy home in which he once convalesced still stands on West Washington Street.

[4] David S. Heidler, and T. Jeanne, Editors, *Encyclopedia of the American Civil War: A Political, Social, and Military History* (New York: W. W. Norton, 2000), 988.

wounded scores of foundering Yankees as they tried to ford the river. Hundreds of other Federals were captured. The battle changed nothing. Evans lost 33 Confederates killed and another 116 wounded or missing. Stone's brigades were practically halved, with 49 Yankees killed, 158 wounded (including Oliver Wendell Holmes Jr.) and more than 700 captured or missing.

Slightly Out of the Way: Shepherdstown, West Virginia

Once known as Mecklenburg, this West Virginia (formerly Virginia) town lent its name to the two-day clash that occurred just to its east, along the Potomac River, on September 19–20, 1862. Wounded victims of the Battle of Shepherdstown and its massive predecessor filled virtually every building in the area. At least 100 Confederates killed outside of Shepherdstown were buried in Elwood Ceme-

tery, where some 300 Southerners—including Stonewall Jackson's aide, Henry Kyd Douglas—now lay.

Today, visitors can walk through the cemetery as part of a day spent in town, which has been named a Historic District in the National Register of Historic Places. Shepherdstown is also the home of the **George Tyler Moore Center for the Study of the Civil War.** Founded in 1993, the center is now located on German Street in the **Conrad Shindler House,** one of countless town buildings that served as makeshift hospitals following the Battle of Antietam. The house was purchased by actress Mary Tyler Moore and donated to then-Shepherd College in 1996, as a tribute to her father George Tyler Moore, a Civil War enthusiast. For information on the center and its programs, call 304-876-5429.

History enthusiasts will also want to visit the **Historic Shepherdstown Museum,** at the corner of Princess and East German Streets.

Set in the restored **Entler Hotel,** a two-story brick holdover from the Civil War era, the museum boasts several rooms, a re-creation of a Victorian sitting room, a 1905 mail wagon, and a number of American Indian and Civil War artifacts and exhibits, among other items. The museum is open April through October, 11:00 a.m. to 5:00 p.m. Saturday and 1:00 to 4:00 p.m. Sunday. Admission is free. Further information about the museum and historic downtown Shepherdstown can be found at www.historicshepherdstown.com.

Historic Sites

Antietam National Battlefield
5831 Dunker Church Road
Sharpsburg
(301) 432-5124
www.nps.gov/anti
Today, the serene landscape of Antietam National Battlefield looks much as it did when the battle began. In recent years, the park has reacquired about 2,000 acres of the battle-field's original countryside, reforested its west and north woods, added some 8,000 feet of historically accurate fencing, and refurbished several of the park's original structures. In addition to 2 ½ miles of new park trails and a renovated visitor's center and museum, the park is now also home to the Pry House Field Hospital Museum, an extension of the National Museum of Civil War Medicine, in Frederick. General McClellan made the house the headquarters of his Union forces, which was visited by Abraham Lincoln two weeks after the battle. The park is open 8:30 a.m. to 6:00 p.m. daily (5:00 p.m. during winter months), and closed on Thanksgiving, Christmas, and New Year's Day. A three-day pass for adults costs just $4 per person or $6 per family; facilities are wheelchair accessible. Located off Route 65, the park is easily accessible from any direction.

Antietam National Cemetery
Antietam National Battlefield
5831 Dunker Church Road
Sharpsburg

Antietam National Cemetery Entrance NATIONAL PARK SERVICE

JUMP OFF TO THE NORTH

(301) 432-5124
www.nps.gov/anti
The final resting place for 4,776 Union soldiers who were killed in the battles of Antietam, Monocacy, and in other nearby conflicts, Antietam National Cemetery is now one of the 130 cemeteries that make up the National Cemetery System. At the center of the cemetery stands a 44-foot, 7-inch granite statue of a Union infantryman, facing homeward to the north to commemorate the fallen soldiers.

Ball's Bluff Battlefield and National Cemetery
Route 15 at Battlefield Parkway
Leesburg, VA
(703) 779-9372
www.nps.gov/nr/travel/journey/bnc.htm
Although Ball's Bluff is located in Virginia, it's just a quick drive down Route 15 from Frederick. Surrounded—much like Manassas Battlefield—by the trappings of the modern world (one must drive through a residential development to reach it), Ball's Bluff Battlefield and National Cemetery is nevertheless nicely tucked away in dense woods. A ¾-mile walking path takes visitors from the parking lot to the edge of the steep bluff down which Union troops fled at battle's end. Aside from the steep hill itself, the highlight of the battlefield is its National Cemetery, a neatly groomed, walled-in burial site containing twenty-five graves representing fifty-four of the battle's victims. Only one of these men—James Allen of the 15th Massachusetts—has been identified. Admission is free.

Barbara Fritchie House and Museum
154 West Patrick Street
Frederick, MD
(301) 698-8992
Barbara Fritchie was immortalized in a John Greenleaf Whittier poem as the woman who challenged Confederate troops in the streets of Frederick: "Shoot if you must, this old gray head," Fritchie reportedly shouted from an upstairs window, "but spare your country's flag." This reconstruction of Fritchie's original

house is open for tours by appointment.

The Kennedy Farmhouse (John Brown's Headquarters)
2406 Chestnut Grove Road
Sharpsburg
(202) 537-8900 (tour information)
www.johnbrown.org
Located just 6 miles from Harpers Ferry, this small farm proved to be just what John Brown needed when he went house hunting in 1859. Under the alias "Isaac Smith," Brown lived here with his followers as they prepared for their 1859 campaign to free slaves. With the help of federal funds and private donations, co-owner South Lynn spent some twenty painstaking years restoring the old farmhouse to its original appearance. Despite the historic significance of the building, which has been declared a National Historic Landmark, its maintenance and operation (still looked over by Mr. Lynn) depends on public support.

Landon House/Maryland Museum of Civil War History
3401 Urbana Pike
Urbana, MD
(301) 874-3914
www.marylandmuseum.org
Landon House was the site of General J. E. B. Stuart's Sabers and Roses Ball, held September 8, 1862, before serving as a field hospital. Modern-day Civil War enthusiasts now know the site, located just outside of Frederick, as the Maryland Museum of Civil War History. The Maryland Museum boasts exhibits that focus on the role that the border state played during the war, plus live performances, costumed interpreters, and ghost walks and "Sabers and Roses" shows every Friday night, beginning at 8:30 p.m. Tickets for tours and shows are $10; a combination ticket costs $15.

Monocacy National Battlefield
4801 Urbana Pike
Frederick, MD
(301) 662-3515
www.nps.gov/mono

General Lew Wallace LIBRARY OF CONGRESS

The Monocacy National Battlefield Park opened a new 7,000-square-foot visitor center in 2007, transforming the occasionally overlooked park into a compelling experience for Civil War enthusiasts who want to explore the "battle that saved Washington." In addition to the new exhibits and electronic maps, the park also opened four new walking trails, making acres of the historic grounds more accessible to the public. A self-guided driving tour follows the events of July 9, 1864. Admission is free. It's open daily 8:30 a.m. to 4:30 p.m. Labor Day through Memorial Day; till 5:00 p.m. during the summer.

Mount Olivet Cemetery
515 South Market Street
Frederick, MD
(301) 662-1164
www.mountolivetcemeteryinc.com
Francis Scott Key, Barbara Fritchie, Maryland's first governor, Thomas Johnson, and some 800 Union and Confederate soldiers lie in Mount Olivet Cemetery, which is open from dawn to dusk daily.

National Museum of Civil War Medicine
48 East Patrick Street
Frederick, MD
(301) 695-1864
www.civilwarmed.org
The vastness of Civil War battlefields and the study of regiments, corps, and flanking movements can easily make one forget about war's human cost. For that reason alone, the National Museum of Civil War Medicine is one of those places that everyone—not just Civil War enthusiasts—should visit. The museum, which opened in 1996, filled a huge void in the field, and has since added a satellite building (the Pry House Field Hospital Museum) on the Antietam Battlefield.

The museum completed a $3-million renovation in 2003, including a complete redesign of its exhibits and the addition of a new one. Installed in 7,000 square feet of space on two floors are lifelike displays that tell the story of Civil War medicine. Boasting an unmatched collection of medical artifacts, they cover the role of the surgeon, from his own sparse training through the examination of recruits (usually superficial); the dangers of camp life (an exhibit that contains the war's only known surviving surgeon's tent); field-dressing and battlefield care; nursing; and a new exhibit on the embalming of the dead.

The National Museum of Civil War Medicine is wheelchair accessible; admission is $6.50 for adults and $4.50 for children. It also offers group tours, which take about ninety minutes and should be arranged in advance. The museum (which also boasts a research room and a one-of-a-kind gift shop) is open (except for New Year's Day, Easter, Thanksgiving, and December 24–25) Monday through Saturday 10:00 a.m. to 5:00 p.m. and Sunday 11:00 a.m. to 5:00 p.m.

Rose Hill Cemetery
(301) 739-3630
600 South Potomac Street
Hagerstown, MD
In the decade that followed the Civil War, some 2,000 Confederate soldiers killed at Antietam or South Mountain were reinterred here. Only 346 of the men were ever identified.

South Mountain State Battlefield
6620 Zittlestown Road
Middletown, MD
(301) 432-8065
www.dnr.state.md.us
Part of the South Mountain Recreation area, the site of the September 14, 1862, Battle of South Mountain is now maintained and operated by the nonprofit group Friends of South Mountain State Battlefield. Only the key sections of the park—Turner's Gap, Fox's Gap, and Crampton's Gap—currently feature roadside markers, interpretive signage, or monuments. But with some financial assistance, the group hopes to add museums at the north and south ends of the battlefield.

Accommodations

Hill House Bed & Breakfast
12 West Third Street
Frederick, MD
(301) 682-4111
www.bbonline.com/md/hillhouse/index.html
This circa-1870 restored Victorian town house is a great place to stay if you're looking for easy access to downtown Frederick's antiques shops and historical sites. The impeccably restored inn boasts four guest rooms furnished with original art, antiques, and period accents like four-poster and canopy beds. Guests also enjoy private bathrooms and a full southern Maryland breakfast each morning. $105-$150

Hollerstown Hill
4 Clarke Place
Frederick, MD
www.hollerstownhill.com
Staying at Hollerstown Hill is much like staying in a dollhouse. Tucked away in a quiet Frederick neighborhood, the circa-1900 Victorian even boasts its own collection of antique dolls, tastefully displayed around the house in the company of other period antiques. There are four large guest rooms, each with wireless Internet, private bath, and one with its own private porch. After a busy day of sightseeing, you can wage battles of your own in a game room stocked with board games, a pool table, and even a Civil War chess set. $115-$125

The Inn at Antietam Bed and Breakfast
220 East Main Street
Sharpsburg
(301) 432-6601
www.innatantietam.com
Few people get the chance to sleep in such comfort on a Civil War battle site, especially one as important as Antietam National Battlefield. But that's just what the Inn at Antietam Bed and Breakfast offers in five distinct suites that range in price and degree of luxury. Each suite features central air-conditioning, private baths, and old-time comfort. Others (such as the General Burnside Smokehouse Suite) also

offer a fireplace, wet bar, and TV/VCR. Common areas include a small library, a parlor (with a baby grand piano), a solarium, and a wraparound porch from which residents can take in the area's unmatched scenery. $120-$185

Inn at Buckeystown
3521 and 3619 Buckeystown Pike
Buckeystown, MD
(301) 874-5755
www.innatbuckeystown.com
Just south of Monocacy, this award-winning inn offers a central location from which to explore Antietam, Frederick, Harpers Ferry, and northern Virginia. Built in 1897, the historic mansion was converted to a luxurious five-bedroom guesthouse in 1981. In the rooms, you'll find sparkling chandeliers (and even working fireplaces in three of the rooms), plus glorious gardens and a wraparound porch that's perfect for savoring a glass of wine (it's strictly bring-your-own-bottle, so be sure to stop by a local winery on your way). For a late afternoon pick-me-up, the inn also offers a delightful high tea service. $115-$275

Jacob Rohrbach Inn
138 West Main Street
Sharpsburg
(301) 432-5079
(877) 839-4242
www.jacob-rohrbach-inn.com
The Jacob Rohrbach Inn is a historical treasure, built more than fifty years before the outbreak of the Civil War. The five-bedroom inn lies within walking distance of the battlefield park and even stocks bicycles for guests who wish to explore the park on two wheels. Before you set out for the day, feast on a delicious multicourse breakfast, prepared with herbs and produce grown on the property. Although the house itself is more than 200 years old, it boasts a full suite of modern amenities like wireless Internet and cable TV, and owners Joanne and Paul Breitenbach are eager to assist with historical information, along with recommendations for sightseeing

and entertainment. Children 10 and up are welcome. $104-$185

Thomas Shepherd Bed and Breakfast
Corner of Duke and German Streets
Shepherdstown, WV
(888) 889-8952
www.thomasshepherdinn.com
Those who take the quick 4-mile drive from Sharpsburg to Shepherdstown will find comfortable accommodations at the Thomas Shepherd Inn, which happens to be the only bed-and-breakfast in town. Built in 1868, the Federal-style inn is one of the few buildings in town that was not used as a hospital following the Battle of Antietam.

Located at the end of Shepherdstown's main thoroughfare, the Thomas Shepherd Inn offers convenience (within walking distance of everything in town, and driving distance of Harpers Ferry, etc.), comfort (six delightful, air-conditioned rooms, private baths), friendly service (homemade breakfast served each morning, etc.), and—considering that owners Jim Ford and Jeanne Muir have Shepherdstown's B&B market cornered—surprisingly reasonable prices. $115-$175

Restaurants

Blue Moon Café
Corner of Princess and High Streets
Shepherdstown, WV
(304) 876-1920
www.bluemoonshepherdstown.com
The Blue Moon menu boasts just about every American staple one can imagine, including gourmet pizzas, fine dinners, hearty sandwiches and salads, and vegetarian meals. You'll take a trip around the globe just by perusing the menu: vegan chick pea curry is listed on the same page as "Jessie's Meato Escondido," a roast beef sandwich topped with feta cheese, fresh spinach, onions, and cucumbers, served on ciabatta bread slathered with herbed cream cheese. The casual environment is just as diverse, with seating in three different dining rooms and outside along the water. It's open Monday through Thursday 11:00 a.m. to

9:00 p.m., and Friday and Saturday 9:00 a.m. to 10:00 p.m., and for breakfast and lunch Sunday 9:00 a.m. to 4:00 p.m. Average dinner entrée price: $10-$15.

Cacique
26 North Market Street
Frederick, MD
(301) 695-2756
www.caciquefrederick.com
You might not think that Frederick would be a hot bed for haute cuisine, but the town has practically become a suburb of Washington, D.C., and it's attracted its share of residents with sophisticated palates. At Cacique, Spanish and Mexican cuisine sit side by side—a cultural faux pas, perhaps, but diners give a thumb's up to Spanish dishes like paella or mussels prepared in Andalucian fashion as well as traditional Mexican cuisine. Cacique is open daily for lunch and dinner. Average dinner entrée price: $15-$20.

Captain Bender's Tavern
111 East Main Street
Sharpsburg
www.captainbenders.com
Captain Bender's is a great local gathering place. It's named for Raleigh Bender, a boatsman on the C&O Canal in the nineteenth century, who also managed a tavern on the site of his modern-day namesake. You can always count on a cold beer, a thick burger, or a generous salad, plus an assortment of panini and pizzas. The restaurant even appeals to heartier appetites with the "death dog," a foot-long hot dog topped with chili, cheese, diced onion, and sour cream. It's open daily for lunch and dinner. Average dinner entrée price: $10-$15.

The Cozy Restaurant
103 Frederick Road
Thurmont, MD
(301) 271-4301
(301) 271-7373
www.cozyvillage.com
Part of the historic Cozy Inn, the Cozy Restaurant is the oldest family-owned restaurant in

Maryland, established in 1929. It's a good choice for groups, specializing in fine American dining in its eleven, uniquely styled rooms, in addition to lavish buffet dinners and fantastic baskets of food to go. There's also a pub serving traditional bar food and Willy's Beer, prepared especially for the inn. It's just a few short miles from the famous presidential retreat at Camp David, and there's a museum on-site stocked with gifts from members of the press and visiting dignitaries. It's open for lunch and dinner weekdays and for breakfast, lunch, and dinner on weekends. Average dinner entrée price: $15-$20.

Jennifer's
207 West Patrick Street
Frederick, MD
(301) 662-0373

There's something friendly and inviting about this Frederick pub, a mainstay for more than two decades. A popular draw for locals, Jennifer's décor is cozy and inviting; exposed brick walls, a large oak bar, and even a fireplace. For lunch, sample salads, sandwiches, or pizza, while dinner brings tasty creations like hot and crunchy chicken with honey-pecan butter or lamb chops. The restaurant also offers a spa menu for light eaters. It's open Monday through Saturday for lunch and dinner and Sunday for dinner. Average dinner entrée price: $10-$15.

Monocacy Crossing
4424A Urbana Pike
Frederick, MD
(301) 846-4204

If you feel like dining off the beaten path, you won't be disappointed with Monocacy Crossing. One of Frederick's top-rated restaurants, it delivers with fantastic food, attentive service, a well-thought-out wine list, and a gorgeous setting. Seafood creations like steamed mussels and clam chowder are fresh and perfectly seasoned, or sample the season's bounty with creations like the Eggplant Napoleon, with layers of fried slices of eggplant, roasted peppers, zucchini, and mushrooms, topped with marinara sauce. On a pleasant day, sit on the outdoor patio to dine al fresco. Average dinner entrée price: $20-$25.

The Tasting Room
101 North Market Street
Frederick, MD
(240) 379-7772
www.tastetr.com

As Frederick's first wine bar, The Tasting Room touts the most extensive, diverse wine list in Frederick—and in most of the D.C. exurbs—along with chic décor that's clearly designed with the young professional set in mind. Located on the corner of Church and Market Streets in downtown Frederick's restaurant district, the stylish restaurant and its patrons look like they'd feel right at home in Manhattan. (Even if you don't dine here, you can peer inside through its floor-to-ceiling windows.) Cosmopolitan flavors also take center stage on the menu prepared by chef and owner Michael Tauraso. Select from starters like Greek lamb, bruschetta, or tuna crudo with sesame-lime dressing, then go for a sophisticated entrée like the Kobe-style Berkshire pork loin, crusted with a blend of coriander and pepper, or local rockfish. Average dinner entrée price: $25-$30.

INTO THE VALLEY

HARPERS FERRY/ WINCHESTER

This tour focuses on Harpers Ferry, West Virginia, and Winchester, Virginia, two key transportation hubs over which Union and Confederate forces clashed throughout the war.

HARPERS FERRY

"Harpers Ferry," Indiana Corporal Edmund Brown wrote after the war, "was a fitting place to begin an advance against the rebellion."[1]

There was no doubting the area's strategic importance, located as it was on the Baltimore and Ohio Railroad line at the gateway to the vital Shenandoah Valley—a natural north-south invasion route packed with forage for man and beast. It was a town worth fighting for, even after Confederate soldiers burned its Federal arsenal and armory and dragged off its valuable gun-making machinery early in the Civil War. The town would change hands at least eight times before Major General Philip Sheridan finally secured it for the Union in 1864. By then, its once-vital armory was a blackened brick shell of its former self—almost, but not quite, lost to history.

Until October 1859, this small town located at the confluence of the Shenandoah and Potomac Rivers was known simply as the home of the historic, old arsenal, and for the stunning natural beauty that surrounded it. By then, "the Hole," as the site was first known, had its first European residents and its namesake business—a ferry service across the Potomac operated by Philadelphian Robert

Harper. Authorized by President George Washington, the Harpers Ferry Arsenal opened in 1801, joining the U.S. Armory at Springfield, Massachusetts, in producing arms for the young American military. In sixty years of production, Harpers Ferry machinery turned out some 600,000 guns—including the Model 1803 flintlock and the Model 1841 percussion rifle, the nation's first. Meanwhile, sectionalism and the slavery issue tore at the United States until a grim, old westerner marched east to transform a town and a nation.

A cold mist swirled through Harpers Ferry in the evening darkness of October 16, 1859. Outside the brick buildings of the U.S. Armory, a lone sentry named Daniel Whelan paced, unaware that revolution was unfolding in the flickering blackness around him.

In the blink of an eye, it seemed, a motley group of armed men had surrounded the startled Whelan, taken him prisoner, and forced their way into the Federal compound he guarded. Whelan listened in stunned silence as the grey-bearded leader of his assailants stepped forward and announced his presence before his god.

"I come here from Kansas," John Brown declared, "and this is a slave state; I have possession of the United States armory, and if the citizens interfere with me, I must only burn the town and have blood."

Thus began Kansas abolitionist John Brown's first step in his mission to free America's slaves. Harpers Ferry would thenceforth forever be linked—depending on one's viewpoint—with violent abolitionist extremism or with the American slave's fight for freedom.

Brown's long-planned assault on slavery was doomed almost from the start. Leading an invasion force of just twenty-one men, Brown had pinned his hopes for reinforce-

---

[1] Time-Life Books, *Voices of the Civil War: Shenandoah, 1862,* (Alexandria, VA: Time-Life Books, 1997), 29.

---

ment on slaves and free blacks in the area. His raid was to be the spark that ignited a massive slave rebellion and brought about the end of the "peculiar institution." Having armed his new recruits from his own arms stores, Brown would lead them into surrounding hills to begin a guerilla war.

None of this would happen, a fact that grizzled old "Osawatomie Brown" may have recognized after two of his minions shot and mortally wounded Shephard Hayward—a free black employed by the Baltimore and Ohio Railroad. Hayward, who, out of curiosity, had stepped off a B&O train as it stopped on the edge of town, was shot in the back as he tried to avoid two armed strangers in the early-morning darkness of October 17.

Very little else went right for Brown's "Army of Liberation." Men dispatched to spread word of the operation and recruit volunteers returned with just a handful of mostly reluctant and confused slaves and their masters, now Brown's prisoners. The sun slowly rose as Brown waited in vain for the legions of black volunteers to appear, and as word of the raid spread. By early morning, hundreds of irate Virginians had converged on the village, guns in hand, eager to deal with the hated abolitionist invaders. Gunfire erupted; three locals fell dead, along with eight of Brown's men. Brown—now more or less trapped in the arsenal's engine room—tried unsuccessfully to negotiate for passage out of town in exchange for his hostages. No one was listening.

At dawn on October 18, Lieutenant J. E. B. Stuart delivered to Brown a surrender request from his superior, Colonel Robert E. Lee, who had reached the site during the night with a contingent of U.S. Marines. Brown refused; marines subsequently rushed the engine house, knocked down its doors, and captured what was left of Brown's army. A handful of marines were wounded during the struggle, as was the elder Brown. One of Brown's sons was dead; a second was mortally wounded.

In a November 23 letter to a Reverend McFarland, Brown wrote:

Christ told me to remember them that were in bonds as bound with them, to do towards them as I would wish them to do towards me in similar circumstances. My conscience bade me do that. I tried to do it, but failed. Therefore I have no regret on that score. I have no sorrow either as to the result, only for my poor wife and children. They have suffered much, and it is hard to leave them uncared for. But God will be a husband to the widow and a father to the fatherless.[2]

After a whirlwind trial through which the injured defendant remained prone on a cot, Brown was convicted of treason and murder, and was sentenced to hang.

On December 2, 1859, John Brown rode to his death sitting atop his own coffin in the back of a wagon. A brand new gallows—surrounded by 800 armed men, reporters, and curious eyewitnesses—awaited him. Without fear or apprehension, Brown mounted the gallows, and, a few minutes later, dropped to his death.

The approach of the Civil War magnified Harpers Ferry's importance—and its vulnerability. Dominated by high ground on three sides, it was practically indefensible.

On April 17, 1861—just three days into the war—an approaching force of Virginia militia and volunteers compelled Lieutenant Roger Jones to set the armory afire and evacuate his tiny Federal garrison. Southern troops arrived too late to claim some 15,000 rifles from the flames, but they managed to save the machinery that turned the guns out. This they shipped to Richmond, where it was soon put to use arming Confederates.

Harpers Ferry was back in Federal hands in September 1862, when Confederate General Robert E. Lee launched his first invasion of the North. Looking to open a supply route

[2] John Brown and Frank B. Sanborn, *The Life And Letters Of John Brown, Liberator Of Kansas And Martyr Of Virginia*, (Whitefish, MT: Kessinger Publishing, LLC), 2007.

Harpers Ferry NATIONAL PARK SERVICE

through the Shenandoah Valley, Lee sent Stonewall Jackson west to remove the one impediment to his plan—a Yankee garrison at Harpers Ferry, now 12,500 men strong. Charged with holding the town to the last extremity was fifty-eight-year-old Union Colonel Dixon Miles, a gray-bearded, elderly looking, army lifer whom events would soon prove had been caught in the wrong place at the wrong time.

Jackson—who had spent the summer defeating Union armies throughout the Shenandoah Valley—sent one column under General John Walker to take Loudoun Heights, and another under General Lafayette McLaws to deal with Federal defenders on Maryland Heights. Jackson would complete the encirclement by occupying Bolivar Heights, in the arsenal's rear.

The issue was only briefly in doubt. Walker quickly accomplished his task. McLaws's Confederates somehow managed to haul cannon and ammunition up Maryland Heights, where, on the morning of September 14, they faced off against Colonel Thomas Ford's 1,600 Bluecoats. Ford's artillerists held their own against McLaws's gunners, but his green infantry—many of whom had not yet mastered even the basics of soldiering—soon broke before the hardened Rebels. The shaken Union soldiers raced back over the Potomac and into town, ceding the heights—and, unwittingly, victory—to Jackson.

Jackson's forces opened fire and quickly forced a Union surrender. Some 1,300 Union cavalrymen managed to escape the trap, but Jackson captured everyone and everything else, including 13,000 rifles and 70 cannon. Jackson's hard-driving foot soldiers impressed their captives: "They were silent as ghosts," one Yankee recalled, "ruthless and rushing in their speed; ragged, earth colored, disheveled and devilish, as tho' they were keen on the scent of the hot blood that was already streaming up from the opening struggle at Antietam, and thirsting for it."[3]

---

[3] Gerald Linderman, *Embattled Courage: The Experience of Combat in the American Civil War* (New York: Free Press, 1989), 66.

The town changed hands several times prior to the summer of 1864, when Union Major General Philip Sheridan finally secured the Shenandoah Valley for the Union. But by then the once-prized arsenal and armory was little more than burned-out brick and mortar, valueless, save for posterity.

WINCHESTER, VA

For the residents of Winchester, Virginia, any day that passed without the rattle of muskets or the thundering hoofbeats of passing cavalry was a gift. Laid out at the northern end of the Shenandoah Valley, it stood in the way of Union and Confederate armies traveling up or down the Valley Pike, or rumbling off on one of the several other roadways that passed through town. It was also home to a Baltimore and Ohio Railroad terminal. Due to its importance as a transportation hub, this small town of 4,500 changed hands more than seventy times in four years of war, and witnessed three significant Civil War battles. It was the seat of hearty Confederate support, especially after Stonewall Jackson made the town the headquarters of his Shenandoah Valley District in November 1861.

In the spring of 1862, George McClellan's Army of the Potomac trudged slowly up the Virginia Peninsula, moving inexorably toward the Confederate capital of Richmond. While Albert Sidney Johnston then Robert E. Lee dealt with McClellan, Stonewall Jackson was left to prevent Union forces in the Shenandoah Valley from slipping west to reinforce the Yankee commander. After chasing John C. Fremont out of the valley, Jackson moved north in pursuit of Nathaniel Banks's Union army. On May 23, Jackson's men overran a small Federal force at Front Royal; two days later, Jackson assaulted Banks's army in the hills south of Winchester. Withstanding fierce resistance and devastating Federal artillery fire, Jackson sent Banks's army retreating through the town and north across the Potomac.

Even worse results befell Union Major General Robert H. Milroy a year later, during Lee's second invasion of the North. Dismissing reports of Lee's rapid advance, Milroy waited until his garrison at Winchester was almost completely encircled. By the time he ordered a withdrawal, Richard Ewell's Corps was on hand to cut off his retreat and sweep up prisoners.

Confederate forces in the Shenandoah Valley continued to plague the Union until August 1864, when Lieutenant General Ulysses S. Grant—now in overall command of Union armies—sent Major General Philip Sheridan to eliminate the problem. Sheridan was a born fighter—aggressive and opportunistic—and he hustled his 40,000-man Army of the Shenandoah into the valley in pursuit of General Jubal Early's audacious little Army of the Valley, which had threatened Washington a few weeks earlier. On September 19, Sheridan's 37,000 Federals attacked Early's 17,000, dug-in troops east of Winchester, slamming into the Confederate center and Early's left. After an afternoon of fighting, Union cavalry from the north and infantry from the east forced Early into retreating south down the pike to Strasburg. After losing again to Sheridan two days later at Fisher's Hill, Early—and the Confederates—were all but finished in the valley.

Historic Sites

Harpers Ferry National Historical Park
Route 340
Harpers Ferry
(304) 535-6029 (Visitor Center)
www.nps.gov/hafe
Visiting Harpers Ferry today is like taking a step back in time; it is a place that every American should see. Only the small engine house building in which John Brown made his last stand in 1859 (now known as John Brown's Fort) remains from the old arsenal. Little sign remains of the army garrisons (usually Union) that were once stationed here, first to protect the arsenal and then to protect the Ohio and Baltimore Railroad that ran through town. But despite what has been lost, the town (only part of which is owned by the

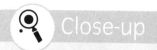

John Brown

John Brown, it seemed, was destined to fight slavery. The son of strict Calvinists, Brown was born in Torrington, Connecticut, on May 9, 1800. His father, Owen, was a modestly successful farmer, cobbler, tanner, and some-time agent of the Underground Railroad. Growing up in Ohio, young John Brown was barely a teen himself when he witnessed slavery's senseless horrors. They transformed Brown—like his father—into an enemy of those who practiced it.

As an adult, Brown's steadfast faith and unyielding hatred of the "pecu-liar institution" drove him—through the frustration of some twenty busi-ness failures—until that zeal overruled everything else in his life. In 1855, Brown followed several of his sons (out of twenty total children) to the plains of Kansas, which the previous year's Kansas-Nebraska Act had trans-formed into a battleground between pro- and antislavery proponents.

On May 21, 1856, pro-slavery raiders swept through the Free Soil town of Lawrence, Kansas, and left it in flames. The following day in Washington, D.C., South Carolina Representative Preston Brooks smashed Massachusetts Senator Charles Sumner into unconsciousness with his cane—in response to Sumner's ringing "Crime against Kansas" speech. Enraged by these unan-swered attacks, Brown vowed to sweep the land of pro-slavery men. "I have no choice," he explained to a reluctant follower. "It has been ordained by the Almighty God, ordained from eternity, that I should make an example of these men."[4]

Late on the night of May 24, Brown led a handful of devoted followers from his Kansas home to the banks of Pottawatomie Creek, where he directed the slaughter of five pro-slavery men. Never formally charged for his role in the "Pottawatomie Creek Massacre," Brown spent the next three years battling pro-slavery Missourians and raising money to fund an excur-sion to incite slave rebellion in the South. Quietly backed by New England abolitionists, Brown purchased weapons and—using the alias "Smith"—rented the ramshackle Maryland farm from which he launched the calami-tous raid on Harpers Ferry that ended without a single slave freed.

Even as he lay bleeding in the hands of his captors, Brown answered his inquisitors with an intelligence and serenity that surprised and impressed even his staunchest foes. His willingness to kill for the antislavery cause shocked and frightened Southerners (and many Northerners). But his courage and dedication made him a martyr to abolitionists. Frederick Dou-glass, who had declined Brown's invitation to participate in the raid, remembered his friend with simple eloquence: "I could live for the slaves; John Brown could die for them."

---

[4] Alice Nichols, *Bleeding Kansas* (London: Oxford University Press, 1954), 113.

National Park Service) remains very much a nineteenth-century settlement. A house built by Robert Harper, who established a ferry service here in 1761, still stands in the lower town. Antiques and gift shops and restaurants line the quaint streets, along with historic buildings and museums. Depending on the season, costumed interpreters are on hand for demonstrations and to answer questions.

Visitors should begin their visit at the Cavalier Heights Visitor Center (which houses a small gift shop and restroom facilities), where they can park and board buses into town. The buses are wheelchair accessible and leave every fifteen minutes. Book hounds will want to stop by the Park's Bookshop on Shenandoah Street, in the lower part of town. At nearly 3,800 beautiful acres—unhindered by the urban sprawl that threatens other parks—Harpers Ferry National Historical Park also features a number of beautiful hiking trails through the hills above town; maps for these can be found online and at the visitor center. The park also contains a library and research room, which is open by appointment.

Harpers Ferry National Historical Park is open daily 8:00 a.m. to 5:00 p.m.; it is closed on Thanksgiving, Christmas Day, and New Year's Day. Admission is $4 for adults (17 and older) arriving on foot, bicycle, or motorcycle; a vehicle pass is $6 for a single, private vehicle.

Jefferson County Museum
200 East Washington Street
Charles Town, WV
(304) 725-8628
jeffctywvmuseum.org
Jefferson County is proud of its Civil War heritage, and with good reason. While still part of Virginia, the county provided more troops to the Confederate cause than any other locality except for Richmond. Despite its Southern sympathies, Charles Town was also the hometown of Martin Delany, the highest-ranking African-American officer during the Civil War. The museum's most prized Civil War relic is the flag that once flew with J. E. B. Stuart's Horse

Artillery. The museum is open 11:00 a.m. to 4:00 p.m. Tuesday through Saturday from April through November. Admission is $3.

John Brown Gallows Site
515 South Samuel Street
Charles Town, WV
Under the sunny, late morning sky of December 2, 1859, a crowd of reporters, curious onlookers, and soldiers gathered in a field to witness the final moments of John Brown—the Kansas abolitionist whose raid on Harpers Ferry had further polarized a nation. Today, a private home occupies the ground on which Brown went to the gallows. But although only a historical marker outside that property remains to explain what took place on the site, it remains a solemn place worth visiting. The Jefferson County Courthouse, where Brown was tried, is also located close by.

John Brown Wax Museum
168 High Street
Harpers Ferry
(304) 535-6342
www.johnbrownwaxmuseum.com
It's hard to miss the John Brown Wax Museum, and visitors to the town definitely should not. The museum's wax figures of Brown, his followers, and the marines sent in to arrest them are eerily human, especially considering how near Brown's party once was to this site. The museum is open seven days a week 9:00 a.m. to 5:00 p.m., from mid-March through mid-December. Admission is $7 for adults, $6 for seniors, and $5 for children 6–12.

Winchester Area Attractions

Civil War Orientation Center
20 South Cameron Street
Winchester, VA
www.shenandoahatwar.org
If you're planning to explore the Civil War sites of the Shenandoah Valley, this Orientation Center and interactive Web site will help you plan your route. Visit online at home to gather information and ideas, and then stop

Major General Philip Sheridan LIBRARY OF CONGRESS

by the Orientation Center as you start your journey.

Fort Collier Civil War Center
922 Martinsburg Pike
Winchester, VA
(540) 667-5572
www.fortcollier.com
In 1861, Confederate General Joseph E. Johnston ordered the construction of a series of defensive earthworks around Winchester, at the northern end of the Shenandoah Valley. For three years they remained unused, until September 19, 1864, when hundreds of Union cavalrymen stormed over and through the Confederate-filled works north of town, all but ending the Third Battle of Winchester. Today these fortifications—known as Fort Collier—remain a sight to see, especially with the addition of a new, self-guided walking tour and detailed interpretive signage. The site is open from dawn until dusk.

Kernstown Battlefield
610 Battle Park Drive
Winchester, VA
(540) 662-1824
www.kernstownbattle.org
Now a registered National Historical Landmark, this site of two Civil War clashes (in 1862 and 1864) is now being looked after by the Kernstown Battlefield Association. Ongoing preservation efforts have led to the purchase of more than 300 acres of the battle area and the addition of road markers and interpretive signage. A small visitor center is open on weekends from May through October. Admission is free.

Museum of the Shenandoah Valley
901 Amherst Street
Winchester, VA
(202) 662-8756
www.shenandoahmuseum.org
This beautiful new $20 million museum opened in 2005 to tell the story of the culture and history of the Shenandoah Valley. While the Civil War isn't a primary focal point of the

curriculum, it's worth a visit for anyone who's planning to explore the region in-depth. The museum is open 10 a.m. to 4 p.m. Tuesday through Sunday, except major holidays. Admission varies depending on which tours you take.

Old Court House Civil War Museum
20 North Loudoun Street
Winchester, VA
(540) 542-1145
www.civilwarmuseum.org
Built in 1840 and used as a hospital and prison during the Civil War, this building served Frederick County until 1995; in 2003 it reopened to the public as a small but interesting museum with exhibits that feature some 3,000 objects. Located in the heart of Winchester's Old Town Walking Mall, it is definitely worth a look. It's open Wednesday through Saturday 10:00 a.m. to 5:00 p.m. and on Sunday 1:00 to 5:00 p.m. Admission is $3 for 5 and up, free for 4 and under.

Stonewall Jackson's Headquarters Museum
415 North Braddock Street
Winchester, VA
(540) 667-3242
winchesterhistory.org/Qstore/stonewalljackson.htm
This is another valley must-see, especially for fans of Stonewall Jackson. Lieutenant Colonel Lewis T. Moore of the 4th Virginia Infantry owned this house, which he loaned to General Jackson for use as a headquarters during the winter of 1861–1862. Maintained today by the Winchester-Frederick County Historical Society, the museum presents Jackson's office almost exactly as he left it. Many of Jackson's personal belongings—including his personal prayer table and prayer book—are on display.
    The museum is open 10:00 a.m. to 4:00 p.m. Monday through Saturday, and noon to 4:00 p.m. Sunday, from April 1 through October 31. During the winter the museum is open 10:00 a.m. to 4:00 p.m. Friday and Saturday and noon to 4:00 p.m. Sunday. Admis-

sion is $5.00 for adults, $4.00 for seniors, and $2.50 for students. Visitors can also buy a block ticket good for admission to the Jackson Museum along with the Abram's Delight Museum and George Washington's Office Museum.

Tours

Harpers Ferry Ghost Tours
217 Lower Clubhouse Drive
Harpers Ferry
(304) 725-8019
www.harpersferryghost.20m.com/about
.html
With so much history afoot in Harpers Ferry, you can expect to hear a good ghost story or two. This guided walking tour is offered on Saturday nights in April and May and on Friday and Saturday nights from June through November. Tours begin at the Old Town Café in Harpers Ferry and cost $5 per person. Reservations are required in October.

Winchester Walking Tours
1360 South Pleasant Valley Road
Winchester, VA
(540) 542-1326
www.visitwinchesterva.com
Stop by the Winchester Visitor Center to pick up a copy of a guide to Winchester's Civil War history, outlined in an easy-to-follow self-guided walking tour.

Accommodations

The Angler's Inn
867 West Washington Street
Harpers Ferry
(304) 535-1239
www.theanglersinn.com
There's no doubt that The Angler's Inn was designed with fishermen in mind, and with good reason. Harpers Ferry is located at the confluence of the Potomac and the Shenandoah Rivers, home to some of the best smallmouth bass and trout fishing in the country. But even if you're sticking to dry land, the inn is an excellent choice for an overnight or weekend stay. Located less than a mile from

the national park, this 1880 guesthouse is a favorite among travelers. There are four beautiful guest rooms, each with private sitting room and private bath. Its wraparound porch is perfect for reading and for savoring complimentary cookies and soda. Another draw: one of the best breakfasts you'll ever taste, featuring entrées like omelets cooked to order, luscious waffles, and spiced bacon. $90-$165

Fuller House Inn and Carriage House
220 West Boscawen Street
Winchester, VA
(540) 722-3976
(877) 722-3976
www.fullerhouseinn.com
"Location is our specialty," innkeeper Debra Johnson says of the Fuller House Inn, speaking of the downtown Winchester location of this charming inn, constructed in 1780. There are two rooms in the main house, outfitted with DVD players, refrigerators, and private baths, and guests enjoy complimentary wine and cheese and a delectable room service breakfast every morning. For extended stays, the Fuller House can also connect you with three additional properties: an 1854 Carriage House, a historic pre–Civil War house, or a downtown apartment. $165

The George Washington Hotel, A Wyndham Historic Hotel
103 East Piccadilly Street
Winchester, VA
(540) 678-4700
www.wyndham.com/hotels/DCAGW
/main.wnt
Wyndham Hotels took over the management this vintage 1924 grand hotel and completed an extensive renovation in 2008. The result: a stunning ninety-room historic hotel loaded with modern conveniences and genteel service befitting its elegant setting. On the premises, there's a unique Roman-bath-inspired indoor swimming pool and a popular restaurant, The Dancing Goat, featuring an open kitchen and outdoor dining in season. $130-$250

The Herds Inn
688 Shady Elm Road
Winchester, VA
(866) 783-2681
www.theherdsinn.com
The Herds Inn stands out among the appealing B&Bs in this region, and with good reason. It's a working dairy farm that serves up a one-of-a-kind rural experience. Guests check into a hand-built log home and watch (and join in, if they wish) the day-to-day farm activities. There's no shortage of activity; the farm is home to sheep, buffalo, goat, peacocks, chickens, turkeys, rabbits, dogs, and, of course, cows—and they're eager to interact with guests. The inn accepts only one party at a time and offers a perfect setup for families. $125-$145

The Inn at Vaucluse Spring
231 Vaucluse Spring Lane Road
Stephens City, VA
(540) 869-0200
(800) 869-0525
www.vauclusespring.com
The Inn at Vaucluse Spring is not your typical B&B. It's a fifteen-room B&B complex, spread across a hundred rolling acres near a limestone spring. Six guest houses make up the property, voted one of the region's most romantic inns by *Washingtonian* magazine, and there's really something for everyone. Discerning travelers can luxuriate in an elegant manor house, while outdoors enthusiasts will feel right at home in a cozy log house dating to the 1850s. The rooms and houses come equipped with fireplaces, Jacuzzi tubs, porches, rocking chairs, and common areas perfect for savoring a glass of wine or curling up with a good book. $145-$275

The Jackson Rose Bed & Breakfast
1141 West Washington Street
Harpers Ferry
(304) 535-1528
www.jacksonrose.com
Before Thomas J. Jackson earned the nickname "Stonewall," he used this 1795 Federal-style mansion as a headquarters in spring 1861. He wrote to his wife, admiring the beautiful roses that grew in the garden outside his house. Jackson's second-story room is one of four rooms available to guests at this B&B, and for Civil War buffs, it's one of the most sought-after rooms in Harpers Ferry. Regardless of which room you check in to, you'll enjoy beautiful antique furnishings, private baths, and a to-die-for breakfast featuring entrées like vegetable frittatas, French toast, fresh-baked muffins, and scones. $110-$140

Killahevlin Bed and Breakfast
1401 North Royal Avenue
Front Royal, VA
(540) 636-7335
(800) 847-6132
www.vairish.com
Killahevlin Bed and Breakfast is located on "Richardson's Hill" in Front Royal. The house was built in 1905 by William Carson, an Irish immigrant who was largely responsible for getting Skyline Drive built. The house is on the National Register of Historic Buildings and the Virginia Landmarks Register. Two of Mosby's Rangers were hanged on the property, and although the tree from which they were hanged was cut down and its wood sold to raise money for the Confederacy, the last remaining seedling from that tree remains on the grounds. Two Civil War crucibles were recovered by Mr. Carson from the site of a forge in Riverton, and are here on the property serving duty as flower pots. Owners and innkeepers Tom and Kathy Conkey offer warm Irish hospitality in their beautiful inn. Guests relax in sumptuous whirlpool tubs and queen-size beds while taking in breathtaking views of the mountains. Downstairs, there's a private Irish pub, open twenty-four hours a day to guests, stocked with a delightful assortment of wine and beer—all you care to drink! $189

Long Hill Bed and Breakfast
547 Apple Pie Ridge Road
Winchester, VA
(540) 450-0341
(866) 450-0341
www.longhillbb.com
Make a reservation at an inn located on
"Apple Pie Ridge Road" and just try not to
crack a smile. Innkeepers George and Rhoda
Kriz claim that the ridge was named by Civil
War soldiers who knew they could count on
the Quakers who had settled in the area for
food and shelter. The hospitality tradition lives
on today in this three-room B&B. Rooms are
charming and comfortable, equipped with
whirlpool tubs, spacious closets, and other
amenities. In cooperation with local historian
Mac Rutherford, Mr. and Mrs. Kriz offer Civil
War Driving and Civil War Walking Tour packages (in addition to a Ghost Tour package).
Rates start at $95 per night; Civil War pack-
ages start at $130 per night.

The Lost Dog Bed and Breakfast
211 South Church Street
Berryville, VA
(540) 955-1181
www.TheLostDog.com
"We don't have any local big box stores and
only a few neon signs," innkeeper Sandy
Sowada says of Berryville, "so our charming
main street with its barber shops, flower
shop, bank, drug store (with a soda fountain),
retail stores, used book store, and restaurants
all have that 1950s atmosphere."
    As for her inn, Ms. Sowada says: "My bed
and breakfast (circa 1884) has three distinctive guest rooms, all with private bathrooms.
We serve a full country breakfast featuring
local eggs, produce, and meats, but we will
cook for special diets with advance notice. We
are located in the heart of the historic district,
and our gardens offer something in bloom
throughout the growing season. And of
course, opportunities for outdoor exercise
and visiting Civil War battlefields abound."
$95–$175

Restaurants

The Anvil Restaurant
1290 West Washington Street
Harpers Ferry
(304) 535-2582
www.anvilrestaurant.com
Longtime visitors to Harpers Ferry and residents of the area can tell you all about the
Anvil. It's a local institution, known for its
fresh seafood (including West Virginia's celebrated trout), plus pastas, pizzas, and satisfying salad. The atmosphere is comfortable and
casual, perhaps even a bit rustic, with an inviting outdoor patio that's perfect for relaxing
after a busy day on the Civil War trail. It's
open for lunch and dinner Wednesday
through Sunday. Happy Hour is a special
treat, with fifty-cent draft beers. Average dinner entrée price: $10-$15.

Battletown Restaurant and
Grey Ghost Tavern
102 West Main Street
Berryville, VA
(540) 955-4100
www.thebattletowninn.com
This quaint Berryville inn and eatery takes
home the prize for the "most Civil
War–sounding restaurant name" in the Winchester region. The menu tries to balance the
North and the South, serving traditional Virginia recipes as well as New American and
continental cuisine. It's open Tuesday through
Sunday for lunch and dinner. Stop in for an
ice-cold beer or a refreshing iced tea while
passing through town, or check into the inn
for a unique overnight stay. Average dinner
entrée price: $20-$25.

Brewbaker's Restaurant
168 North Loudoun Street
Winchester, VA
(540) 535-0111
www.brewbakersrestaurant.com
Brewbaker's is a great choice for casual fare like
zesty wings, juicy burgers, and seafood classics
like crab cakes and crab balls. The kitchen
shows off its playful side in creations like the

Harpers Ferry NATIONAL PARK SERVICE

"Chicken Everything": chicken simmered in olive oil, along with mushrooms, onions, broccoli, sun-dried tomatoes, and crushed red peppers, and tossed with rigatoni and parmesan cheese. Or, there are the delightful pork loins, marinated in Montreal steak seasoning and served with an apricot merlot sauce with steamed vegetables. It's open for lunch and dinner, Tuesday through Saturday. Average dinner entrée price: $10-$15.

Cork Street Tavern
8 West Cork Street
Winchester, VA
(540) 667-3777
www.jesara.com/corkstreettavern.htm
This no-frills Old Town Winchester eatery is housed in an 1830s building that survived heavy shelling during the Civil War as the city was passed back and forth between Union and Confederate command. Locals and visitors gather here for barbecue ribs (considered the best in the Shenandoah Valley), along with tangy barbecue pork sandwiches and Reubens. It's open daily for lunch and dinner. Average dinner entrée price: $10-$15.

One Block West
25 South Indian Alley
Winchester, VA
(540) 663-1455
www.obwrestaurant.com
Upscale dining finds its home in Winchester in chef/owner Ed Matthews's stylish eatery, which takes its name from its location, one block west of the town's historic strip. The casual, comfortable eatery shows off the freshest flavors of the Shenandoah Valley in an inventive menu that changes daily. Matthews browses local farmers markets for fresh ingredients like seafood, wild mushrooms, cheeses, and succulent cuts of bison, lamb, and duck. Look for delectable concoctions like caramelized sea scallops with local bok choy and grilled veal porterhouse with pancetta and sun-dried tomato cream. It's open Tuesday through Saturday for lunch and dinner. Average dinner entrée price: $25-$30.

Secret Six Tavern
186 High Street
Harpers Ferry
(304) 535-1159
After a long day of sightseeing, grab a table at Secret Six Tavern and soak up the breathtaking view of the town and the railroad that travels just below. True to the town's historic traditions, the restaurant takes its name from the John Brown era. A group of Northern aristocrats who called themselves the "Secret Six" silently lent their support to Brown's efforts to use force and arms to rid the nation of slavery. Included in this elite group of citizenry: the editor of the *Atlantic Monthly*, a Unitarian minister, a noted physician, an educator, and two philanthropists. Average dinner entrée price: $15-$20.

Village Square Restaurant
103 North Loudoun Street
Winchester, VA
(540) 667-8961
www.villagesquarerestaurant.com
At Village Square, Chef Daniel Kalber shows his eye for fresh and local cuisine. On the menu, you'll find interesting new interpretations of classic creations like diver scallops Oscar with lump crab meat and couscous pilaf or tequila-lime marinated duck breast with wild rice chiles rellenos and roasted corn salsa. The restaurant forms part of downtown Winchester's dining and entertainment strip. It's open daily for lunch and dinner. Average dinner entrée price: $25-$30.

Violino
181 North Loudoun Street
Winchester, VA
(540) 667-8006
www.violinorestaurant.com
Violino has staked out a position in the minds (and stomachs!) of Winchester area residents and visitors for good Italian food, good Italian wine, and warm Italian hospitality. If you're lucky, you might even catch chef and owner Franco Stocco emerging from the kitchen to belt a classic aria. While regulars love the

familylike atmosphere, first timers are usually here for the food—and they won't be disappointed. Try the classic Italian fare or sample Stocco's original creations like the Ravioli della Nonna Emilia, filled with Swiss chard and fresh goat ricotta cheese, served in a walnut sauce; a baked Portobello topped with mushroom, parmesan, and rosemary puree; or a savory rib eye prepared in a Barolo wine reduction and served with roasted potatoes. It's open Monday through Saturday for lunch and dinner. Average dinner entrée price: $20-$25.

THE CENTRAL VALLEY

NEW MARKET/STAUNTON

This tour focuses on the central Shenandoah Valley, ground over which Union and Confederate troops often marched on the way through the corridor.

Discussions of the May 15, 1864, Battle of New Market often begin and end with colorful talk of the charge of the Virginia Military Institute (VMI) Corps of Cadets, which Confederate General John C. Breckinridge had called into service and sent into battle with great reluctance. It was an electrifying moment, at a crucial time of the battle. Even Union soldiers spoke with admiration of the young, gray-coated, youths' disciplined advance into galling Federal fire. Spectacle aside, the stout performance of the young cadets helped seal a Confederate victory of great strategic importance, one that bought time and resources for Robert E. Lee's hard-pressed Army of Northern Virginia.

By the spring of 1864, Union armies had been trying unsuccessfully for more than two years to wrest control of the Shenandoah Valley from the Confederacy. Now President Abraham Lincoln had given command of Union armies to Lieutenant General Ulysses S. Grant, who came east armed with a plan to end the war. His strategy called for a general advance by all Union armies. In the East, Grant would carry the brunt of the offensive against Lee in central Virginia, while Benjamin Butler marched up the James River and Franz Sigel—hopefully—took control of the troublesome valley. Sigel, whose military résumé was dotted with failures, was a courageous fighter but a poor general. His embarrassing flight from Wilson's Creek in 1861 had cost many Union lives and sealed a Confederate victory in the war's first major battle in the west. But

politicking and his popularity with the Union's thousands of German soldiers had kept him in uniform for three years, and now Grant had reluctantly assigned him a job no other Yankee general had been able to do.

Dogged by John Mosby's Confederate raiders, Sigel showed little urgency as he moved his 6,500 men south up the valley, prompting in his non-German-speaking troops "the most supreme contempt for General Sigel and his crowd of foreign adventurers."[1] Marching north to meet him was a patched-together force under Major General John C. Breckinridge, a 43-year-old Kentuckian with a square jaw and sweeping moustache. Breckinridge lacked the formal military credentials of his Federal counterpart; he had had just a smattering of military experience during the Mexican War. But he was a capable, intelligent leader; by 1861 he had already been elected James Buchanan's vice president and served in the U.S. Senate. He was no Sigel. One aide (who happened to be the son of U.S. Senator Henry Clay) called the general "the truest, greatest man I was ever thrown in contact with."[2]

It was Breckinridge's job to protect Southern communications and transportation in the valley, while guarding the left flank of Robert E. Lee's army, now locked in mortal combat to the east with Grant's persistent Federals. That meant keeping Sigel—and any other Union force—from crossing the valley into the Blue Ridge gaps to north-central Virginia. The best way to do that, Breckinridge wisely reasoned, was to attack.

Early on May 15, Breckinridge reached the outskirts of New Market with a force of per-

---

[1] William C. Davis, *The Battle of New Market* (Mechanicsburg, PA: Stackpole Books, 1993), 43.
[2] Davis, 17.

haps 5,000 men, including cavalry and 222 VMI cadets. After exchanging artillery fire with a few Union guns, Breckinridge pushed his two infantry brigades toward a thin Yankee line running west from the Valley Pike, north of town. The Federals were already falling back to a second position around noon when Sigel—who had been sending units up the pike piecemeal throughout the morning—finally reached the battlefield from Woodstock, 20 miles to the north. Even now his small army was incomplete.

By 2:00 p.m., Breckinridge had secured New Market and was on the move, northward down the pike toward the first of two battle lines laid out by Sigel. Helped by accurate artillery fire, the Confederates sent Sigel's skirmishers then his entire first line scampering north; only some of the Bluecoats rallied at the new Yankee position. Brigadier General Gabriel Wharton's Virginians seemed about to sweep through Sigel's right when they ran into a fence planted across a rise called Bushong's Hill. The Confederates stalled, as Yankee lead poured into their ranks. As the 62nd Virginia pulled back and reformed, a gap opened between the regiment's left and the dangling right flank of the 51st Virginia to the west. To avert disaster, Breckinridge now ordered up the anxious cadets, who had to this point been held in reserve.

In remarkable order, the boys marched forward into withering Yankee fire—slowed for just a moment—then, with cheers ringing around them, moved into the vacant slot alongside the shattered 62nd. Shortly after this, Sigel's cavalry commander, Major General Julius Stahel, led 2,000 Yankee horsemen charging down the pike in driving rain toward the Confederate right—and into hell. What canister blasted from each side of the pike did not hit, Virginia infantrymen did. The Federal charge quickly disintegrated, and confused Yankee horsemen raced for the rear.

With the momentum of the battle suddenly changing again, a flustered Sigel decided to charge Breckinridge's left. By now, however, the VMI boys had stabilized the

Rebel line east of the pike; Breckinridge, in fact, even had another regiment, the 26th Virginia, coming up from reserve. Having disposed of Stahel's cavalry, even Brigadier General John Echols's two regiments had moved up on the right. In poor order, Sigel's three regiments came forward—then one by one reversed course in the face of heavy artillery and rifle fire.

With Breckinridge's lines advancing and Yankee infantrymen and artillerists withdrawing in haste, the day's result became obvious. Only the awful weather and a brave rear guard defense offered by Captain Henry DuPont's single Federal battery saved Sigel's Bluecoats from slaughter. Meanwhile Brigadier General Jeremiah Sullivan arrived north of New Market with two Ohio regiments too late for the battle, but in time to cover yet another shameless retreat by Sigel, who withdrew eight miles to Mount Jackson.

Sigel had matched his Kentucky counterpart in bravery, but in little else. Grant, shocked by word of Sigel's loss and retreat, now could not get rid of the German fast enough. "By all means," he wrote to Henry Halleck, "I would say appoint General [David] Hunter, or anyone else, to the command of West Virginia." The hapless Sigel was briefly reassigned to Harpers Ferry then relieved for good on July 8.

Sigel later blamed his failure in the valley on Lee, who, he claimed, had "the advantage of a central position" that left him "always ready and able to turn the scales in his favor." But Lee—as Sigel well knew—was then locked in a death struggle with Grant and in no position to send bodies of troops anywhere. Siegel suggested the campaign could've been carried out in May 1964 with 20,000 troops, needed twice that by August.

BATTLE OF CEDAR CREEK

For three years, Confederate generals had run circles around the likes of Nathaniel Banks, John C. Frémont, and Franz Sigel in the Shenandoah Valley. During the past few

John C. Breckinridge

Only the Civil War, it seems, could have halted the political rise of John C. Breckinridge, the Kentuckian who climbed from the state legislature to the vice presidency by the age of thirty-five. The unsuccessful presidential candidate of Southern Democrats in 1860, Breckinridge was still serving in the U.S. Senate a year later when his Southern sympathies aroused suspicion. Rather than wait for his impending arrest, Breckinridge fled south and, as he put it, exchanged "a term of six years in the U.S. Senate for the musket of a soldier."[3]

LIBRARY OF CONGRESS

In a Confederate uniform, Breckinridge quickly proved that some politicians, at least, could make good generals. A born leader, he quickly gained the respect of his men and peers, developing his skills on the battlefields of Shiloh and Chickamauga before taking over the Confederate Western Department of Virginia in 1864. Following his reputation-making victory at New Market, Breckinridge reinforced Lee in the Wilderness, and then served under Jubal Early during his raid on Washington and subsequent defeat at Winchester. As the war wound down, Breckinridge moved to Richmond to become Jefferson Davis's secretary of war—far too late to be of much use. This once-rising star in American politics then spent four years in exile before returning home to Kentucky, where he died in 1875.

---

[3] David Stephen Heidler, *Encyclopedia of the American Civil War: A Political, Social, and Military History* (New York: W. W. Norton, 2002), 278.

weeks, Jubal Early had even knifed through the valley to threaten Washington. Now, on August 7, 1864, thirty-five-year-old Major General Philip Sheridan took command of the 40,000-man Army of the Shenandoah with orders to secure the valley once and for all.

A fighting general with a strong dislike of his enemies, Sheridan quickly struck at Early's much smaller force. Sheridan's veterans whipped Early's men at Third Winchester on September 19 and again two days later at Fisher's Hill. Convinced by early October that Early was beaten, Sheridan began to move north again—all the while burning anything that might aid his enemy. And after Union cavalry under George Armstrong Custer and Wesley Merritt smashed their Confederate counterparts at Tom's Brook on October 9, Sheridan believed he had accomplished his mission.

Sheridan, in fact, was absent from the army on the morning of October 19 when Early launched a surprise attack on the encamped Federals along Cedar Creek, southwest of Winchester. By mid-morning, Early's divisions had scattered much of three Union corps, and the Confederate commander was sure of victory. But Union cavalry slowed the Confederates, and Brigadier General Horatio Wright (commanding in Sheridan's absence) managed to establish a rallying point in a wood north of Middletown. Meanwhile, Sheridan—galloping at full speed from Winchester—reached the new Union line, received an update from Wright, and began preparations for a counterattack. First, though, the diminutive general rode slowly by the tightening Union ranks, reassuring each unit of success and rekindling the fighting spirit within each veteran. The awful morning was forgotten. Major Aldace F. Walker wrote later: "Cheers seemed to come from throats of brass, and caps were thrown to the tops of the scattering oaks; but beneath and yet superior to these noisy demonstrations, there was in every heart a revulsion of feeling, and a pressure of emotion, beyond description. No

more doubt or chance for doubt existed; we were safe, perfectly and unconditionally safe, and every man knew it."[4]

What at first looked like a morale-boosting victory for the South was about to end instead with Jubal Early's Confederates beaten and driven out of the Shenandoah Valley for good. Aside from some brief, afternoon skirmishing, the Cedar Creek battlefield remained quiet until 4:00 p.m., when Sheridan's reinvigorated army trod vigorously out of the woods west of the pike. Sheridan's right crashed into Early's left—then, along with the rest of the advancing Federal line, ground to a halt before Confederate ranks blasting away from behind stone walls. Thirty minutes into the fight, however, George Custer's division of blue-clad troopers—followed by William Dwight's infantry—slammed into Early's left and rolled up the Confederate lines. "Regiment after regiment; brigade after brigade," John Gordon later recalled, "in rapid succession was crushed, and, like hard clods of clay under a pelting rain, the superb commands crumbled to pieces."[5] Just like that, the day-long affair turned. Where Union soldiers and wagon trains had clogged the pike heading north that morning, now the Confederates did the same streaming south. With Early's army went Southern hopes of further use of the valley, which had supplied Lee's legions for four long years.

Other Points of Interest

Cross Keys/Port Republic
Stonewall Jackson closed out his 1862 Valley Campaign with a pair of victories in lesser-known battles, at Cross Keys on June 8 and Port Republic on June 9. Currently, there are no visitor facilities at the sites, much of which remain private property. But there are interpretive highway markers and battlefield signs in the vicinity.

---

[4] Thomas A. Lewis, *Guns of Cedar Creek* (Strasburg, VA: Heritage Associates, 1997), 254–255.
[5] Lewis, 234.

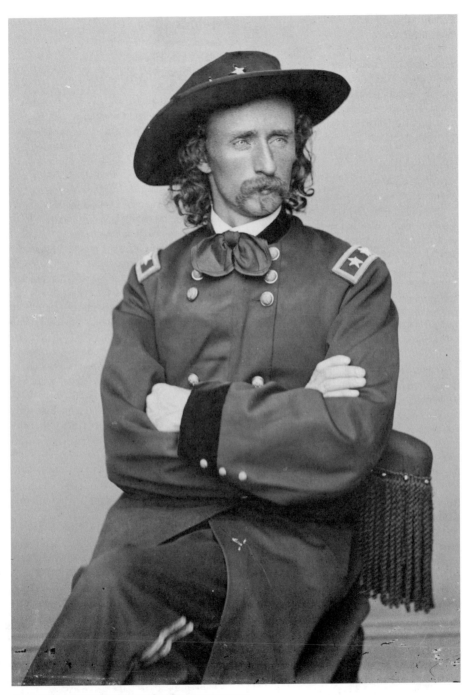

Major General George Armstrong Custer LIBRARY OF CONGRESS

Fisher's Hill Battlefield
Toms River, VA

There are no visitor facilities on the site of the September 22, 1864, Battle of Fisher's Hill, in which Union Major General Philip Sheridan bested General Jubal Early's Confederates for the second time in three days. You can, however, follow a self-guided walking tour with trail markers on site.

Gordonsville, VA
www.hgiexchange.org

Gordonville's Exchange Hotel was used as a hospital during the Civil War and now houses a small museum. You won't find the massive exhibits of larger historic sites here, but it is worth a visit if you are in the area. It is open until 4:00 p.m. each day except Wednesday. Gordonsville visitors will also want to drop by the Gordonsville Presbyterian Church to see the pew in which Stonewall Jackson often prayed, and tour Maplewood Cemetery, where some 700 Southern soldiers were buried.

Shenandoah Valley/Skyline Drive
www.shenandoahatwar.org

The valley's natural beauty, inviting hiking trails, and other outdoor recreation opportunities are the reasons that most visitors visit the Shenandoah Valley. Travel on the Blue Ridge Parkway, also known as "Skyline Drive," and you're on the doorstep of more than one hundred Civil War sites. From the drive's northernmost entry point in Front Royal, you can drive past points of interest like Luray Gap, where Stonewall Jackson announced that his command had become the Second Corps of Lee's Army of Northern Virginia, and Lacey Springs, the site of a cavalry clash between Union General Custer and Confederate General Thomas L. Rosser. As you drive through the park, be sure to stop at a few of the scenic overlooks. Not only will you be rewarded with a breathtaking view of the rolling hillside, you'll also understand the strategic importance of the towns and mountain passes during the Valley Campaigns of 1862 and 1864. Admission to Skyline Drive is $15; park entry is valid for seven days.

Historic Sites

Cedar Creek Battlefield
8437 Valley Pike
Middletown, VA
(540) 869-2064
(888) 628-1864
www.cedarcreekbattlefield.org

Now part of the new Cedar Creek and Belle Grove National Historical Park, the Cedar Creek Battlefield remains under the care of the nonprofit Cedar Creek Battlefield Foundation. Founded in 1989 to stave off development on a key section of the original battlefield, the group sponsors annual reenactments to help fund ongoing preservation efforts. In recent years the group has been able to add a modern visitor center, bookshop, and exhibits to the building that houses the foundation's offices. Efforts are now focused on restoring the Solomon Heater House, around which Confederate and Union forces once swirled.

Located at the intersection of Routes 81 and 66 (Route 11—the old Valley Pike—runs through the park), the visitor center is open Monday through Saturday, 10:00 a.m. to 4:00 p.m., and Sunday 1:00 to 4:00 p.m. (between April 1 and October 31). It is open by appointment during the winter.

New Market Battlefield State Historical Park and Hall of Valor Museum
8895 Collins Drive
New Market, VA
(866) 515-1864
www.vmi.edu/newmarket

This 300-acre park includes the hilly ground over which Union and Confederate forces clashed on May 15, 1864; the Jacob Bushong Farm; and the Hall of Valor Civil War Museum. Travelers should begin their visit with a trip through the Hall of Valor Museum, the exhibits of which explore the war in Virginia and the Battle of New Market—especially the role of the Virginia Military Institute cadets in that fight. While exploring the battlefield, visitors will want to look over the farm, which includes two Bushong family homes; a blacksmith shop; a henhouse; a loom and meat storage house; and a bake oven among its buildings, and remains a well-preserved reminder of nineteenth-century life. The park is open 9:00 a.m. to 5:00 p.m. daily, and closed Thanksgiving, Christmas Day, and New Year's Day.

Stonewall Jackson Museum at Hupp's Hill
33229 Old Valley Pike
Strasburg, VA
(540) 465-5884
This is a stop better suited for Civil War buffs with like-minded kids. Adjacent to the Cedar Creek Battlefield, the Hupp's Hill grounds offer a walking tour of Confederate entrenchments and Union gun positions, while the site's central building uses exhibits and photographs to tell the story of Stonewall Jackson and the war in the Shenandoah Valley. But the Hupp's Hill staff focuses much of its efforts on children, offering summer camps each summer and encouraging kids to try on uniforms, handle reproduction weapons, and learn from Civil War games and living history workshops.

The museum, which also has a gift shop, is open 10:00 a.m. to 5:00 p.m. April through October; and 10:00 a.m. to 4:00 p.m. November through March. It is closed Thanksgiving, December 24–25, New Year's Day, and Easter. Admission is $5 for adults, $4 for children (one child under 6 is free with each adult admission).

Tours
While New Market isn't packed with must-see attractions, the town is proud to tell its story with walking tours that illustrate how the Civil War impacted life in a small Virginia town. The Apple Blossom Inn (see Accommodations section) organizes one-and-a-half hour walking tours of the town, offered Tuesday, Friday, and Sunday from March through November. The cost is $10 for adults, $5 for children. Call 540-325-9529 or log on to www.appleblossom inn.net/new-market-walking-tours.html for more information.

Accommodations
Apple Blossom Inn
9317 North Congress Street
New Market, VA
(540) 740-3747
www.appleblossominn.net
If you're traveling through New Market and like the idea of having a historic house all to yourself, the Apple Blossom Inn is just the ticket. The two-bedroom, one-and-a-half bathroom layout is perfect for a traveling family or two couples touring the battlefields together. Built in 1806, the house comes equipped with a parlor, a full kitchen, a music room, a cozy porch with a swing, and a peaceful garden. You'll also enjoy a full cooked breakfast in the morning. The inn is the departure point for themed walking tours that bring New Market's Civil War history to life. $99 for one to two guests, $122 for three guests, and $145 for four guests.

Cross Roads Inn Bed and Breakfast
9222 John Sevier Road
New Market, VA
(540) 740-4157
(888) 740-4157
www.crossroadsinnva.com
Larry and Sharon Smith's spacious and inviting Cross Roads Inn is pure Virginia in its country charm and hospitality. You'll be greeted with complimentary hors d'oeuvres at check in, and you can help yourself to coffee and hot chocolate from the pantry of the 1925 house at any time of day. Rates are very reasonable, and rooms feature private baths, air-conditioning, antique furnishings, and other amenities; a number of specials are offered. Guests will enjoy the six-room inn's common areas (including a fireplace in the living room), gardens, outdoor spa, and relaxing front porch. Reservations are recommended. $75-$135

Franz Sigel

The personification of what ailed Union generalship for much of the Civil War, Franz Sigel could thank his powers of persuasion for lasting in command as long as he did. Born in Germany in 1824, Sigel was a young army officer during the German revolutions of 1848–1849, then, with thousands of other Germans, fled to the United States. Settling in St. Louis, Missouri, among that city's broad German population, Sigel attracted the notice of politician Frank Blair and Captain Nathaniel Lyon in 1861. These two staunch Unionists enlisted Sigel's help in recruiting and training German recruits, most of whom were passionately pro-Union. Sigel soon found himself with a prominent position in Lyon's small Army of the West. Determined to crush secessionist fervor in Missouri, Lyon quickly secured the northern part of the state, and then went after Sterling Price's much larger Western Army south of Springfield. Presented by Sigel with a plan to divide the army and attack Price from two sides (with the second wing under Sigel's command), Lyon reluctantly acquiesced, hoping his decision would stiffen the resolve of his German troops in the coming battle.

At Wilson's Creek on August 10, Sigel's wing collapsed in short order, leaving Major Samuel Sturgis (Lyon had been killed leading a charge) to fashion a difficult withdrawal for the small Union army. Sigel escaped on horseback to Springfield. Replaced by Samuel Curtis, Sigel resigned in a huff. Given another command, Sigel fought at Pea Ridge, Arkansas, and then joined the carnival of Union commands trying to track Stonewall Jackson in the Shenandoah Valley. After fighting at Second Bull Run and several weeks of speech making in support of the Republican Party, Sigel quit the army again. Once again his political skills earned him a new command—this time as head of the Union Department of West Virginia, in which position he managed to lose at New Market in 1864. Finally, after vacating Martinsburg and Harpers Ferry in the face of Confederate General Jubal Early, Sigel was finished. Grant, busy enough with Robert E. Lee in Virginia, wrote Henry Halleck in Washington: "All of General Sigel's operations from the beginning of the war have been so unsuccessful that I think it advisable to relieve him from all duty; at least until present troubles are over. I do not feel certain at any time that he will not, after abandoning stores, artillery, and trains, make a successful retreat to some safe place."[6] Relieved of the burden of duty for which he was not fit, Sigel went on to a modestly successful career in politics and publishing, and died in New York City in 1902.

---

[6] Frank Vandiver, *Jubal's Raid: General Early's Famous Attack on Washington in 1864* (University of Nebraska Press, 1992).

The Inn at Narrow Passage
US 11 South
Woodstock, VA
(540) 459-8000
(800) 459-8002
www.narrowpassage.com
The Inn at Narrow Passage is one of Virginia's longest-operating guesthouses, welcoming travelers since the 1740s. It takes its name from a dangerous nearby passage in the road, only wide enough for one wagon to cross at a time and constantly threatened by Indian attacks. During the 1862 Valley campaign, Stonewall Jackson even checked in, using the inn as a headquarters. From here, he famously ordered Jedediah Hotchkiss to "make me a map of the valley." Today's guests can take advantage of historic guest rooms outfitted with wood floors, porches, and spectacular views of the Shenandoah River and Massanutten Mountains. A lavish breakfast is served fireside in the main dining room. $115-$165

Piney Hill Bed & Breakfast
1048 Piney Hill Road
Luray, VA
(540) 778-5261
(800) 644-5261
www.pineyhillbandb.com
From the moment you arrive at Piney Hill, you'll understand why it was named one of the top B&Bs in the country by TripAdvisor. Built in the early 1800s, the farmhouse offers a luxurious respite after a busy day of touring. Sip a glass of wine as you read a book on the wraparound porch, or take advantage of the outdoor Jacuzzi and the breathtaking views of the surrounding mountains. If you're looking for more of an intimate experience, check into the Rosebud Cottage, also located on the property. It's a cozy 500-square-foot house that's perfect for a romantic getaway, outfitted with a screened-in porch and a gas fireplace; gourmet breakfast is delivered in a picnic basket to your doorstep every morning. $135-$195

Rosendale Inn
17917 Farmhouse Lane
New Market, VA
(540) 740-4281
www.rosendaleinn.com
Presidential history buffs will find themselves right at home at the Rosendale Inn, located at the foot of Massanutten Mountain. Franklin Delano Roosevelt used the beautiful farmhouse as his retreat from the White House, and Mrs. Woodrow Wilson was also a guest at the B&B. Spacious rooms come furnished with period antiques and private bathrooms. Most have their own in-room fireplaces. Guests can also park themselves in rocking chairs on the veranda to soak up the picturesque scenery. $105-$150

South Court Inn Bed & Breakfast
160 South Court Street
Luray, VA
(540) 843-0980
www.southcourtinn.com
A magnificently restored 1870s farmhouse, the South Court Inn is a popular choice among travelers who are exploring the beautiful Shenandoah Valley, its wineries, and quaint antiques shops. Perfect for a romantic escape, most of the inn's rooms feature whirlpool tubs, and innkeepers Tom and Anita Potts are happy to help you arrange in-room massages, roses, champagne, and other extras. You'll wake up to a delicious and decadent breakfast of banana-stuffed French toast, soufflés, and other treats that you wouldn't normally make for yourself. Room rates range from $125-$175, or, for a little more privacy, you can rent the Susie Hodges Cottage, starting at $189 for a one-night stay or $150 per night for a two-night stay.

The Staunton Choral Gardens Bed and Breakfast
216 West Frederick Street
Staunton, VA
(540) 885-6556
www.stauntonbedandbreakfast.com
A bit south of this tour's more notable attrac-

tions, the Staunton Choral Gardens is right on the way to Lexington and within easy reach of Appomattox and other central Virginia Civil War sites. And like almost every other property in the valley, it has its own Civil War story connected to it. According to owner Carolyn Avalos, Robert E. Lee—whose daughters attended a private school across the street— regularly boarded his horse Traveler in the inn's carriage house when he took a train from Staunton.

Naturally noted for its beautiful gardens, Staunton Choral Gardens offers warm, comfortable rooms, free high-speed, wireless Internet service, and other modern amenities. Adjacent to the inn's main building is the historic carriage house, now "a luxurious, two-story suite," owner Carolyn Avalos says, "very inviting and quite unique—all redone but keeping the charm." The inn is located within walking distance of all the town's attractions, which can also be reached via free trolley service. $75-$200

Stonewall Jackson Inn
547 East Market Street
Harrisonburg, VA
(540) 433-8233
(800) 445-5330
www.StonewallJacksonInn.com
Civil War buffs will no doubt be attracted to an inn named after one of the war's most legendary figures. At this Harrisonburg bed and breakfast, each of the ten guest rooms is named for another prominent Civil War figure, from Grant to Sheridan to Pickett. The rooms are decorated with period antiques and replicas, as well as works by local artists. You'll also enjoy a private bath, wireless Internet, and cable TV in each guest room, and a scrumptious breakfast featuring Virginia ham, Virginia apples, and locally produced sausage. The circa-1885 mansion itself is architecturally unique, a combination of a Queen Anne mansion and a New England–style cottage. $129-$169

Jacob Swartz House
574 Jiggady Road
New Market, VA
(540) 740-9208
(877) 740-9208
www.jacobswartz.com
This private two-bedroom farmhouse, built in 1852 by cobbler Jacob Swartz, is loaded with Civil War history. When Virginia seceded from the Union in 1861, Swartz enlisted in the Confederate Army. His shoe-making services were deemed invaluable, however, and he was sent back home to make boots and equipment for the Southern forces. The Battle of New Market broke out just across the river from the family's home. In December 1864, Federal troops under the command of George Custer raided the house and Swartz's cobbler shop, taking food and supplies. Today the house is a pleasant country retreat, equipped with a wood-burning stove, fully stocked kitchen, and private screened porch overlooking the Shenandoah River. Rates start at $125 (double occupancy).

Restaurants

A Moment to Remember
55 East Main Street
Luray, VA
(540) 743-1121
www.a-moment2remember.com
If you're staying in Luray or paying a visit to its attractions, stop for breakfast, lunch, or dinner at A Moment to Remember. Start your day with an omelet made with fresh Virginia ham or a stack of buttermilk pancakes, feast on salads or sandwiches for lunch, and enjoy a selection of seafood entrees for dinner. Or, stop by between meals for an invigorating espresso drink or a light bite. It's open Monday through Saturday for breakfast, lunch, and dinner. Average dinner entrée price: $15-$20.

Jalisco Authentic Mexican Restaurant
9403 Congress Street
New Market, VA
(540) 740-9404
You might be surprised to find authentic Mexican fare in a little town like New Market, but you won't be disappointed by the zesty flavors, generous portions, and friendly service. The extensive menu is chock-full of combination platters, grilled specialties, and vegetarian selections, which taste even better when paired with a traditional margarita (or one flavored with strawberry or peach). It's open daily for lunch and dinner. Average dinner entrée price: $10-$15.

Mill Street Grill
1 Mill Street
Staunton, VA
(540) 886-0656
www.millstreetgrill.com
If you travel as far south as Staunton, stop for a bite at the Mill Street Grill. Don't be surprised to see a waiting line at this casual pub-style eatery; it's no secret that Mill Street serves the best fall-off-the-bone ribs for miles around. Choose from baby back pork ribs, beef ribs, prime rib, or a combination of the above, expertly seasoned and served with fresh coleslaw, your choice of potato, and fresh bread accompanied by the flavored butter of the day. If you're not in the mood for ribs, you can feast on other grilled and fried creations, including chicken, seafood, steak, and more. Portions are generous, but there's also a "light side" menu with several tempting lower calorie selections. Average dinner entrée price: $15-$20.

Mrs. Rowe's Restaurant and Bakery
74 Rowe Road
Staunton, VA
(540) 886-1833
www.mrsrowes.com
If you're traveling to Staunton and are hungry for a home-cooked meal, stop by Mrs. Rowe's for all-American classics. The menu is loaded with Southern favorites like sweet potato pie,

fried chicken, meatloaf, collard greens, and other tasty dishes. If you've got a sweet tooth, you won't want to miss the homemade pies, cakes, and sweets. If you're eating on the run, order dinner to go. It's open daily from 7:00 a.m. to 8:00 p.m. (9:00 p.m. during the summer). Average dinner entrée price: $10-$15.

Publik House Restaurant
9386 Congress Street
New Market, VA
(540) 740-2699
www.publikhouserestaurant.com
Housed in a building once used as a Confederate headquarters, the Congress St. Publik House offers fine dining and an accommodating menu of eclectic dishes, including American and vegetarian meals. If you're in the market for a lighter bite, sip a beer and snack on casual fare in the Old Cross Ordinary, a traditional pub located on the property. There's also a wine shop featuring wines from local wineries. Average dinner entrée price: $25-$30.

Southern Kitchen
9576 South Congress Street
New Market, VA
(540) 740-3514
It would be hard to top Southern Kitchen for hearty American fare such as fried chicken and pie, all of which are served in generous helpings. Owned and operated by the Newland family since 1955, the diner-style eatery is a favorite of visitors to the valley. You'll find regional specialties like peanut soup and honest-to-goodness Virginia ham, plus seafood selections like flounder, rainbow trout, and fried shrimp. It's open daily from 7:00 a.m. to 9:00 p.m. Average dinner entrée price: under $10.

Southern Station Diner
915 East Main Street
Luray, VA
(540) 743-6001
This family-friendly diner is a good bet for travelers staying in Luray. Traditional breakfast

fare like pancakes and Eggs Benedict is available all day. The restaurant is clean, service is friendly, and the restaurant is well equipped to entertain small children with a box of toys, books, and puzzles. It's open daily for breakfast, lunch, and dinner. Average dinner entrée price: under $10.

Wayne's 2 Worlds, Café and Emporium
9478 South Congress Street
New Market, VA
(540) 740-3783
This unassuming New Market eatery offers a casual and comfortable environment with a style all its own and a menu that defies comparison. In addition to American staples like burgers and chicken salad, Wayne's offers kielbasa, coconut shrimp bisque, and other European-based dishes. For hungry battlefield troopers on the go, Wayne's is an ideal stop on the way out or for lunch. It is not open for dinner, however. Wayne's is open seven days a week for breakfast at 7:00 a.m. Lunch is served 11:00 a.m. to 3:00 p.m.; Sunday brunch is served 11:00 a.m. to 3:00 p.m. Average entrée price: under $10.

HIGH TIDE

HARRISBURG/GETTYSBURG

This tour focuses on sites related to the 1863 Gettysburg Campaign.

What began as an ambitious undertaking in the wake of another crushing Confederate victory ended with Southern generals pondering what might have been.

The time seemed right—at least to General Robert E. Lee, commander of the vaunted Army of Northern Virginia. He and his trusted corps commanders had just engineered a stunning rout of Major General Joe Hooker's Army of the Potomac in the Battle of Chancellorsville (May 1–4,1863). That Union army was on its heels, Lee felt, and surely ill prepared for a massive counterthrust. Further, a strike into Pennsylvania might loosen Major General Ulysses S. Grant's grip on Vicksburg, Mississippi, where Lieutenant General John C. Pemberton's besieged Confederate army was on it last legs.

The potentially spectacular possibilities did not end there. An invasion of the North, Lee believed, would secure badly needed recruits from Maryland; possibly frighten Northern leaders into peace talks; and, most of all, present an opportunity to crush a Yankee Army on its turf, and win European recognition for the South. Lee's indefatigable army was on a high, and eager to take the battle to the enemy. "Like the rest of the army generally, nothing gave me much concern so long as I knew Gen. Lee was in command," Edward Porter Alexander, Lee's fine artilleryman, wrote after the war. "I am sure there can never have been an army with more supreme confidence in its commander than that army had in Gen. Lee. We looked forward to victory under him as confidently as to successive sunrises."[1]

Lee would eventually find that all was not as he thought, beginning with his opponent. In spite of his lapse at Chancellorsville, "Fighting Joe" Hooker was not about to let Lee's army waltz into the North unguarded. Since replacing Ambrose Burnside atop the Army of the Potomac, he had instituted a series of organizational changes that were already benefiting the army. Foremost among these changes was his restructuring of the Federal cavalry into one corps, under Major General Alfred Pleasanton. The Union Cavalry Corps, already brimming with talented young officers, would come of age during the upcoming campaign and help deal the South a terrible blow.

Lee launched his campaign on June 3, marching his Army of Northern Virginia north to Culpeper then west into the Shenandoah Valley. Hooker sent cavalry to track him, and on June 9, Pleasanton's Federals barreled into Major General J. E. B. "Jeb" Stuart's camp at Brandy Station. The day-long engagement that followed left Stuart's men with the battlefield, but their commander embarrassed. The Federal cavalry had surprised him and fought him generally on even terms. No longer could Union cavalrymen be laughed off as mere pickets or messengers; they were a fighting force that Stuart would now have to deal with.

Lee, meanwhile continued north, capturing an unprepared Union garrison at Winchester and crossing the Potomac. Hooker followed, screening Washington and Baltimore even while engaged in a battle of wills with the War Department over a perceived lack of support. On June 28—with a potentially titanic confrontation between the two

---

[1] Scott Bowden and Bill Ward, *Last Chance for Victory: Robert E. Lee and the Gettysburg Campaign* (New York, NY: Da Capo, 2003), 93.

armies in the offing—a frustrated Hooker offered his resignation, which was promptly accepted. His replacement was the sleepy-eyed George Gordon Meade—yet another capable corps commander seemingly set up for a great fall. Hearing of the change, Robert E. Lee remarked that "Meade will commit no blunder in my front, and if I make one, he will make haste to take advantage of it."[2]

Lieutenant General Richard Ewell's II Corps was perched on the doorstep of Harrisburg, ready to pounce on Pennsylvania's capital when Lee received word of the Army of the Potomac's presence north of the Potomac. Lee postponed the Harrisburg operation and consolidated his strung-out army west of Gettysburg, a small transportation hub with a population of about 2,400.

Still unsure of Meade's exact position (Jeb Stuart's cavalry, which was supposed to be screening on Lee's right, had circled far to the east and lost touch with the army), Lee allowed Major General Henry Heth to take his division into Gettysburg after a cache of shoes rumored to be stored there, although the exact reason for taking this route has been disputed. Marching southeast down the Chambersburg Pike early on July 1, Heth's men heard the popping sound of carbine fire: they had run into John Buford's two brigades of dismounted Union cavalry, screening for Meade and stretched across the pike in a defensive position. First contact had been made.

The skirmish quickly exploded into a serious fight, as Confederate reinforcements flowed toward the town from the west and north. Buford's outgunned horsemen held their ground until General John Reynolds's I Corps arrived to bolster his position. The highly respected Reynolds, however, soon fell from his horse, killed by a Rebel bullet. Gradually the Union lines north and west of town bent, then broke, sending regiments scrambling headlong back through town. Rebel infantry charged in pursuit, as Union officers tried desperately to rally their disorganized units on high ground south of town.

Joining Major General Oliver Otis Howard (XI Corps commander) on Cemetery Hill, Major General Winfield Scott Hancock (II Corps commander) led the effort to bring order out of disaster. Here—with advantages in numbers and initiative and plenty of daylight left—the Confederates lost a crucial opportunity to seize the hills (Culp's and Cemetery) below town. "There was not an officer, not even a man, that did not expect that the war would be closed upon that hill that evening," one Confederate later wrote. But "some one made a blunder that lost the battle of Gettysburg, and, humanly speaking, the Confederate cause."[3] Pressed to attack, Jubal Early deferred to his corps commander Richard Ewell, who was disinclined to undertake any further offensive without specific orders from Lee. But when he received a message shortly after 5:00 p.m. in which Lee "wished him to take the Cemetery Hill if it were possible," he decided that it was not.

Meanwhile, newly minted army commander George Meade had been eyeing for his army an excellent defensive position to the south along Pipe Creek. Now, however, he sent word for the army to dig in where it was. Yankees spent the night felling trees, digging rifle pits, and maneuvering heavy cannon into firing positions. As the sun rose on July 2, the opposing armies had jostled into the positions from which they would fight for the next two days. Lee's forces stretched south along Seminary Ridge; five of the seven corps of Meade's Army of the Potomac were hunkered down in a classic and formidable defensive position, on high ground stretching in a fish-hook shape from Culp's and Cemetery Hills south along Cemetery Ridge to a pair of hills called the Little and Big Round Tops. Rolling farmland separated the armies.

Anchoring the left end of the Union lines was the III Corps of Major General Daniel Sick-

---

[2] Albert A. Nofi, *The Gettysburg Campaign: June–July 1863* (Conshohocken, PA: Combined Books, 1993), 53.

[3] Glenn Tucker, *High Tide at Gettysburg: The Campaign in Pennsylvania* (New York: Bobbs Merrill, Inc., 1958), 178.

les, a hot-tempered New Yorker and military neophyte fresh out of the U.S. House of Representatives. Sickles had in 1859 played the lead in one of the nation's most infamous and celebrated scandals. Catching his beautiful young wife in an elaborate tryst with the handsome U.S. Attorney Philip Barton Key—the son of Francis Scott Key, author of "The Star Spangled Banner"—the enraged Sickles chased Key down in Washington's Lafayette Square and shot him to death. In the trial that followed, Sickles' lawyer—future Secretary of War Edwin Stanton—got his client off with the first successful use of the insanity defense. Sickles then forfeited much of the public's sympathy for him by reuniting with his adulteress wife.

At Gettysburg, Sickles decided to push his III Corps forward into an angular position onto higher ground along the Emmitsburg Road, which bisected the battlefield, a position that he felt offered his men a defensive advantage. It also opened a gaping hole between his men and Hancock's II Corps to his right, an ominous fact that Meade himself pointed out to Sickles late that morning. By then it was too late to do much about it.

On Seminary Ridge, meanwhile, Lee had decided to try and capitalize on the success of July 1. If executed properly, he believed, a coordinated attack should rupture the Union lines. Lieutenant General James Longstreet—commander of I Corps and Lee's most trusted subordinate (in the wake of Thomas J. "Stonewall" Jackson's mortal wounding at Chancellorsville)—believed otherwise. He followed his orders, but—as many of his detractors would later argue—took too long in doing so. By the time Longstreet launched his July 2 attack on the Union left, up the Emmitsburg Road, Meade's V Corps (under Major General George Sykes) had reached the area. As Sickles' divisions tumbled back under the weight of Major General Lafayette McLaws' onrushing Rebels, Sykes' men—along with Federals sent over from the right—moved forward to plug the gap. Sickles fell with a shattered leg, which was later amputated. (Sickles

later had his shattered leg bones preserved in a miniature coffin. They can still be seen today—with the cannonball that smashed them—in an exhibit in Washington, D.C.'s National Museum of Health and Medicine.) Meanwhile, only heroic fighting from outgunned Maine and Pennsylvania infantrymen saved Little Round Top from falling to Texas and Alabama troops of John Hood's Confederate division. It was here that a little-known Maine professor named Joshua Lawrence Chamberlain earned everlasting fame for ordering a decisive bayonet charge as each side reached exhaustion.

The struggle for Little Round Top nearly resulted in disastrous repercussions for Meade, who responded to that emergency by stripping Culp's Hill of most of Major General Henry Slocum's XII Corps and sending it south to support his softened left flank. But the Confederates were not yet through for the day: Jubal Early nearly overran Cemetery Hill before Yankee reinforcements finally stopped him. And as dusk deepened, Major General Edward Johnson sent his division crashing up the wooded hillside of Culp's Hill—now defended by just 1,300 New Yorkers under Brigadier General George Sears Greene. Greene, an 1826 West Point graduate and renowned engineer, was a grandson of Revolutionary War hero Nathanael Greene, and a skilled fighter himself. Fighting tenaciously from behind formidable breastworks, his men held off Johnson's 5,000 attackers until Slocum's XII Corps returned in the middle of the night. The thickened Union lines shattered a follow-up assault ordered by Johnson before dawn.

As the sun rose on July 3, thousands of tired, hungry, and filthy soldiers stirred, wondering what the day would bring. Meade, after polling his corps commanders, had already decided to remain in position to receive an attack. Lee, meanwhile, was more determined than ever to break though the blue line facing him from across the fields south of town. Again overruling Longstreet's request for a turning movement south of the

Round Tops, Lee ordered an attack on Meade's stretched-out center. Ordered to direct the assault, the I Corps commander told an officer: "I don't want to make this attack. I believe it will fail—I do not see how it can succeed—I would not make it even now, but that Gen. Lee has ordered it and expects it."[4]

Nevertheless, at 1:00 p.m. on July 3, the hills of Adams County shook with the sound of Lee's booming cannon, some 150 guns under the direction of Lee's skilled young artillerist, Major Edward Porter Alexander. Union batteries responded for a time, then Major General Henry Hunt silenced them to conserve ammunition for a charge that now appeared inevitable. Alexander quieted his own guns some time later, passing word to Longstreet that he had barely enough shells left to support his advance. Reluctantly, Lee's husky corps commander gave the order for the assault on Meade's center—an attack soon to be dubbed Pickett's Charge.

Dashing Major General George Pickett commanded one of the attacking force's three divisions; Johnston Pettigrew and Isaac Trimble led the others. At 3:00 p.m., the roughly 13,000 men in gray and butternut set out to carry the heights ahead of them. It was a magnificent sight, even to the anxious Federals watching their approach. But for veterans of Fredericksburg, where hundreds of Yankees had fallen before Rebel rifles on Marye's Heights, it also meant a chance to avenge fallen friends.

The advancing Confederate lines were in no-man's-land now, too far from their target to charge, and far from the safety of the woods they had left. Now the quiet Yankee guns began to roar again—from every angle. Shells exploded above the attackers, shredding unit flags and soldiers alike. Dressing their lines in the midst of hell, the Confederates lurched forward. Now hundreds of Yankee muskets in the center of the blue lines

went off at once—filling the air with smoke and the battlefield with more dead Confederates. Union artillerists switched to canister, and ripped huge gaps in the slowing, butternut ranks. Confederates surging within feet of the ridge watched in horror as hundreds of Pennsylvanians opened up on them—en masse—from behind a stone wall. "The slaughter was terrible," one Federal recalled.[5] Only at one point did the charging Rebels breach the Union line, led by General Lewis Armistead who led his men forward yelling, "Boys, give them the cold steel! Who will follow me?"[6] Within moments, Yankee reinforcements plugged the hole, and Armistead fell mortally wounded.

By 4:00 p.m., the sloping fields before Cemetery Ridge were filled with dead Confederate soldiers. At least two-thirds of the attacking force was a casualty. Survivors of the shattered charge were streaming back to the safety of the woods, to sporadic Union taunts of "Fredericksburg! Fredericksburg!" Even Lee's vaunted cavalry, which under J. E. B. Stuart had circled Meade's army in an attempt to attack it from the rear, had been turned back, east of town, by Federal troopers under Major Generals David Gregg and George Custer. Robert E. Lee now turned to his subordinates to prepare for a Union counterattack. Pickett, for one, seemed too overwhelmed to move. "General Lee, I have no division now, Armistead is down, Garnett is down, and Kemper is mortally wounded." Lee persevered: "Come now, General Pickett, this has been my fight and upon my shoulders rests the blame. The men and officers of your command have written the name of Virginia as high today as it has ever been written before."[7] The Battle of Gettysburg was over.

Three days of fighting had produced some 50,000 casualties, including 3,155 dead Federals and 4,427 dead Confederates. The losses were especially hard for Lee, with a much smaller army, to take; they proved dou-

[4] Noah Andre Trudeau, *Gettysburg* (New York: Harper Perennial, 2003). 474–475.

[5] Trudeau, 499.
[6] Trudeau, 507.
[7] Trudeau, 521.

James Buchanan

Few presidents have been as qualified for their position as Pennsylvania lawyer James Buchanan, who occupied the Oval Office as the nation took its last steps toward civil war (1857–1861).

Born in the Pennsylvania wilderness on April 23, 1791, Buchanan graduated from Dickinson College in 1809 and passed the bar three years later. He began his political career as a state assemblyman then served in the U.S. House of Representatives (1821–1831); as minister to Russia (1832–1833); in the U.S. Senate (1834–1845); as President James K. Polk's secretary of state (1845–1849); and as minister to England (1852–1857). Thirty-six years of government service thoroughly schooled Buchanan in the ins and outs of domestic and foreign policy, and prepared him for his final job. A man of great integrity, he believed in the law, reason, and compromise. He was, a friend said, "wedded to the Constitution."[8]

Buchanan's handling of the brewing sectional crisis ultimately obscured an otherwise accomplished presidency. His own belief that both secession and federal "coercion" were unconstitutional made finding a solution to the problem imperative. He steadfastly pursued compromise between the North and South, while reasonable discussions of the slavery and states rights issues turned increasingly into passionate screaming matches, even fighting. In 1860 and 1861, compromise was out of vogue.

With a mixture of relief and sadness, Buchanan handed the reins of government to Abraham Lincoln on March 4, 1861. He retired to his Pennsylvania farm—from where he quietly backed his successor's efforts to restore the union. He died in 1868.

[8] Philip Shriver Klein, *President James Buchanan: A Biography,* (University Park, PA; Pennsylvania State University Press, 1962), 428.

bly painful for the South the next day when word of Vicksburg's surrender (to Grant) zipped over telegraph wires. Lee at least managed to preserve his remaining forces: With Meade slow to pursue, the Army of Northern Virginia slipped across the swollen Potomac River into Virginia on July 14, leaving Abraham Lincoln to fume over another lost opportunity.

Widely seen as the turning point of the Civil War, the Battle of Gettysburg did not signal the end of the Confederacy. But with Union victories in the West and Grant's ascension to command of all Union armies

in March 1864, Lee would never again have the resources or freedom to strike into the North again.

Historic Sites

American Civil War Museum (formerly the National Civil War Wax Museum)
297 Steinwehr Avenue
(717) 334-6245
www.e-gettysburg.com
Opened in 1962, the museum lacks the depth and power of its counterpart in Harrisburg (see listing below), but it does a good job of

re-creating scenes from the battlefield and the surrounding town with its lifelike dioramas. Visitors can immerse themselves in the battlefield action through the feature presentation in the Battleroom Auditorium, listening to battle cries and cannon fire. At the end of the presentation, you can even listen as Lincoln delivers his immortal address. The museum is open daily from March through December. Admission is $5.50 for adults, $3.50 for students, and $2.50 for children.

General Lee's Headquarters
401 Buford Avenue
(717) 334-3141
www.civilwarheadquarters.com
Constructed in 1834, this stone house was located at the center and rear of Lee's battle lines at the time of the battle, making it an ideal location for the Confederate officer's headquarters. It's now home to a small Civil War museum featuring artifacts and stories from the battle. The museum is open daily from March through November 9:00 a.m. to 5:00 p.m., with extended hours in the summer. Admission is $3 for adults.

Gettysburg National Cemetery
Baltimore Pike
Abraham Lincoln dedicated this haunting burial ground, now home to more than 7,000 soldiers and their loved ones, during his Gettysburg Address on November 19, 1863. It's open dawn to dusk; admission is free.

Gettysburg National Military Park
97 Taneytown Road
(717) 334-1124, ext. 431
www.nps.gov/gett/
No other Civil War battlefield is quite like the one that dominates Gettysburg, Pennsylvania. The epic proportions and importance of the July 1–3, 1863, battle is reflected today in the number of individual and unit monuments (more than 1,300) that grace its 6,000 acres. Roads provide ready access to all the park's crucial areas, from Little Round Top to Culp's Hill. Visitors can sit among the boulders of the

Devil's Den, where Yankees and Rebels once stalked each other; trace the path taken by the legions of Pickett, Trimble, and Pettigrew during their fateful charge of July 3; visit the cramped home (the Lydia Leister house) in which George Meade and his corps commanders met on the night of July 2; and trace the opposing lines along Seminary and Cemetery Ridges.

Gettysburg's visitor center remains among the best of any National Military Park, and features the Gettysburg Museum of the Civil War. The museum's artifact-based displays practically burst with minié balls, cartridge boxes, bayonets, swords, uniforms, and other equipment left on the battlefield. Exhibits touch on everything from campaign life for soldiers and officers to the proper use of artillery, and they boast enough military arms to fill an arsenal. Here visitors will also find a thirty-minute Electric Map program (for a small fee), a large bookstore and gift shop, and National Park Service rangers to answer questions and help arrange two-hour battlefield tours by licensed guides. The park also offers audiotapes (or CDs) for private driving tours, and private companies run bus tours. See the Tours section of this chapter for more details.

Still one of the park's feature attractions is the Cyclorama Center, whose interior is dominated by the 360-degree, 359-by-27-foot painting of Pickett's Charge. The painting is currently undergoing restoration, and only a portion of the painting is on view. The center itself, which also offers exhibits of relics and artwork related to the Battle of Gettysburg and the Gettysburg Address, remains open. Visitors should also walk through the Soldiers' (or Gettysburg) National Cemetery, the burial site of Union soldiers dedicated so movingly by President Abraham Lincoln on November 19, 1863. (Most Confederate victims of the battle were buried in Richmond's Hollywood Cemetery.)

Today, Gettysburg National Military Park is in the midst of change. The park is putting the finishing touches on a new $103 million visitor

 Close-up

George Sears Greene

While the performances of Federal commanders such as Ambrose Burnside, Franz Sigel, George McClellan, and John Pope made the terms "Union general" and "mediocre" synonymous, a few lower-level officers helped keep Union armies fighting. It's surely no coincidence that several of these men—including the up-and-coming Colonel Joshua Lawrence Chamberlain—fought at Gettysburg. At sixty-two years old, George Sears Greene could hardly be called "up and coming." But since entering the war as colonel of the 60th New York in January 1862, he had exhibited a sensible, hard-driving, fighting style lacking in more senior—or politically connected—Yankee officers. Promoted to brigadier, he served under one flawed army commander after another—Nathaniel Banks in the Shenandoah Valley, McClellan at Antietam, Joe Hooker at Chancellorsville—until George Gordon Meade left him to defend the Army of the Potomac's right flank with his single brigade at Gettysburg. Of the grizzled Greene, with whom he had served in the antebellum army, James Longstreet said "there was no better officer in either army."[9]

Born in Apponaug, Rhode Island, in 1801 in a little red house that local roads, telephone wires, and businesses have today all but squeezed from existence, Greene inherited the fighting spirit of his grandfather, Nathanael Greene—once George Washington's second in command. Greene's sons extended the family's fighting tradition: Two served in Union armies, while a third—Samuel Dana Greene—served as Commander John Worley's executive officer on the USS *Monitor* during its fateful clash with the CSS *Virginia*.

Army life was not new to Greene, who had not only graduated from West Point in 1823, but taught engineering and mathematics there for four years. After several years in the field, Greene resigned his commission in the stale, peacetime army to pursue civilian work as an engineer. He soon made a national name for himself, developing New York's Croton Water Works and the Central Park Reservoir, and serving as superintendent of the Providence, Warren, and Bristol Railroad. The graying Rhode Islander was working in the Empire State when the war began, and he received his new commission from that state.

In October 1863, a Confederate bullet smashed through Greene's mouth at Wauhatchie, Tennessee, ending his service in the field. But he recovered to serve on courts-martial duty and march in the Grand Review. With the war over, the robust old fighter resumed his life as a civil engineer, while compiling his family's rich genealogy. He died at the age of ninety-seven. Today, a boulder carried north from Culp's Hill marks his gravesite, not far from the house in which he was born. And along the slope of Culp's Hill, a statue of Greene still looks out over the ground that he and his tiny brigade so ably defended.

---

[9] Eric Ethier, "George Sears Greene: Gettysburg's Other Second Day Hero," *Rhode Island History* 53, no. 2 (May 1995): 65.

center and museum—one designed to be less obtrusive built on ground that was not central to the battle. It is scheduled to open in spring 2008; the old one will be torn down. Meanwhile, the battlefield continues to fight off the ugly infringements of souvenir stands and convenience stores in an otherwise lovely town. Recent years have seen the removal of ugly obstructions like the 300-foot National Tower. Efforts to restore the battlefield to its original appearance (at the time of the battle) have included the removal of hundreds of acres of trees; the replanting of many more acres of trees, thickets, and orchards; and the addition of historic fencing that once divided local farms.

The park is open daily, free of charge, 6:00 a.m. to 10:00 p.m., April 1 to October 31, and 6:00 a.m. to 7:00 p.m., November 1 to March 31. The park visitor center is open daily 8:00 a.m. to 5:00 p.m., with summer hours 8:00 a.m. to 6:00 p.m. daily; it is closed Thanksgiving Day, Christmas Day, and New Year's Day. The Cyclorama Center is open daily 9:00 a.m. to 5:00 p.m.; it is closed Thanksgiving Day, Christmas Day, and New Year's Day.

Jennie Wade House Museum
777 Baltimore Street
(717) 334-4100
www.jennie-wade-house.com
Gettysburg native Mary Virginia "Ginnie" Wade was baking bread for Union soldiers on July 3, 1863, when a stray bullet crashed through her home and killed her. Just twenty years old, Miss Wade was the only civilian killed in town during the Battle of Gettysburg. The home today looks practically—and eerily—as it did in July 1863 (with the exception of its gift shop). Admission is $7.25, or you can stop by the adjacent Battlefield Tour Center (778 Baltimore Street) to purchase a combo ticket including a Battlefield tour and attractions admissions, starting at $41.50.

The National Civil War Museum
One Lincoln Circle at Reservoir Park
Harrisburg, PA
(717) 260-1861
www.NationalCivilWarMuseum.org
With so much to see 40 miles south at Gettysburg, building a Civil War museum in Harrisburg once seemed, to some observers, a bad idea. True, the state capital had once been home to Camp Curtin—a Union training depot that trained and sent 300,000 soldiers into Federal armies. But no serious fighting had taken place here: the outbreak of fighting at Gettysburg forestalled General Richard Ewell's plan to attack the city, and it was never threatened again. But when it opened in 2001, this fabulous, 65,000-square-foot museum turned heads, and made Harrisburg the ideal jump-off point for an excursion to Gettysburg.

The brainchild of former mayor Stephen R. Reed—who started collecting for the museum during the mid-1990s—the National Civil War Museum boasts two floors of state-of-the-art exhibits, based on its 24,000-piece artifact collection, which dates from 1850 to 1876. (Highlights of the collection include the kepi worn by Confederate General George Pickett at Gettysburg; a bible once carried by Robert E. Lee; one of the gauntlets Stonewall Jackson was wearing when he was shot at Chancellorsville; and Ulysses S. Grant's sword belt.) The museum strives to tell the "complete" story of the Civil War. "We wanted to tell the story, not just of the battles," Reed said, "but of the people who lived and worked, and fought and died, during the war years. And we wanted to take an unflinching look at slavery, the root cause of the conflict."

Tours of the museum's seventeen exhibit galleries begin on the second floor, starting with "A House Divided." They naturally describe the military campaigns of the conflict, while also exploring "The Peculiar Institution: American Slavery," "Making of Armies," "Civil War Music," "Lincoln: War and Remembrance," and other topics. Interactive battle maps and audio posts bring each exhibit to life, and a small theater offers the sixteen-minute, prize-winning film, *A Nation Endures* every twenty minutes

The National Civil War Museum is open Wednesday through Saturday 10:00 a.m. to 5:00 p.m., and Sunday noon to 5:00 p.m. Admission is $8 for adults, $7 for seniors, and $6 for students. The museum is wheelchair accessible.

The Rupp House
451 Baltimore Street
(717) 334-7292
www.friendsofgettysburg.org
This interactive museum re-creates the culture of nineteenth-century Gettysburg through interactive, hands-on exhibitions and activities led by guides and volunteers in period clothing. The Rupp House (in which the museum is located) was built in 1868 to replace a lavish house that sustained serious damage during the battle. It's open Friday, Saturday, and Sunday only in April and May and September through December; call ahead for additional days and hours during the summertime. Admission is free; donations go to support battlefield preservation efforts.

Shriver House Museum
309 Baltimore Street
(717) 337-2800
www.shriverhouse.org
A welcome addition to Gettysburg and the museum community is the Shriver House Museum, a relatively new facility dedicated to telling the story of Gettysburg civilians who witnessed the epic 1863 battle. Built in 1860 by George Washington Shriver, the house was caught in the middle of the first day's fighting. Evidence of Confederate sharpshooters firing from the attic included eyewitness reports of soldiers knocking portholes in the attic's sides. Restoration efforts (which continue today) turned up bullets and stains that were recently proven to be blood. It appears certain that at least one Rebel was killed in the Shriver House attic.

The building today looks about as it did when George, his wife, Hettie, and their two

small children lived there in 1861, shortly before George joined the Union cavalry. Between stops at Gettysburg's military sites, visitors should tour the restored rooms of the Shriver House (along with the nearby Jennie Wade House) to get an inkling of how civilians lived in the midst of war. The museum is open from April through November, Monday through Saturday 10:00 a.m. to 5:00 p.m. and noon to 5:00 p.m. Sunday. Closed in January (except for groups by appointment), the Shriver House is open Saturday and Sunday noon to 5:00 p.m. during December, February, and March. Admission is $7.25 for adults, $6.00 for seniors, and $5.00 for kids under 12.

Soldier's National Museum
777 Baltimore Street
(717) 334-4890
The building that now houses the Soldier's National Museum was the headquarters for Union General Oliver O. Howard during the battle. It later became the Soldier's National Orphanage and now houses a popular collection of Civil War battle dioramas and more than 5,000 artifacts. Admission is $7.25, or purchase a combo ticket at the Battlefield Tours depot across the street.

U.S. Army Heritage and Education Center
950 Soldiers Drive
Carlisle, PA
(717) 245-3971
www.carlisle.army.mil/ahec
Long known simply as Carlisle Barracks, the home of the U.S. Army War College and Military History Institute and Museum is now part of the new U.S. Army Heritage and Education Center. Charged with "Telling the Army Story—One Soldier at a Time," this one-of-a-kind complex is destined to become one of the nation's most compelling historical attractions.

Founded by Englishman John Stanwix in 1757, Carlisle Barracks has since been home to a series of army schools, most notably the Carlisle Indian Industrial School, for American Indians. Here a young Jim Thorpe got his first

Gettysburg National Park NATIONAL PARK SERVICE

taste of football, playing for the Carlisle Indians—once one of the nation's great football
powers. The site is best known, of course, for
its research facilities: anchored by a massive
collection of books (some 325,000), manu-
scripts (11,000,000, largely unofficial papers,
unit histories, and private papers), photographs (1,700,000), and maps (19,500), the
Military History Institute has long been the

premier site for the study of army history. In
2005 it was moved into a new 67,000-square-
foot building—the first of several structures
that will eventually house a visitor and education center, a state-of-the-art conservation
facility, and the long-awaited Army Heritage
Museum. The visitor and education center is
slated to open in 2008; the other sites should
be completed by 2011.

Already, the site has opened its new Army Heritage Trail—a unique, 1-mile, outdoor walk through American military history. Fantastic recreations along the trail address every major American war, and include a Revolutionary War redoubt, a section of the Antietam battlefield, a Civil War winter encampment, and a portion of D-Day's Omaha Beach. The trail alone makes a visit here a must. The Army Heritage and Education Center is open Monday through Friday 9:00 a.m. to 4:45 p.m., except on federal holidays. It is wheelchair accessible, and admission is free. Security is tight, however, so calling ahead is advised.

Other Points of Interest

The Coster Avenue Mural and Amos Humiston Monument

Late on the afternoon of on July 1, 1863, two Confederate brigades slammed into Colonel Charles R. Coster's thin line of 1,200 Yankees on the northeastern outskirts of Gettysburg. Coster's left and right flanks collapsed, and his center regiment—the 154th New York Volunteers—was forced to follow its brother regiments in flight back through town.

One hundred twenty-five years later a crucial moment of this struggle appeared in vivid color on the back of a warehouse at the end of a Gettysburg side street. The moving and detailed 80-foot mural was the work of Rhode Island artist and 154th New York Regimental historian Mark Dunkelman (with Johan Bjurman), who designed the image as an homage to the soldiers who fought in Kuhn's brickyard. (A monument to the 154th New York also stands nearby.) Recently restored, the Coster Avenue mural remains one of Gettysburg's neat, little-known treasures.

In his Coster Avenue painting, Dunkelman included the image of young Sergeant Amos Humiston, a member of the 154th New York whose lifeless body was found on the outskirts of town shortly after the battle. An ambrotype of three children found clutched in his hand was the only clue to Humiston's identification, which was determined only after his wife saw the photograph in a newspaper four months later. In 1993, Dunkelman (who later explored Humiston's story in his 1999 book *Gettysburg's Unknown Soldier: the Life, Death, and Celebrity of Amos Humiston*) joined Gettysburg residents and interested supporters in dedicating a monument and plaque to Humiston in front of the Gettysburg Fire Station, at 35 North Stratton Street. Even today, a visit to this small memorial makes the war seem terribly personal.

Eisenhower National Historic Site
97 Taneytown Road
(717) 338-9114
www.nps.gov/eise

While there's no direct link to the Civil War, American history buffs may be interested to tour the weekend retreat of the World War II leader and president, which is adjacent to the National Military Park. The Eisenhowers lived on this estate and farm from 1961 until the former president's death in 1969. The house is open daily 9:00 a.m. to 4:00 p.m. Guests must park at the National Military Park and ride a complimentary shuttle to the farm entrance. Admission is $6.50 for adults, and $4.00 for children under 12.

Tours

From ghost walks to double-decker buses to bicycles, there are dozens of ways to tour Gettysburg—and dozens of companies ready to show you around. If you're not sure where to begin, start at the National Battlefield Park visitor center. You can arrange a private guided tour with a park ranger ($45 for two hours for up to six passengers; see www.gettysburgtourguides.org) or purchase a CD ($19.95) for an audio driving tour.

Companies specializing in general battlefield tours are listed below.

Gettysburg Battlefield Bus Tours
778 Baltimore Street
(717) 334-6296
www.gettysburgbattlefieldtours.com

Historic Battlefield Bus Tours
55 Steinwehr Avenue
(717) 334-8000

Gettysbike Bicycle Tours
240 Steinwehr Avenue
(717) 752-7752
www.gettysbike.com

Ghost Tours

With all of the suffering and tragedy that occurred in this historic town, it's not surprising to hear talk of hauntings. More than 200 buildings that were standing at the time of the war remain intact today, setting the perfect scene for some truly spine-tingling tales. There are many companies providing ghost tours; there's not much difference in the content, delivery, or price. If you're visiting during the busy spring and summer season, however, you may want to bear in mind that street traffic on major thoroughfares like Baltimore Street and Steinwehr Avenue may leave you straining to hear the ghastly tales.

Civil War Hauntings Candlelight Ghost Walks
240 Steinwehr Avenue
(717) 752-5588
www.cwhauntings.com

Farnsworth House Civil War Mourning
Theater and Haunted History Walks
401 Baltimore Street
(717) 334-8838
www.farnsworthhouseinn.com

Ghostly Images of Gettysburg
548 Baltimore Street
(717) 334-4100
www.gettysburgbattlefieldtours.org

Ghosts of Gettysburg Candlelight
Walking Tours
271 Baltimore Street
(717) 337-0445
www.ghostsofgettysburg.com

Visitor Center
Gettysburg Convention and Visitors Bureau
102 Carlisle Street
(717) 334-6274

Accommodations

Battlefield Bed and Breakfast Inn
2264 Emmitsburg Road
(717) 334-8804
(888) 766-3897
www.gettysburgbattlefield.com
Five minutes from the Gettysburg Battlefield visitor center, this 1809 farmhouse has appeared in several "Best of" lists; it's easy to see why. The inn caters to the Civil War "crowd," and guests will feel almost as if they lived in town through the battle. The eight-guest room (each named after a regiment that fought at Gettysburg) inn is situated on 30 acres of farmland, surrounded by original campaign ground. The innkeepers host daily Civil War history presentations while staff in period costumes serve a home-cooked breakfast each morning. Each room also offers a private bath and air-conditioning. Rates are a tad higher than other local inns, but for good reason. Reservations are highly recommended. $175-$225

Best Western Gettysburg Hotel
One Lincoln Square
(717) 337-2000
(866) 378-1797
We normally don't include chain hotels in this guide, but you can't stroll through downtown Gettysburg without noticing the Best Western. Established in 1797, the hotel saw its share of action in 1863, earning a listing on the National Register of Historic Places and Historic Hotels of America. At Willis House, located across the street, Abraham Lincoln penned the Gettysburg Address. The accommodations are roomy, outfitted with modern amenities like wi-fi and cable television. $100-$300

President Abraham Lincoln LIBRARY OF CONGRESS

Blue Sky Motel
2585 Biglerville Road
(717) 677-7736
(800) 745-8194
www.blueskymotel.com
This no-frills, old-fashioned country motel won't win any awards, but it's clean, convenient, and unbeatably affordable. Even during peak season, you'll pay less than $100 per night. The low price includes a pool, free coffee, and access to friendly, knowledgeable owners who are eager to help you plan your visit to Gettysburg's attractions. $29-$89

Brafferton Inn
44 York Street
(717) 337-3423
(866) 337-3423
www.brafferton.com
A bullet lodged in the mantel of one of the Brafferton's rooms tells you all you need to know about this building's history. Built in 1786, this unique residence was transformed into an inn two centuries later. Today it is one of three York Street structures that make up the Brafferton Inn. Amenities and rates vary, but all eighteen rooms in the house and the adjoining carriage house reflect quiet, nineteenth-century comfort. Some have luxurious touches like whirlpool tubs and gas fireplaces. $90-$209

The Brickhouse Inn
452 Baltimore Street
(717) 338-9337
(800) 864-3464
www.brickhouseinn.com
Owners and Innkeepers Tessa Bardo and Brian Duncan stress cleanliness and convenience; their inn is within easy walking distance of Gettysburg's shops, restaurants, and attractions, and it offers off-street parking. The Brickhouse is also known for comfort and relative tranquility—despite its central location—provided in part by the inn's spacious gardens. "The Welty House—where we have five of our rooms—is a genuine historic house," the owners say. "It was occupied by

Confederate forces at the end of the battle's first day and still bears bullet holes in its walls." Each room is named for one of the states represented in the battle and furnished with antiques and family heirlooms. All rooms showcase the house's original hardwood floors, and some even feature private porches with rocking chairs. $99-$164

The Gaslight Inn
33 East Middle Street
(717) 337-9100
(800) 914-5698
www.thegaslightinn.com
For another historic experience, check into this elegant nine-room inn, which dates to 1872. Each room comes with a private bath, most with Jacuzzi tubs, steam showers, and some with fireplaces. Eager to set the mood for a romantic escape, the inn will also help guests arrange special indulgences like an in-room massage, flowers, and chocolate-covered strawberries. Guests can also take advantage of personalized concierge service to help arrange sightseeing activities, dining and other diversions, and a tasty full-cooked breakfast each morning. $114-$195

James Gettys Inn
27 Chambersberg Street
(888) 900-5275
www.jamesgettyshotel.com
Named for the town's founder, the James Gettys Inn sits in the heart of downtown Gettysburg. During the Civil War, it was known as the Union Hotel and was used as a hospital. Twenty-five years later, it hosted 250 guests for the official battle commemoration. Each spacious guest room includes a well-stocked kitchenette, private bath, and separate living area. In lieu of breakfast service, fresh pastries, juice, and fruit are brought to each guest room the night before, and rooms are equipped with coffee makers and supplies. $120-$250

Gettystown Inn/ Dobbin House
89 Steinwehr Avenue
(717) 334-2100
www.dobbinhouse.com
Dating back to 1776, Gettysburg's oldest and most historic building overlooks the Gettysburg National Cemetery, where Lincoln delivered the Gettysburg Address. Prior to the Civil War, the house was a well-known "station" on the Underground Railroad, used to conceal runaway slaves. While many Gettysburg visitors stop here to dine at the Dobbin House, a popular colonial tavern-style restaurant, you can also spend the night at the nine-room Gettystown Inn. Rooms are comfortably furnished with antiques and old-fashioned beds. Breakfast at the adjacent restaurant is included. You can also arrange to stay at the Little Round Top Farm, a five-bedroom farmhouse set on twelve acres with a pond and a walking path to the spot where the 20th Maine infantry preserved the Union position on the hill. $90-$150; Little Round Top Farm is $1,500 per week.

Herr Tavern & Publick House
900 Chambersburg Road
(717) 334-4332
(800) 362-9849
www.herrtavern.com
The Herr Publick House witnessed some of the first action of the battles of Gettysburg. On the morning of July 1, Confederate forces drove the Union cavalry back toward Gettysburg along the road that passed in front of the 1815 inn and tavern. Although the inn sustained damage during the battle and during a windstorm more than a century later, the original building has been painstakingly restored to its nineteenth-century appearance. Owner Steven Wolf has also added eleven more guest rooms to share the experience with more travelers. There's a fine-dining restaurant, a casual tavern, and even a limited-service spa on site as well. $109-$209

Restaurants

Blue Parrot Bistro
35 Chambersburg Street
(717) 337-3739
www.blueparrotbistro.com
Housed in a Civil War–era building, this eclectic downtown bistro serves modern American and Mediterranean fare. Start with hummus or baba ghanoush, and then sample the grilled platter: a French pork chop, lamb chop, and venison steak, served with ratatouille and garlic mashed potatoes. Or, choose a flavorful pasta dish or a juicy hamburger. Wash it down with a Pennsylvania beer. The bistro is open Tuesday through Saturday for lunch and dinner. It's also open on Sunday from May through October. Average dinner entrée price: $15-$20.

Farnsworth House Inn
401 Baltimore Street
(717) 334-8838
www.farnsworthhouseinn.com
The restored Farnsworth Dining Rooms—decorated in honor of Gettysburg commanders George G. Meade and Robert E. Lee—offer a menu filled with hearty Northern and Southern dishes, such as Virginia ham, Yankee pot roast, and Maryland-style crab cakes. Outdoor dining is also available. The Farnsworth House is also a bed-and-breakfast, and it boasts a real countrified tavern filled with memorabilia from the movie *Gettsyburg*. If you're a fan of the macabre, you may also want to check out the house's cellar stories. Ghost-seekers descend into the cellar and gather around a coffin to hear a scary litany of local ghost lore. The tavern opens for lunch daily at 11:30 a.m., featuring a number of Pennsylvania favorites. Average dinner entrée price: $20-$25.

Gina's Place
16 East Hanover Street
(717) 337-2697
If you're in the mood for Italian, locals will tell you that Gina's is the best in town. Don't be

surprised if Gina herself greets you when you walk in the door, and then sits down with you to take your order. She's also the culinary genius behind the house-made pasta, fresh bread, and other tasty Italian creations. If you're traveling with a large group, inquire about the bountiful all-you-can-eat family-style meals, a bargain at $25 per person. Average dinner entrée price: $15-$20.

Gingerbread Man
217 Steinwehr Avenue
(717) 334-1100
www.thegingerbreadman.net
When you step inside the Gingerbread Man, you'll quickly realize why it's one of the most popular restaurants in town. Service is efficient and friendly, and there's something for everyone on the menu: pasta platters, sizzling fajitas, fresh salads, gyros, steaks, seafood—even nine specialty hamburgers and six specialty grilled chicken sandwiches. Many agree that the prime attraction is, however, the dessert. Fresh strawberries over warm shortcake doused with whipped cream, decadent chocolate peanut butter pie, and, of course, homemade gingerbread, topped with lemon sauce or whipped cream. Catering to the touring crowd, the restaurant also offers "Blue and Grey Belly Boxes," portable meals that are perfect for a day on the town or the battlefield. Average dinner entrée price: $10-$15.

Historic Cashtown Inn
1325 Old Route 30
Cashtown, PA
(717) 334-9722
www.cashtowninn.com
Also a bed-and-breakfast, and formerly a stagecoach stop—and the headquarters of Confederate General A. P. Hill—the circa-1797 building that now houses the popular Cashtown Inn still looks as if dusty riders should be tying their steeds up out front. But don't be fooled; the inn's lunch (melts, clubs, crab cakes, etc.), dinner (filet mignon, quail, seafood dishes), wine, and dessert menus are upscale and eclectic. It's open Tuesday

through Saturday for lunch and dinner. Average dinner entrée price: $20-$25.

Olivia's
3015 Baltimore Pike
(717) 359-9357
This family-owned eatery is located a few miles from Lincoln Square, but you'll find it's worth the trip. The menu blends Mediterranean classics like stuffed grape leaves, pastitchio, spanakopita, and baked lasagna with innovative twists and fresh local ingredients. On a pleasant day, ask for a seat on the outdoor terrace. It's open for lunch and dinner Tuesday through Sunday. Average dinner entrée price: $10-$15.

Spiritfield's Pub & Fare
619 Baltimore Street
(717) 334-9449
If you stop at the Gettysburg Tour Center to plan your activities or visit the Jennie Wade House, you're bound to notice Spirtifield's, located just across the street. True to its name, you'll find burgers and standard pub fare, with crab cakes, muffalata sandwiches, and other interesting bites thrown in. On a pleasant day, sit on the porch and sip a glass of sangria. Average dinner entrée price: $10-$15.

Slightly Out of the Way: Chambersburg, Pennsylvania

Although no major battles were fought here, Chambersburg likely suffered more during the Civil War than any other Northern town. The residents of this small village were still caring for soldiers wounded in the Battle of Antietam when Major General "Jeb" Stuart's cavalry looted and burned several of its buildings. Confederate raiders torched another portion of the town a year later during the Gettysburg Campaign. And on July 30, 1864, Chambersburg suffered the wrath of Lieutenant General Jubal Early, who—angered by Union devastation of parts of the Shenandoah Valley, and General David Hunter's burning of the Virginia Military Institute—sent General John McCausland's cavalry to extort reparations from the Pennsylvania town. When no money was forthcoming, McCausland evacuated the town and set it afire.

Today, visitors to the town should stop first at the Chambersburg Heritage Center, the hub of Franklin County tourism and a historic attraction in its own right. Housed in a beautifully renovated, wheelchair-accessible marble bank building built in 1915, the center is the place to go for information, travel brochures, and tips on local driving tours. It also offers a gift shop and restrooms.

Before venturing out into the town's National Historic District, visitors should also peruse the Heritage Center's extensive exhibits, which detail the town's role in the Civil War and the Underground Railroad. Serious Civil War buffs will also want to ask about the Chambersburg Civil War Seminars—an annual series of talks sponsored by the Greater Chamber of Commerce and hosted by Ted Alexander, the Chief Historian at Antietam National Battlefield.

Between Memorial Day and Thanksgiving, the Chambersburg Heritage Center is open Monday through Friday, 9:00 a.m. to 5:00 p.m.; Saturday 10:00 a.m. to 4:00 p.m.; and Sunday noon to 3:00 p.m. During the off-season, the center closes at 2:00 p.m. and is closed on Sunday. For more information call 717-264-7101, or visit the center's Web site at www.chambersburg.org.

BLOODED PLAINS

MANASSAS

This tour focuses, in general, on sites related to the 1861 and 1862 battles at Manassas.

FIRST MANASSAS

If it wasn't quite the war's *first* battle, it was surely going to be the biggest; and thousands of gung-ho soldiers on each side expected it to be the last. Experienced military men—such as Lincoln's aging General-in-Chief Winfield Scott—knew better. Still the nation's reigning military hero at the age of seventy-four, Scott had advocated a slow strangulation of the South, rather than a risky attempt at a quick fix. But military exigencies were no match for political and popular pressure. Newspapers across the North were already demanding that the Rebels be crushed. The *New York Tribune* was blaring the headlines: FORWARD TO RICHMOND! FORWARD TO RICHMOND! Influential publisher Horace Greeley insisted that the national army should prevent the new Confederate Congress from convening there on July 20.[1] Equally aggressive-minded Southerners insisted that any Federal thrust be met headlong, and naturally, blunted.

And so on July 16, 1861, crisply uniformed, forty-two-year-old Brigadier General Irvin McDowell set out from northern Virginia with a raw army of 35,000 with which to attack Brigadier General P. G. T. Beauregard's equally green army of 22,000 Confederates laying in wait behind a muddy Virginia stream called Bull Run. The polished McDowell was a Mexican War veteran and an 1838 graduate of

West Point, where he had also spent four years teaching cadets tactics. Now he would find out if green volunteers could carry out his orders on a battlefield. Winfield Scott, for one, doubted it.

McDowell's opponent was an old West Point acquaintance who had finished second, compared to his twenty-third, in a class of forty-five. Beauregard—who had resigned as superintendent of West Point in January before directing the Rebel attack on Fort Sumter—was already a hero across the South, and a much-hated villain in the North. Deployed to protect the vital rail junction at Manassas, Beauregard's army counted only about 21,000. Another 12,000 Confederates, however, under General Joseph E. Johnston, were within reinforcing distance in the lower Shenandoah Valley. McDowell was counting on Major General Robert Patterson's small army to keep Johnston where he was.

Crossing Bull Run creek before dawn on July 21, McDowell opened the battle with an attack on the left of Beauregard's long lines. Each side sent in reinforcements, but the Rebel line caved in, sending Confederates south across a stream and up a rise called Henry House Hill. Blue-clad regiments followed, pressing Bernard Bee's brigade. Here, however, the Confederates stiffened, spurred on by the appearance of Brigadier General Thomas J. Jackson's supporting brigade on the hill's far side. Minutes before his own death, Bee bellowed the words that would make a legend: "Look! There is Jackson standing like a stone wall! Rally behind the Virginians!"

For two hours, McDowell's Yankees marched up Henry House Hill into the teeth of a desperate Confederate defense. Robert Patterson had not, as it happened, prevented Johnston's escape, and the infusion of his

---

[1] James McPherson, *Battle Cry of Freedom: The Civil War Era* (London: Oxford University Press, 2003), 334.

Rebel troops gradually turned the tide of battle. Late in the afternoon, Johnston and Beauregard took to the offense, launching a stunning blow against the tiring Yankees on McDowell's left flank. That was all it took. The frustrated Federals took to their heels, retreating back across Bull Run and onto the Warrenton Turnpike. Panic followed, and McDowell's army fled all the way back to Washington, D.C. The shocking victory cost the Confederates 387 killed and some 1,600 wounded. McDowell lost 460 men killed, 1,100 wounded, and another 1,300 missing.

In the wake of the debacle, Walt Whitman thought of Abraham Lincoln, whose young administration had been saddled with such crushing news, and wrote with admiration:

The president recovering himself, begins that very night—sternly, rapidly sets about the task of reorganizing his forces, and placing himself in positions for future and surer work. If there were nothing else of Abraham Lincoln for history to stamp him with, it is enough to send him with his wreath to the memory of all future time, that he endured that hour, that day, bitterer than gall—indeed, a crucifixion day—that it did not conquer him—that he unflinchingly stemm'd [sic] it, and resolv'd [sic] to lift himself and the Union out of it.[2]

SECOND MANASSAS

The strategic situation in the east hadn't changed much thirteen months later, when armies of blue and gray met at Manassas for a rematch. Early that summer, George McClellan had driven his grand, new Army of the Potomac to the gates of the Confederate capital before a change in Confederate command, heavy rains, and McClellan's own demons conspired to push his befuddled army all the way back down the Virginia Peninsula.

Exasperated with the timid and difficult McClellan, Abraham Lincoln relieved the general of his army and assigned two of its corps to Major General John Pope, a forty-year-old West Pointer who had made a name for himself with a couple of minor victories on the Mississippi.

Pope spent most of August awaiting the arrival of McClellan's men and shifting his own 50,000 troops around central and northern Virginia in response to Robert E. Lee's movements north. Failing to detect Stonewall Jackson's lightning march past his right flank, Pope reacted only after Jackson defeated Nathaniel Banks at Cedar Mountain, cut the Orange and Alexandria rail line at Bristoe, and sacked the Union supply base at Manassas Junction. Marching his 65,000 men northeast up the Warrenton Turnpike, Pope discovered Stonewall Jackson's 24,000 Confederates dug into an abandoned railroad bed in a wood north of Manassas. On August 29, Pope—failing to concentrate his forces properly—pitched into Jackson's in a series of attacks, all of which were repulsed. Finally, he launched Major General Fitz John Porter's command at Jackson's right, only to find James Longstreet's newly arrived corps entrenched there.

The following day, Pope renewed his attacks with the same results, until Longstreet, followed by Jackson, ordered massive counterattacks. Pope's army folded up, and in an eerie repeat of the previous year's fight here, retreated east up the turnpike behind a solid rear-guard defense. Lee's victory cost him 9,200 casualties, including nearly 1,500 killed and 7,600 wounded. Pope's losses amounted to 1,724 killed, 8,372 wounded, and nearly 6,000 missing or captured. The revolving door atop the Army of the Potomac whirled again, spinning Pope all the way to The Plains and bringing George McClellan back for another tour.

---

[2] Robert U. Johnson, *Battles And Leaders Of The Civil War: Volume I: From Sumter to Shiloh* (New York, Castle Books, 1956), 193.

Major General John Pope LIBRARY OF CONGRESS

John Singleton Mosby

From his base in Warrenton—some 20 miles southwest of Manassas—John Singleton Mosby spent much of the war terrorizing Union forces from the Potomac River to the lower Shenandoah Valley. The success of Mosby's Rangers in raiding Federal supply lines, cutting communications, and diverting Union troops from other campaigns earned for his stomping grounds the designation "Mosby's Confederacy," and for the slippery Mosby—who was never caught—the moniker "Gray Ghost."

From early in his life, the intelligent but aggressive Mosby seemed destined either for great success or a quick end. Born in Powhatan County, Virginia, in 1833, he enrolled at the University of Virginia in Charlottesville in 1850. The following year Mosby found himself in jail after shooting a fellow student during an argument. But his incarceration proved to be a lucky break: Pardoned after seven months, he began studying law with the man who had prosecuted him. Eventually he passed the Virginia bar and opened a law office in Bristol, Virginia.

The outbreak of the war spurred Mosby to enlist in the Confederate cavalry, and he soon found himself serving under Major General J. E. B. Stuart. Chaffed by the regulations of regulated army life, Mosby got permission to form a detachment of Partisan Rangers in December 1862. By dividing his command (which was never bigger than 800 men) and striking several targets quickly and simultaneously, Mosby often froze his opponents, who could never tell when or where his horsemen would attack again. This way he was able to paralyze much larger Union commands—even disrupt whole campaigns.

In spite of repeated Union efforts to track and capture or kill him, Mosby survived the war and went on to even greater success—working for the U.S. government. He even took time to protest against the violence of another field of battle—the football gridiron.

Historic Sites

Ben Lomond Historic Site
10311 Sudley Manor Drive
Manassas, VA
(703) 792-4060
Currently under restoration, this home was built in the 1830s and sustained considerable damage during the battles at Manassas. During the first battle, it was used as a hospital. On the walls, you'll still see graffiti messages from wounded soldiers.

Brandy Station Battlefield
19484 Brandy Road (Graffiti House)
Brandy Station, VA
(540) 727-7718
www.brandystationfoundation.com
The biggest cavalry battle ever fought on this continent took place at Brandy Station, Virginia, on June 9, 1863, when Major General Alfred Pleasonton's Yankee troopers piled into Major General J. E. B. Stuart's Confederate camp. Some 17,000 horsemen took part in the day-long affair, which ended in Confederate victory. Stuart, however, had been surprised and fought to a standstill—an indication of the vastly improved Federal cavalry.

Today the Brandy Station Foundation (which, along with the Civil War Preservation Trust [CWPT], owns the preserved sections of the original battle site) maintains and operates the battlefield with the help of donations, grants, and fund-raisers. A recent success here was the CWPT purchase of a small but crucial 18.9-acre section of the original battlefield.

Whether by driving tour or prearranged guided tour (April through November 4), there is much to see here today, starting with the Graffiti House. In this building, soldiers from each side scrawled messages or their names here while recovering from wounds. The building also serves today as a museum and park visitor center, offering exhibits, information, tours, and lectures.

Not yet an official park, the Brandy Station battlefield is therefore open free of charge. The Graffiti House is open free of charge 11:00 a.m. to 4:00 p.m. Wednesday,

Friday, Saturday, and Sunday from April through November. It is open on Wednesday and Saturday during the winter.

The John Singleton Mosby Museum and Education Center
33 North Calhoun Street
Warrenton, VA
(540) 351-1600
www.mosbymuseum.org
Museum planners hope to unveil the completed John Singleton Mosby Museum and Education Center in Warrenton in spring 2008. Located in the same complex as the newly opened Warrenton-Fauquer County Visitor Center, the museum's mission will be to tell the story of Colonel John Mosby, Warrenton, and the county from the 1850s through 1880. Workers have already finished renovating the inside of the building, and are now busily raising money to fund improvements to its interior. Eventually, the site will include the museum inside the Spilman-Mosby House, set adjacent to the county visitor center.

The building now known as Brentmoor, the Spilman-Mosby House was built in 1859 by Judge Edward M. Spilman. Spilman sold the house to former Partisan Ranger John Keith, who in turn sold it to Mosby, who had used Warrenton as a base of operations for much of the war. Mosby, in turn, sold the house to another Confederate veteran, longtime friend Eppa Hunton. The building is now on the National Register of Historic Places.

Liberia Plantation House
8601 Portner Avenue
Manassas, VA
(703) 368-1873
va-manassas.civicplus.com/index
.asp?ID=419
Once a thriving plantation with as many as ninety slaves, Liberia was used by Brigadier General P. G. T. Beauregard as a headquarters during the summer of 1861. A year later, Union Major General Irvin McDowell made the building his own headquarters, driving the owners, the Weir family, away for the remainder of the war.

General Pierre Gustave Toutant Beauregard LIBRARY OF CONGRESS

As of summer 2007, a thorough restoration of Liberia was under way, limiting its accessibility to special tours and events, so be sure to call ahead.

The Manassas Museum
901 Prince William Street
Manassas, VA
(703) 368-1873
www.manassasmuseum.org
The 7,000-square-foot Manassas Museum is the hub of all things historical in Manassas, including a number of small Civil War sites not part of the Manassas Battlefield. Permanent and changing exhibits and videos tell the story of Northern Piedmont history, with a special focus on the Civil War and its effect on the community. The museum also contains a research library and excellent gift shop. Information about other area sites (see below) that fall under the jurisdiction of the Manassas Museum System can also be found here. The museum is open year-round, Tuesday through Sunday 10:00 a.m. to 5:00 p.m., and is wheelchair accessible. Admission is free for children under 6; $2 for kids 6–15 and seniors over 60; and $3 for adults.

Manassas National Battlefield Park
Route 234 (Visitor Center)
Manassas, VA
(703) 361-1339
www.nps.gov/mana
For now, at least, only the ghosts of the men who died here occupy the battlefields of Manassas, quietly guarding the few cannon and monuments that honor their exploits. Outside these serene plains wait the land-grabbing minions of modern society, ready to spring onto this prime real estate and plant yet more strip malls and condominiums. Perhaps no major Civil War site faces the squeeze of encroaching "civilization" quite like Manassas National Battlefield does. It is surrounded by suburban sprawl, which, in places, extends to the very edge of its original breastworks.

Despite the ever-present threat outside its boundaries, this 5,000-acre park looks and feels much the same (aside from one very busy, four-lane intersection) today as it did 140 years ago. Much of it feels secluded from the twentieth century. The recent removal of power lines from the Brawner Farm and partial restoration of the Henry and Thornbury Houses have helped. The park has also added a new picnic area and is in the midst of building a new visitor center.

Before setting out on a walking tour of the park, visitors will want to check out its small museum, which offers exhibits, a short film (for $3), and a helpful electronic battlefield map. Admission to the park itself is $3 for adults (for a three-day pass); children under 17 are free.

Manassas Railroad Depot
9431 West Street
Manassas, VA
(703) 361-6599
(877) 848-3018
www.visitmanassas.org
The depot is the town's de facto visitor center, where brochures and tourist information can be found. It is also the home of the James and Marion Payne Memorial Railroad Heritage Gallery, a combination of exhibits and artifact displays representing the town's extensive railroad history. Admission is free to the gallery, which is open daily 10:00 a.m. to 5:00 p.m.

Mayfield Earthwork Fort
8401 Quarry Road
Manassas, VA
(703) 368-1873
This 11-acre site was constructed by P. G. T. Beauregard's Confederates during May and June 1861, in anticipation of Union attack. After March 1862, Union soldiers also periodically used the earthworks.

Restoration efforts here concluded in 2001, leaving the addition of an interpretive trail with markers and replica "Quaker guns." The park is open daily from sunrise to sunset and is free of charge. (Restoration is also under way at a second local series of earth-

Manassas National Battlefield Park NATIONAL PARK SERVICE

works known as the Cannon Branch Fort. For an update on its status, contact the Manassas Museum.)

The Museum of Culpeper History
803 South Main Street
Culpeper, VA
(540) 829-1749
www.culpepermuseum.com
If you're traveling southwest, continue on to

Culpeper, another charming Virginia town that's brimming with Civil War history. From Manassas, it's about an hour to this town, tucked away in the scenic Blue Ridge Mountains. The Culpeper Museum offers a fantastic overview of the county's historic past. Located at the entrance to the Culpeper Historic District, this unassuming facility (which was originally known as the Culpeper Cavalry Museum) now focuses on the history of

Culpeper County. In addition to impressive indoor and outdoor displays related to Native American and Colonial history, the museum boasts an entire gallery dedicated to the Civil War. The Museum of Culpeper History is open Monday through Saturday 10:00 a.m. to 5:00 p.m. Admission is $3 for nonresidents.

Old Jail Museum
Court House Square
Warrenton, VA
(540) 347-5525
Consisting of two structures built in 1808 and 1823, this beautifully preserved old jail now houses a series of exhibits about the Revolutionary War, Native American history, the Civil War, and local favorite John Singleton Mosby. The Old Jail Museum is open Tuesday through Sunday 10:00 a.m. to 4:00 p.m. It's free of charge, but donations are welcome.

Other Points of Interest

Aldie Mill
Aldie, VA
(703) 327-6118
Located just west of Route 15 on U.S. Route 50, the small town of Aldie witnessed the passing of troops on June 17, 1863, as they marched toward Gettysburg. Mosby's men also fought near Aldie Mill in 1861. The early nineteenth-century mill is open for tours noon to 5:00 p.m. Sunday, April through October. Tours are free, but donations are welcome.

Blackburn's Ford
North of Manassas off Route 28
Soldiers got their first taste of battle on this ford on Bull Run. On July 18, Union troops approached the ford during a reconnaissance trip only to find Confederate forces waiting. The Southern forces stood their ground, setting the tone for the major battle that was about to transpire.

Marshall, VA
Mosby's raiders fought and finally, on April 21, 1865, disbanded in this small town west of Manassas and Haymarket. Confederate loyal-

ists silently cheered here as they watched Stonewall Jackson pass through on his way to the Battle of Second Manassas.

Piedmont Station
Delaplane, VA
It was at this train station west of Manassas that soldiers from the Army of the Shenandoah boarded a train on their way to Manassas Junction on July 19, 1861. Colonel Thomas J. Jackson was among the travelers; two days later, he would earn his nickname "Stonewall" at the First Battle of Manassas. The troops' 30-mile trip east is believed to be the first instance in which troops were moved into combat on railroad.

Rectortown, VA
Another small town in this Civil War history-rich corner of Virginia, it was here that General George McClellan was relieved of his command of the Union forces and replaced by General Ambrose Burnside in November 1862 after McClellan's failure to destroy Lee's army at Antietam.

Signal Hill
Manassas Park, VA
This small, independent town just outside of Manassas was once home to a Confederate signal station. On July 21, 1861, a Confederate signal officer named E. P. Alexander first spotted a Union cannon and forces closing in on the Confederate line. He sent a signal to Nathan "Shanks" Evans, who held the command near the Run Bridge. It is believed to be the first time "wigwag" signaling—a system of coded flag movements—was used during combat.

Thoroughfare Gap
West of Manassas, off Interstate 66
Confederate forces led by Stonewall Jackson traveled through this mountain pass on their way to fight in the Second Battle of Manassas. Confederate General James Longstreet followed with his troops, but they were met with resistance from Union forces under the com-

mand of General James B. Ricketts. The Union forces failed to stall Longstreet's advance, thus enabling the Second Battle of Manassas to take place. You can still see the ruins of Chapman's Mill, a Confederate meat curing and distribution center, which witnessed much of the battle.

Warrenton Cemetery
Warrenton, VA
In this cemetery, located across the street from the visitor center, there's a memorial honoring the more than 600 Confederate soldiers who died in the region's makeshift hospitals. It's also home to Mosby's grave.

Tours

Virginia Civil War Trails
This brochure offers a detailed walking trail and driving trail connecting many of Manassas's Civil War sites. You can pick up a copy of the brochure at the historic railroad depot or the Manassas Museum, or log on to www.civilwartrails.org to view an interactive map and pick up some tips for organizing your visit. On the same Web site, you'll also find a guide to the Route 50 corridor and sites in Warrenton and Fauquier County.

Accommodations

Bennett House Bed & Breakfast
9252 Bennett Drive
Manassas, VA
(800) 354-7060
www.virginiabennetthouse.com
If you're looking for a place to stay in Manassas, an area increasingly threatened by urban sprawl, your options are largely confined to national and international chain hotels. For something a little more unique, however, Bennett House is your best bet. The impeccably kept bed-and-breakfast offers tranquil, home-style comfort (as well as antique-filled rooms, central air, and in-room cable and VCRs) in the heart of Old Town Manassas. Mornings are memorable, as innkeepers Jean and Curtis Harrover offer a full country breakfast. The inn

has just two rooms, so visitors should make a reservation well in advance. $115-$150

Black Horse Inn
8393 Meetze Road
Warrenton, VA
(540) 349-4020
www.blackhorseinn.com
If you don't mind a bit of a drive from the battlefield, treat yourself to a stay at the award-winning Black Horse Inn in Warrenton, about thirty minutes west of Manassas—a town with unspoiled scenery and Civil War attractions of its own as well. The circa-1850 mansion served as a hospital during the Civil War and was frequently visited by the Black Horse Cavalry. Today, the nine-room inn is among the finest in northern Virginia. Many of its rooms are outfitted with canopy beds, gable ceilings, and Jacuzzi and antique claw-foot tubs; stables are even available for visiting horses. Breakfast and tea service is also included in the room rate. $125-$325

Country Inn & Suites
10810 Battleview Parkway
Manassas, VA
(703) 393-9797
www.countryinns.com
We've done our best to avoid chain accommodations, but in a region where national brands hold sway, it's good to include one of the top players. Country Inn & Suites provides an exceptional value—pleasant amenities, including a complimentary and substantial breakfast, an indoor pool, and whirlpools in many of the rooms—and a great location between the Manassas National Battlefield Park and Old Town Manassas. $149-$169

Fountain Hall Bed and Breakfast
609 South East Street
Culpeper, VA
(540) 825-8200
(800) 298-4748
www.fountainhall.com
While Culpeper is a bit of a drive from the sites of Manassas and Warrenton, you're in

for a treat if you make the trip. Steve and Kathi Walker's Fountain Hall is truly one of a kind. Built in 1859 in the heart of Culpeper, this grand Colonial Revival, complete with glorious walnut staircase, is within walking distance of the Culpeper Museum, National Cemetery, and the fine dining offered downtown. Civil War buffs can easily walk to Brandy Station or the Cedar Mountain area, while the battlefields of Manassas, Fredericksburg, and Spotsylvania are just a short drive away. For old-fashioned relaxation, Fountain Hall features an extensive library and lawn games. $120–$160

The Grey Horse Inn Bed & Breakfast
4350 Fauquier Avenue
The Plains, VA
(540) 253-7000
(877) 253-7020
www.greyhorseinn.com
Innkeepers John and Ellen Hearty welcome guests to this wonderful hunt country retreat in the town of The Plains. Confederate troops marched through the town—amid spies working for both sides—in August 1862 as they ventured to Manassas. There are six bedrooms, including one two-room suite, tastefully decorated to reflect the spirit of this 1880s-era mansion. The picturesque grounds and gardens form the perfect setting to enjoy a book or savor a cup of tea. True to its name, the inn is also popular among horse lovers who flock to The Plains for Virginia's Gold Cup steeplechase race and other equestrian events. $112–$210

Poplar Springs, the INN spa
9245 Rogues Road
Casanova, VA
(540) 788-4600
(800) 490-7747
www.poplarspringsinn.com
What could be more romantic than a town called Casanova? Secluded, charming, and outfitted with one of the region's most inviting spas, Poplar Springs is a fitting match for the town in which it's located. The inn is nes-

tled on 200 private wooded acres, with hiking and biking paths that lend to exploration on foot. Because it's a popular choice for stressed-out Washingtonians eager for an escape, the inn goes overboard to help you relax: think breakfast in bed, prompt valet service, and highly attentive service. While much of the twenty-two-room property is modern construction, the historic Manor House now houses a fine-dining restaurant known for its roaring fire, soothing piano music, and fine cuisine. Don't be surprised to see sweetbreads, venison, elk, and other unusual items on the menu. $240–$550

Westfields Marriott
14750 Conference Center Drive
Chantilly, VA
(703) 818-0300
www.marriott.com/hotels/travel/iadwf-westfields-marriott-washington-dulles/
For luxury accommodations and even a quick round of golf or spa treatment between Manassas and Dulles Airport, this AAA-Four Diamond designated Marriott property is a fine choice. Unlike many of our other recommendations, this 327-room resort is sleek and modern, equipped with modern, business-traveler-friendly amenities like wireless Internet, but also furnished with touches of art and antiques. There's a Fred Couples–designed golf course on the premises, along with a high-end spa. $150-$350

Restaurants

Carmello's & Little Portugal Restaurant
9108 Center Street
Manassas, VA
(703) 368-5522
www.carmellos.com
It may be surprising to find one of the Washington, D.C., metropolitan area's premier Portuguese restaurants in the commuter town of Manassas, but many regional residents with discerning palates have found their way to Carmello's since it opened nearly twenty years ago. On the menu, you'll find a blend of classic northern Italian pasta dishes, along

Brigadier General Thomas McDowell LIBRARY OF CONGRESS

with Portuguese creations like bife pimenta (filet mignon served in port wine with cracked pepper) and vierias (shrimp, scallops, lobster, and artichoke hearts sauteed in garlic and white wine sauce). Pair up your dinner with a bottle of Alvarhino or another Portuguese wine. It's located on Old Town Manassas's primary shopping street, perfect for an after-dinner stroll. Average dinner entrée price: $20-$25.

City Square Café
9428 Battle Street
Manassas, VA
(703) 369-6022
www.citysquarecafe.com
This family-friendly restaurant has served comfortable, casual fare to locals and visitors for more than thirty years. Owners Robert and Susana Barolin serve Mediterranean dishes like chicken parmesan and veal Marsala, along with standard American classics like prime rib and shrimp scampi. Showcasing the flavors of the Barolins's native Uruguay, you'll also find an extensive selection of South American wines on the wine list, along with empanadas on the menu. Average dinner entrée price: $15-$20.

Claire's at the Depot
65 South Third Street
Warrenton, VA
(540) 351-1616
www.clairesrestaurant.com
As the Washington, D.C., metropolitan area continues to expand to the west, once-sleepy towns like Warrenton begin to attract more urban-minded residents, along with high-quality restaurants such as this one. On the menu, you'll find eclectic, modern cuisine. The turn-of-the-century depot in which it's located shows off the flavors of the town's railroad past. Modern twists and regional classics frequently show up on the menu, like scrumptious she-crab soup and oysters served in a cornmeal crust. Dishes are flavorful, crafted with local produce and seasoned with fresh herbs grown on-site, and vegetari-

ans won't be disappointed by the meatless selections. If you dine here in the spring or summer, ask to be seated on the glorious outdoor patio among the seasonal flowers and fountains. Average dinner entrée price: $20-$25.

Foti's Restaurant
219 East Davis Street
Culpeper, VA
(540) 829-8400
www.fotisrestaurant.com
New to the Culpeper restaurant scene, Foti's has quickly become known as one of the area's best eating establishments. This is not a restaurant to walk into straight from a battlefield; it is a first-class, fine-dining house perfect for those looking for superb food and a relaxing night on the town. Wondering about the name? It's a childhood nickname that co-owner Frank Maragos used to answer to, setting the tone for a friendly, familiar dining experience. Main courses include such flavorful creations as crispy seared Tasmanian salmon and lamb three ways. Foti's is open for lunch Tuesday through Friday 11:30 a.m. to 2:00 p.m., and dinner Tuesday through Friday 5:30 to 9:30 p.m. (Saturday dinner from 5:00 p.m.). Reservations are highly recommended. Average dinner entrée price: $20-$25.

Okra's Louisiana Bistro
9110 Center Street
Manassas, VA
(703) 330-2729
www.okras.com
Even discerning Cajun diners take a shine to Okra's, a colorful, friendly eatery in Old Town Manassas. Munch on appetizers like alligator bites and fried okra as you wait for your food and sip an Abita beer or Hurricane. For the main course, you can't go wrong with the jambalaya, teeming with andouille, shrimp and tasso ham, or the zesty crawfish étoufée, flavorful and bursting with vegetables and spices. The restaurant is also a lively place for nightlife with frequent live music acts. It stays open late—until 10:00 p.m. on Sunday, mid-

night on Monday, Tuesday, and Wednesday, and until 2:00 a.m. Thursday and Friday. Average dinner entrée price: $15-$20.

The Rail Stop Restaurant
6478 Main Street
The Plains, VA
(540) 253-5644
www.railstoprestaurant.com

It's no wonder that railroad-themed restaurants are popular in this part of Virginia; the steel tracks played an integral role in the histories of many of the Commonwealth's small towns and cities. In the tiny hamlet of The Plains, the Rail Stop is the place to go for your urban restaurant fix—and possibly even a brush with a celebrity. (Actor Robert Duvall lives nearby and was once co-owner of the restaurant.) Stop in at lunchtime for a satisfying grilled salmon BLT topped with pancetta, arugula, and basil aioli or linger over a tantalizing dinner of pan-seared scallops accompanied by mushroom risotto and smothered in a garlic cream sauce or fresh gnocchi paired with Italian sausage, artichokes, roasted peppers, tomatoes, onions, and fresh mozzarella. It's open Tuesday for dinner 5:30 to 9:00 p.m.; and for lunch and dinner Wednesday through Saturday:11:00 a.m. to 3:00 p.m. for lunch; 5:30 to 9:00 p.m. Wednesday and Thursday and 5:30 to 9:30 p.m. Friday, and 5:00 to 9:30 p.m. Saturday. Sunday brunch is served from 10:30 a.m. to 3:00 p.m. and dinner from 5:00 to 8:30 p.m. Average entrée price: $20-$25.

Sweetwater Tavern
14250 Sweetwater Lane
Centreville, VA
(703) 449-1100
www.greatamericanrestaurants.com

Locals love Sweetwater Tavern—a Fairfax, Virginia–based restaurant with a few locations in the Washington, D.C., metro area, including this one that's just north of Manassas. It's always hopping, and the food, service, and ambience are consistently good. Sample the house-made beers and munch on Southwestern creations like Tex-Mex egg rolls and spicy bean-cheese-guacamole dip, then move on to crowd-pleasing main courses like crispy chicken tenders, juicy burgers, and barbecue ribs. If you're shopping for evening entertainment, you're also likely to find live music and a crowd that appreciates it. Average dinner entrée price: $15-$20.

Virginia Barbeque
9952 Liberia Avenue
Manassas, VA
(703) 369-4227
www.vabbqmanassas.com

If you're looking for great barbecue in the town of Manassas, this is the place for it. Don't let the plain strip mall in which it's located fool you; it's well known in the area for producing fabulous meats in the Virginia, North Carolina, or Texas tradition. Because you're in Virginia, we'd steer you to the specialty: Virginia-style pulled pork, slathered in the spicy tomato-based sauce for which the Old Dominion is known. The restaurant also does an admirable job with traditional barbecue accompaniments, like tangy coleslaw, perfectly seasoned baked beans, and freshly prepared hush puppies. Average dinner entrée price: $10-$15.

POWDER KEG

BALTIMORE

This tour concentrates on the city of Baltimore, an important railroad hub of heavily Southern sentiment during the Civil War.

Bathed in glory by the city's defiant stand against the British in 1814, Baltimore was, by midcentury, a bustling seaport and trade center big enough to rival Washington, D.C., in status. In 1830 the brand-new Baltimore and Ohio Railroad opened, and slowly extended its reach across Maryland, through Harpers Ferry, and by 1853 all the way across western Virginia (now West Virginia) to the Ohio River. It brought new settlers to the Midwest, and returned east with trade goods.

By 1861 Baltimore was a city divided. As in that political powder keg called St. Louis, Missouri, Confederate sympathizers lived side by side with stout Unionists. The ugly riot that darkened the city in April 1861 reflected Maryland's sharply divided loyalties, and helped guide new President Abraham Lincoln in his efforts to keep the state from seceding.

Union officials had already managed to avoid trouble in Baltimore once, when the president-elect passed through the city on his way from Illinois to Washington, D.C., late on February 22. Warned of a plot to assassinate him as he switched trains in Baltimore, Lincoln reluctantly agreed, as he later put it, "to run no risk where no risk was necessary."[1] The intelligence, after all, had come from Allan Pinkerton—founder of the Pinkerton Detective Agency—who presumably knew what he was doing. (Pinkerton's agency would later gain fame on the frontier during its pursuit of the Jesse James Gang. First, however, Pinker-

ton would come under fire for backing George McClellan's ridiculous claims of enemy troop numbers during his brief tenure atop the Army of the Potomac.

With a heavy coat covering his shoulders and an unfamiliar soft hat on his head, Lincoln (along with Pinkerton and Ward Hill Lamon, his personal bodyguard) slipped unannounced from a special train in Baltimore in the wee hours of February 23, transferred to the capital-bound train, and reached Washington without incident. Things took a violent turn a few weeks later, however, after Lincoln—in the wake of the Confederate attack on Fort Sumter—issued a call for 75,000 volunteers with which to suppress the rebellion. For a number of Southern governors, this was the step—they claimed—that pushed them into the Confederate camp. Eastern Maryland was home to a vocal, pro-Southern population. The arrival of Northern troops in Baltimore was bound to cause a fuss.

On April 19—one hundred years to the day after the Battles of Lexington and Concord—the 6th Massachusetts Militia debarked in Baltimore en route, like Lincoln a few weeks earlier, to Washington. A hostile crowd awaited them. When the inexperienced militiamen passed, angry Marylanders unleashed a barrage of stones. In return, the attackers received a volley of musketry. The exchange left four soldiers and a dozen civilians dead on the street.

Things were only slightly quieter two months later when Elisha Hunt Rhodes rolled into town with the 2nd Rhode Island Volunteers. "We arrived in Baltimore after dark and disembarked from the cars to march through the city to the Washington Depot," wrote Rhodes. "Immense crowds met us at the depot and the streets were lined with people

---

[1] David Herbert Donald, *Lincoln* (New York: Simon and Schuster, 1995), 279.

Fort McHenry National Monument NATIONAL PARK SERVICE

who shouted for Jeff Davis and abused us roundly."[2]

Warning a Maryland peace commission to "Keep your rowdies in Baltimore," Lincoln used heavy-handed persuasion to keep the state loyal. Federal authorities arrested Baltimore's mayor when he refused to pledge an oath of loyalty to the Union. A small army of Union troops deployed throughout the city while Lincoln used the media to infuse pro-Union sentiment. Baltimore calmed. Although Maryland soldiers fought for each side during the war, the state remained in the Union.

Historic Sites

Baltimore Civil War Museum at President Street Station
601 President Street
Baltimore
(410) 385-5188
www.mdhs.org/explore/baltcivilwar.html
Managed by the Maryland Historical Society and housed in a historic, 1849 railroad build-

ing, this museum explores the roles and divided sentiments of Baltimore and Maryland in the Civil War, in addition to the local efforts of the Underground Railroad to move slaves north to freedom. The museum's exhibits offer insight into the April 19 riot and other tumultuous 1861 events. It's also a starting point for the Baltimore Riot Walking Trail, which is marked by six interpretive markers. Admission is $4 for adults, $3 for children 13–17, and free for seniors and college students with ID. The museum is open Thursday through Monday from 10:00 a.m. to 5:00 p.m.

Baltimore and Ohio Railroad Museum
901 West Pratt Street
Baltimore
(410) 752-2490
www.borail.org
After a near-disastrous roof collapse that left a number of locomotives and other artifacts

[2] Elisha Hunt Rhodes, *All for the Union: The Civil War Diary & Letters of Elisha Hunt Rhodes* (New York: Vintage, 1992).

badly damaged, the renowned B&O Railroad Museum reopened late in 2004 with expanded visitor services and educational programs. The heart of the 40-acre museum complex, of course, remains its historic loco-motives and its unmatched collection of rail-road artifacts and ephemera dating to 1830. The combination of these marvelous old machines and recognition of their importance in the Civil War (and the expansion of the fron-tier) makes this museum a must-see for adults and kids.

With the exception of federal holidays (when the museum is closed), the Baltimore and Ohio Railroad Museum is open Monday through Friday 10:00 a.m. to 4:00 p.m., Satur-day 10:00 a.m. to 5:00 p.m., and Sunday 11:00 a.m. to 4:00 p.m. Admission is $14 for adults, $12 for seniors, and $8 for children ages 2–12. For $2 more, you can add a visit to the B&O Railroad Museum at Ellicott City Sta-tion, the oldest surviving railroad station in America, dating to 1830. See the "Other Sites of Interest" section.

Reginald F. Lewis Museum of Maryland African American History & Culture
830 East Pratt Street
Baltimore
(443) 263-1800
www.africanamericanculture.org
While the Civil War isn't a primary focal point of this museum, which opened in 2005 at Bal-timore's Inner Harbor, it does an admirable job of recounting the contributions of Mary-land's free and enslaved African Americans before, during, and after the war. It's a must-see for any African-American history enthusiast, tackling topics like family life and community bonds, labor contributions, and cultural and entertainment achievements. It's open Tuesday through Saturday from 10:00 a.m. to 5:00 p.m. and Sunday noon to 5:00 p.m. Admission is $8 for adults, $6 for students and seniors, and free for children under age 6.

USS *Constellation* Museum
Pier 1, Inner Harbor
301 East Pratt Street
Baltimore
(410) 539-1797
www.constellation.org
The last all-sail ship built by the U.S. Navy, the *Constellation* was used to police the coast of Africa to enforce slave trading laws. During the war, it defended Union merchants from Confederate raiders. It's also the only Civil War–era ship that's still afloat. The ship is open daily from May 1 through October 14 from 10:00 a.m. to 4:00 p.m., October 15 to April 30 from 10:00 a.m. to 4:00 p.m., closed Thanksgiving, Christmas, and New Year's. Admission is $8.75 for adults, $7.50 for sen-iors, $4.75 for children age 6 to 14; children age 5 and under free.

Other Sites of Interest

B&O Railroad Museum: Ellicott City Station
2711 Maryland Avenue
Ellicott City, MD
(410) 461-1945
www.ecborail.org
The oldest surviving railroad station in the United States, the Ellicott City Station is a nice complement to a visit to the B&O Railroad museum. Visitors can learn about the rise of railroad transportation in the United States; there's also an exhibition that discusses the importance of the railroad to the Union during the Civil War. It's open Friday and Saturday 11:00 a.m. to 4:00 p.m. and Sunday noon to 5:00 p.m. Admission is $5 for adults (or $2 when combined with a visit to the Baltimore museum).

Druid Hill Park
North and Madison Streets
Baltimore
www.ci.baltimore.md.us/government/recn parks/popups/parks/druid_hill_park.htm
The city's first large municipal park was pur-chased in 1860 at the height of a nationwide movement to develop parks for city dwellers. Early in the war, Union soldiers camped near

the park's entrance. As the war gathered steam, the park became an organizing point for members of the U.S. Colored Troops. Admission is free.

Federal Hill
Baltimore
www.historicfederalhill.org
This park overlooking the Inner Harbor attracts visitors for more than just a postcard-perfect view. After the riot of 1861, Union troops took command of the strategic location under the command of General Benjamin F. Butler, who led troops from Annapolis to Baltimore in the middle of the night on the B&O Railroad. Overnight, the men put up a small fort and aimed their cannons squarely at downtown Baltimore to intimidate would-be dissenters and to keep the city and the state under Union control.

Fort McHenry National Monument and Historic Shrine
2400 East Fort Avenue
Baltimore
(410) 962-4290
www.nps.gov/fomc
Famed for its role in repelling the British attack on Baltimore during the War of 1812, Fort McHenry was garrisoned by Union troops and used during the Civil War as a prison for Confederate soldiers and sympathizers. It's open 8:00 a.m. to 4:45 p.m. daily with extended hours in the summer. Admission is $7.00 for 16 and older; under 16 free.

Lansdowne Christian Church
101 Clyde Avenue
Baltimore
(410) 242-4821
www.erols.com/lanscc
This historic church was built in 1905, a gift from Civil War veteran Charles Hull and his wife, Mary, to honor the fallen Union soldiers. The benefactors required, however, that the church hold a memorial service every May in memory of Hull's brothers-at-arms, making the church the focal point of local Memorial Day observances.

Maryland Historical Society
201 West Monument Street
Baltimore
(410) 685-3750
www.mdhs.org
There's a small gallery in this museum that showcases Civil War artifacts recovered from the battleground border state. You can also watch a short video about the war and its effects on the region. If you're in luck, you'll catch a temporary exhibition with a Civil War theme. The museum is open Wednesday through Sunday 10:00 a.m. to 5:00 p.m. Admission is $4 for adults, $3 for seniors and children 13–17, and free for children under 12.

Mount Clare Museum House
1500 Washington Boulevard
Baltimore
(410) 837-3262
www.mountclare.org
Located in the center of what was once a rich plantation, Mount Clare is a splendid example of Georgian architecture built for one of the city's most celebrated colonial residents, Charles Carroll. During the war, guns and munitions were stored on the grounds of the mansions in a position known as Camp Carroll. Union forces used the western pastures as a cavalry training facility. The mansion is open Tuesday through Saturday 10:00 a.m. to 4:00 p.m. and Mondays by appointment. Admission is $6 for adults, $5 for seniors, and $4 for students (under 18).

Accommodations

Abacrombie Fine Food and Accommodations
58 West Biddle Street
Baltimore
(410) 244-7227
www.abacrombie.net
Locals know this twelve-room B&B best for its fine-dining restaurant, voted "Best Restaurant" by the Baltimore *Sun*, but overnight guests discover clean, comfortable, and reasonably priced accommodations that include free parking and breakfast. Rooms are fur-

Fort McHenry National Monument NATIONAL PARK SERVICE

nished with antiques and replicas that reflect the history and flavor of the historic location. A word of caution: The Abacrombie is housed in a four-story row house, so be sure to pack lightly; you may be climbing steps! $88-$185

Admiral Fell Inn
888 South Broadway
Baltimore
(410) 522-7380

www.harbormagic.com/AdmiralFell/
admiral_fell_default.asp
A Baltimore landmark and one of the National Trust for Historic Preservation's Historic Hotels of America, the stylistically diverse, eighty-room Admiral Fell Inn fits nicely into the Fells Point Historic District. Its nicely appointed, modern rooms and suites (which offer everything from fireplaces and canopy beds to Jacuzzis) look and feel much cozier than most hotel rooms. As you might expect

in a historic hotel, ghost legends abound. Curious guests can sit down for afternoon tea to learn about the spirit-residents or decide for themselves during a one-hour ghost tour of the hotel and grounds. A stone's throw from the Inner Harbor, the quietly classy inn is central to everything in Baltimore. But if you want to stay in for dinner, the inn also boasts its own fine-dining restaurant named True. $179-$250

Aunt Rebecca's Bed & Breakfast
106 East Preston Street
Baltimore
(410) 625-1007
www.auntrebeccasbnb.com
Situated in an 1870 brownstone town house, Aunt Rebecca's is a favorite among visitors to downtown Baltimore, and with good reason. Its innkeepers are warm and welcoming, its prices are reasonable, and the location can't be beat. The three guest rooms are large and comfortable and feature special touches like claw-foot bathtubs. Rates include free parking and a tasty, home-cooked breakfast served to all guests at 8:00 a.m. $100-$125

Brookshire Suites
120 East Lombard Street
Baltimore
(410) 625-1300
www.harbormagic.com/Brookshire/
brookshire_default.asp
If all of the history hunting has left you craving something a little more contemporary, check in to the Brookshire Suites. It's a sister property of historic Admiral Fell Inn, but there's a strikingly different mood at this ninety-seven-room Inner Harbor hotel. Guests enjoy a complimentary hot breakfast served in the Cloud Club, a top-floor dining room with a breathtaking view of the city and its surroundings. Local wines and beers are served by the glass—and free of charge—to guests on weekdays 5:30 p.m. to 6:30 p.m., while summers bring weekly bargain-priced Crab Feasts to let guests try out a Maryland culinary tradition. Guest rooms and suites are roomy,

clean, and comfortable, and many have pleasant views of the harbor. $179-$250

Celie's Waterfront Bed and Breakfast
1714 Thames Street
Baltimore
(410) 522-2323
(800) 432-0184
www.celieswaterfront.com
Located on the historic Fells Point waterfront, Celie's is sunny, comfortable, convenient, unique, and brimming with modern amenities (plus access to the inn's private rooftop deck). The inn's Harbor Front rooms are perfect for romantic getaways, outfitted with four-poster king-size beds, wood-burning fireplaces and hydro-thermal massage tubs. The hotel also boasts two large suites equipped with pull-out couches and kitchens that sleep four to six guests. In-room fridges are stocked with complimentary water and sodas, and continental breakfast is included in the room rate. $139-$340

4 East Madison Inn
4 East Madison Street
Baltimore
(410) 332-0880
www.4eastmadisoninn.com
If you prefer the authenticity of Baltimore's neighborhoods to the built-up modernity of the Inner Harbor, check into this elegant nine-room B&B in Mount Vernon. The cozy rooms are furnished with glorious antiques, ornately carved Victorian furniture, chandeliers, and even fireplaces in some rooms. Guests enjoy modern conveniences like high-speed Internet, free parking, comfortable beds, and a lavish, home-cooked breakfast. $185-$250

Glenda's Bed & Breakfast
2028 Park Avenue
Baltimore
(410) 383-8535
www.bedandbreakfast.com/maryland-
baltimore-glendasbedbreakfast.html
This charming two-room B&B is carved out of a three-story 1886 brick and brownstone row

house with magnificent high ceilings. Although it's tempting to sleep in when you're luxuriating in a cozy bed (and perhaps even enjoying the in-room fireplace), you won't want to miss breakfast prepared by Glenda herself. You'll also be treated to afternoon tea, complete with tasty desserts, served daily 4:00 to 5:00 p.m. While it's not in the heart of the tourist district, it's a short five- to ten-minute drive or bus trip to most points of interest—well worth it for the reasonably priced accommodations and personal service. $120-$130

Inn at Henderson's Wharf
1000 Fell Street
Baltimore
(410) 522-7777
www.hendersonswharf.com
Step inside the Inn at Henderson's Wharf and you'll see why it's consistently rated one of Baltimore's top hotels. Located in Fell Point, where Baltimore dips gently into the Chesapeake Bay and where restaurants and nightclubs abound, the thirty-eight-room inn is warm and welcoming, offering friendly, knowledgeable service and even a complimentary bottle of wine upon check-in. Rooms are luxuriously outfitted with lush feather beds, flat-screen TVs, and, in some cases, exposed-brick walls. Guests can walk to the bars, shops, and restaurants in Fell Point for the evening, then wake up to a delicious breakfast spread—which can also be enjoyed in an outdoor garden patio. $250-$350

Inn at 2920
2920 Elliott Street
Baltimore
(410) 342-4450
www.theinnat2920.com
Most travelers associate B&Bs with antique furnishings and floral bedspreads, but that's not the case at this upscale, contemporary property. The five fashionably furnished rooms have fun and funky names and designs, and some come with a resident beta fish whose name matches the theme of the

room. Valentino, for example, lives in the "Bordello Room," while Columbus stays in the "Room at the End of the World." Guests can luxuriate in Jacuzzi tubs and enjoy high-speed wireless Internet access and gourmet breakfast. From the Canton neighborhood, where the inn is located, it's a twenty- to thirty-minute walk to downtown Baltimore or a quick water taxi ride across the harbor. $155-$225

Restaurants

Aldo's Ristorante Italiano
306 South High Street
Baltimore
(410) 727-0700
www.aldositaly.com
If you want to splurge on a wonderful Italian meal in an inspiring setting, Aldo's is a fine place to do it. Step inside and you'll see why it's considered the most beautiful restaurant in Little Italy. The dining room is outfitted with soaring columns, glorious high ceilings, and intricate woodwork, much of it carved by Chef/Owner Aldo Vitale. The chef hails from the Calabria region of southern Italy and infuses light, Mediterranean cooking traditions into many of his dishes. If you're in the mood for a little indulgence, however, look past the light and healthy seafood dishes and feast on Aldo's Tournedos Rossini, a decadent combination of grilled filet mignon, seared Hudson Valley foie gras, Italian black truffle, porcini, and wild mushrooms sauce, served with four-cheese risotto. It's open for dinner nightly. Men should note that jackets are required. Average dinner entrée price: $25-$30.

Amicci's
231 South High Street
Baltimore
(410) 528-1096
www.amiccis.com
This friendly, laid-back Italian restaurant lacks the formality you'll find in other Little Italy hot spots. The food is simple, fresh, and reasonably priced; there's not much on the dinner

menu that's priced above $18. Choose from classic Italian favorites and comfort foods like lasagna, chicken parmigiana, and house-made gnocchi. Pastas come served with classic sauces or gussied up with sautéed chicken, shrimp, and fresh veggies. Families will also feel right at home in this kid-friendly eatery that's open daily for lunch and dinner. Average dinner entrée price: $12-$18.

Angelina's Restaurant
7135 Harford Road
Baltimore
(410) 444-5545
Opened in 1952, Angelina's is a culinary landmark, the odd marriage of an Italian restaurant and Irish pub. And believe it or not, many diners agree that Angelina's signature crab cakes are the best in town. In addition to the famous cakes, teeming with sweet, tender crab meat and almost no filling, you'll also find Italian specialties, Irish classics like shepherd's pie, fish and chips, and pints of Guinness flowing on draft. In fact, legend has it that Angelina's poured the first Guinness in Baltimore. It's open for lunch and dinner daily. Average dinner entrée price: $12-$18.

The Bicycle, A Global Bistro
1444 Light Street
Baltimore
(410) 234-1900
www.bicyclebistro.com
This trendy Federal Hill favorite has earned a reputation as one of Charm City's most sought-after tables. "Global Bistro" isn't an exaggeration here; the menu is infused with the flavors of India, South America, Italy, France, Thailand—and usually in some combination, prepared in an open kitchen by Executive Chef Nicholas Batey. Starters include sashimi grade tuna served with avocado and a spicy peanut dressing; for the main feature, there's a tantalizing grilled New Zealand rack of lamb, marinated in cilantro-lime dressing and served with grilled pineapple poblano chutney and scallion and roasted garlic mashed potatoes. It's open for dinner Monday through Saturday. Average dinner entrée price: $25-$30.

Della Notte
801 Eastern Avenue
Baltimore
(410) 837-5500
www.dellanotte.com
A popular draw in Baltimore's renowned Little Italy neighborhood, Della Notte features classic Italian cuisine made from the finest veal, poultry, and seafood. The restaurant's diverse menu also offers hearty dishes such as filet mignon, lamb shanks, and Chesapeake Bay rockfish. Breads and desserts are made fresh on the premises. Another bonus: Della Notte offers free parking, a rarity in Little Italy! Reservations are recommended on weekends. Della Notte is open for lunch and dinner seven days a week. Average dinner entrée price: $25-$30.

Helen's Garden Café
2908 O'Donnell Street
Baltimore
(410) 276-2233
www.helensgarden.com
Helen's is the place to go in the Canton neighborhood for salads, sandwiches, pasta dishes, and other light lunch fare. For dinner, you'll find a tantalizing assortment of meat dishes like curried salmon, pork chops au poivre, and Greek shrimp, with dozens of complementary wines available by the glass. The space is charming and inviting, furnished with eclectic pieces of art. It's open Tuesday through Sunday for lunch and dinner. Average dinner entrée price: $20-$25.

MaMa's on the Half Shell
2901 O'Donnell Street
Baltimore
(410) 276-3161
If you're prowling for fresh seafood, MaMa's should be on your radar screen. While the shrimp are succulent and the crab cakes are packed with as much meat as you could hope for, the real draw is the ice-cold jumbo-size

oysters. Sit outside on the patio and savor the flavors of the Chesapeake, best when washed down with a local beer. MaMa's is located in the Camden neighborhood, about a $10 cab ride from downtown. It's open for lunch and dinner daily. Average dinner entrée price: $20-$25.

Nacho Mama's
2907 O'Donnell Street
Baltimore
(410) 675-0898
nachomamascanton.com

For Mexican fare served in a fun, festive atmosphere, stop by this Canton bistro, which adds a Baltimore twist to southwestern classics. Quesadillas are stuffed with shrimp, artichokes and, of course, jumbo lump crab meat. Mexican favorites like tacos, fajitas, and chimichangas are hot sellers, while other diners opt for Mama's classic meatloaf or chipotle-seasoned barbeque baby back ribs. Come during happy hour and you're likely to find a crowd of locals gathered here for after-work margaritas, munching on chips served in hubcaps. It's open daily for lunch and dinner. Average dinner entrée price: $10-$15.

Obrycki's Crab House and Seafood Restaurant
1727 East Pratt Street
Baltimore
(410) 732-6399
www.obryckis.com

In Baltimore, everyone's got an opinion on where you should go for crabs. While some may argue that Obrycki's house-blended seasoning isn't as tasty as the traditional Old Bay seasoning, the popularity of this Fells Point eatery among locals and visitors tells a different story. The restaurant uses only the freshest local seafood, which limits it to seasonal (March through November) operations. If cracking into a crab isn't for you, you can also feast on crab cakes and other regional specialties here. The restaurant is open Monday through Saturday 11:30 a.m. to 11:00 p.m.,

and Sunday 11:30 a.m. to 9:30 p.m. It closes a bit earlier during the fall. Average dinner entrée price: $20-$25.

Phillips Harbor Place
301 Light Street
Baltimore
(410) 685-6600
www.phillipsseafood.com

Phillips must be doing something right. A Baltimore dining destination since 1980, you'll still find long lines packed with tourists and locals during peak season. Don't leave without tasting the specialty of the house: the famous lump crab cakes, flavored with two types of mustard and the signature house seasoning. Or, for a true seafood extravaganza, feast on the all-you-can-eat seafood buffet (adjacent to the main restaurant), which includes steamed crabs and a smattering of side dishes. It's open for lunch and dinner daily. Average dinner entrée price: $25-$30.

Pierpoint Restaurant
1822 Aliceanna Street
Baltimore
(410) 675-2080
www.pierpointrestaurant.com

Although it's been open nearly twenty years, Chef Nancy Longo's Pierpoint Restaurant remains one of the most talked-about restaurants in Baltimore. While it's ever popular with locals, Longo's culinary creations showcase Maryland's bounty, making it a great pick for visitors, too. The Fells Point eatery is cozy and intimate, with room for just forty-four customers; it's best to make a reservation or come on a less-crowded week night. There's also a spectacular open kitchen, allowing diners to watch the team in action as they craft tasty concoctions like Maryland-style cioppino, pork chops, and Moroccan lamb with mango pesto. It's open for lunch Tuesday through Friday (by reservation only), dinner Tuesday through Sunday, and Sunday brunch. Average dinner entrée price: $20-$25.

Samos
600 Oldham Street
Baltimore
(410) 675-5292
www.samosrestaurant.com
Don't judge this well-loved Greektown restaurant for its plain and simple exterior; take a look instead at the long lines of locals who have named this place one of their favorites for authentic Mediterranean fare, served in a casual setting (and equally popular for takeout). Step inside the modest eatery, and you'll be greeted by the mouth-watering smell of gyros turning on a spit and warm pita bread emerging from the oven. Can't decide what to order? For $19.50 per person (minimum two people), you can take a culinary expedition with the "Tour of Samos," a combination platter featuring a Greek salad, calamari, lamb chops, chicken souvlaki, dolomites, spinach pie, garlic shrimp, and gyro. It's open Monday through Saturday 10:00 a.m. to 9:00 p.m. Average dinner entrée price: $15-$20.

THE CAPITAL

WASHINGTON, D.C.

This tour focuses on the nation's capital and the immediate vicinity. The bustling seat of the federal government was, for four years, ringed by forts of earth, wood, and cannon.

Civil War–era Washington, D.C., was a city of contrasts, one part bustling metropolis and one part muddy, frontier boomtown. In its drinking establishments, robust support for both the Union and the new Confederacy was voiced. Politicians and foreign visitors gathered in the ever-popular Willard Hotel to debate the merits of the states' rights. Loud arguments occasionally degenerated into fights in the Senate and House; congressmen armed with pistols and derringers walked the streets prepared to defend their beliefs.

Would-be soldiers seeing the city for the first time had differing impressions. Poor sewage and drainage systems contributed to a rising stench from the Potomac River that summer heat only magnified. And it was hard to think of a city in which pigs roamed the streets as the national capital. (One evening that summer, an army lieutenant chasing a skulker down Pennsylvania Avenue captured his quarry when the man tripped over a cow napping in the street.) Even the capitol was a mess. For nearly a decade, engineers, masons, and carpenters had been busy refurbishing the building; but even now, the iron dome designed to replace the original wooden model remained unfinished. And with war clouds forming, mobilization of a national army would only add to the city's transitory appearance.

Here, on March 4, 1861, a broad mix of locals and out-of-towners packed the shoulders of Pennsylvania Avenue to catch a glimpse of the tall, lanky westerner about to be inaugurated as president. At noon, Abraham Lincoln emerged from the Willard Hotel with his white-haired, careworn, predecessor, James Buchanan, and they climbed into a carriage to make the short trip to the U.S. Capitol. It loomed up behind the gathered dignitaries as if to remind them of the important national work at hand.

From the Capitol's east portico, Lincoln delivered his inaugural address to a crowd gathered below the watchful eyes of soldiers posted atop nearby buildings. In his closing remarks, the former lawyer reached out to the South, where seven states had already seceded from the Union:

"We are not enemies, but friends. We must not be enemies . . . The mystic chords of memory, stretching from every battlefield, and patriot grave, to every living heart and hearthstone, all over this broad land, will yet swell the chorus of the Union, when again touched, as surely they will be, by the better angels of our nature."

The April 12 Confederate bombardment of Fort Sumter, however, shattered any remaining illusions of peace. And after a Rebel Army sent thousands of Yankees fleeing back from Manassas into the capital in July, the threat of a Confederate attack on Washington took on real meaning. Union engineers went to work constructing an elaborate defensive ring around the city—one that by 1865 would include some 160 separate forts and batteries linked by rifle pits in a 37-mile arc. Only once was this ring challenged, and then not seriously. In July 1864, Jubal Early led a force of 14,000 Confederates down (north) the

Clara Barton National Historic Site NATIONAL PARK SERVICE

Shenandoah Valley, past a hastily-gathered Union force at the Monocacy River, and to the northern outskirts of the city. But Early, who was really trying to divert Union troops from Petersburg, quickly retreated back onto home ground. Panicked city residents breathed a collective sigh of relief.

War changed the District. The mud and wandering farm animals remained, but Abraham Lincoln, the man who had done so much to bind the nation back together, was gone, assassinated by John Wilkes Booth within days of Robert E. Lee's surrender. His replacement, Tennessean Andrew Johnson, would soon prove to be a shadow of his predecessor.

But with the war over, thousands of soldiers were returning home—packing up tents and vacating the vast earthworks that had turned the city into an armed, itinerant camp. Black codes were gone, the Thirteenth Amendment had been passed, and free African Americans were assuming a more visible place in Washington society. Peace and hope had returned. Even the capitol dome—long the symbol of a shattered nation—had been finished.

Museums and Attractions

African American Civil War Memorial
U Street and Vermont Avenue NW
Washington, D.C.
(202) 667-2667
www.afroamcivilwar.org
Dedicated in 1998, this memorial honors the more than 200,000 African-American soldiers who fought to preserve the Union. The centerpiece of the memorial is "Spirit of Freedom," a 10-foot statue bearing the likenesses of young black soldiers and a sailor, created by Kentucky artist Ed Hamilton. It was the first major work by an African-American sculptor to earn a place of honor on federal land in Washington, D.C. Surrounding the statue is a granite-paved plaza encircled by walls bearing the names of the men who served. The memorial is located in the Shaw neighborhood, named for Robert Gould Shaw, the white colonel who led the 54th Massachu-

setts Volunteer Infantry's troops, as immortalized in the movie "Glory." Near the memorial, the African American Civil War Memorial Freedom Foundation Museum and Visitors Center (1200 U Street NW) offers further insight into the black experience during the Civil War. It's open weekdays from 10:00 AM to 5:00 PM and until 2:00 PM on Saturday. Admission is free.

Clara Barton National Historic Site
5801 Oxford Road
Glen Echo, MD
(301) 320-1410
www.nps.gov/clba/
The founder of the American Red Cross first made her mark caring for wounded soldiers of the Civil War, both on and off battlefields, earning for herself the moniker "Angel of the Battlefield." A bullet nearly ended her career at Antietam. Clara Barton National Historic Site is open for guided tours daily from 10:00 AM to 4:00 PM, except on Thanksgiving, Christmas, and New Year's Day. Admission is free.

Ford's Theatre National Historical Site
517 10th Street NW
Washington, D.C.
(202) 426-6841
www.fordstheatre.org
There's no American theater that's quite as historic as Ford's. On April 14, 1865, President and Mrs. Lincoln joined Major Henry Reed Rathbone and Clara Harris for a performance of "Our American Cousin." While the president and his party were seated in the presidential box, they were surprised by Confederate activist and actor John Wilkes Booth, who shot Lincoln and stabbed Rathbone before leaping to the stage in an attempt to escape. Lincoln died at 7:22 the next morning at the Petersen House, located directly across the street. The theater closed its doors immediately after the assassination and served as a warehouse, museum, and office building for 90 years before President Eisenhower authorized its restoration in 1954. Ford's reopened in 1968 and has since func-

Ford's Theater FORD'S THEATER NATIONAL HISTORIC SITE, NATIONAL PARK SERVICE

tioned as a working theater known for its productions of American stage classics. At the holidays, however, the historic stage turns into Victorian England for an annual production of "A Christmas Carol."

If you're not able to catch a play, it's still worth the trip to see the theater itself, largely restored to the way it looked in 1865. The lower level houses a museum packed with artifacts, including Booth's 44-caliber Deringer and informative displays discussing the assassination conspirators and their trials. You can also walk across the street to tour Petersen House and see the room where Lincoln died. Ford's Theatre is open from 9:00 AM to 5:00 PM daily (except during matinee performances). (Note: Ford's Theatre and Petersen House are closed for renovation through November 2008). Admission is free.

Frederick Douglass National Historic Site
1411 W Street SE
Washington, D.C.
(202) 426-5961
www.nps.gov/frdo/

The former slave who became one of the giants of the Civil War era purchased this 21-room home in 1877. Known as Cedar Hill, the historic home is located across the Anacostia River, offering a spectacular view of Washington, D.C.'s cityscape to the north. The museum offers exhibits, interpretive programs, and a film which tells the story of Douglass' life. Reopened in February 2007 following an extensive renovation, the glorious home was restored to look as it did in Douglass' day. It's open daily 9:00 AM to 5:00 PM during the warm weather months, and closes an hour earlier during the winter.

International Spy Museum
800 F Street NW
Washington, D.C.
(202) 393-7798
www.spymuseum.org
There's no doubt that this high-touch, high-tech museum has a post-WWII focus, but Civil War spies like Belle Boyd and Rose Greenbow do factor into a few of its exhibitions. Time-travel forward into the twentieth century to see Cold War gadgets like buttonhole cameras, lipstick guns and cipher machines, or to take part in *Operation Spy*, the museum's new hour-long, immersive espionage experience. The museum's hours vary by season, opening as early as 9:00 AM and closing as late as 8:00 PM. Admission is $16 for adults, $15 for seniors/ military and $13 for children.

Library of Congress
Independence Avenue at 1st Street SE
Washington, D.C.
(202) 707-8000
www.loc.gov/visit
While the Library of Congress is the world's largest library, it's more than just a collection of books. Housed in one of Washington, D.C.'s most spectacular spaces, the Library is a treasure-trove of priceless national and international artifacts. Although the exhibited items change, the Civil War is always a theme in the Library's American Treasures gallery, and researchers find it an invaluable resource for deeper investigations into pivotal events in American history. Admission is free.

Lincoln Memorial
The National Mall at 23rd Street NW
Washington, D.C.
(202) 426-6841
www.nps.gov/linc
If you only have time to visit one memorial in Washington, D.C., make it this powerful tribute to the president who worked to keep the country together during the tumultuous war. It's symbolically located across the Memorial Bridge from Arlington National Cemetery, where Robert E. Lee's plantation home looms

in the distance, representing the reunion of the two sides. In another symbolic gesture, the memorial's 36 columns represent the 36 states that were reunited at the time of the assassination. Read a passage from the Gettysburg Address on one side of the marble temple and an excerpt from Lincoln's Second Inaugural Address on the other. Admission is free.

National Archives Building
700 Pennsylvania Avenue NW (entrance on Constitution Avenue between 7th and 9th Streets NW)
Washington, D.C.
(202) 357-5000
www.archives.gov
While the National Archives is best known as the home of the original Declaration of Independence, the Constitution and the Bill of Rights, the National Archives is a must-see for anyone conducting Civil War research. It's here that you'll find draft records, court martial case files, photographs and key pieces of correspondence, including a recently-uncovered letter from Lincoln to his General-in-Chief Henry Halleck in 1863 suggesting that if General George Meade could follow up his victory at Gettysburg with another defeat of Robert E. Lee and his southern troops, the war would be brought to an end. Admission is free.

National Museum of American History
14th Street and Constitution Avenue NW
Washington, D.C.
(202) 633-1000
http://americanhistory.si.edu
Also known as "America's Attic," this popular Smithsonian Institution museum houses artifacts of U.S. history, pop culture, politics, technology and more. American military history, along with social history and presidential lore, are themes that show up in various parts of the vast collection. The museum is closed for renovation through summer 2008, but you can find Civil War-era artifacts like Abraham Lincoln's top hat in a special exhibition drawn from the permanent collection on display at the National

Air and Space Museum (6th Street and Jefferson Drive SW). Admission is free.

National Museum of Health and Medicine
6900 Georgia Avenue NW
Washington, D.C.
(202) 782-2200
www.nmhm.washingtondc.museum
What's now a repository for medical artifacts, anatomical and pathological specimens and other health-related materials started in 1862 as the Army Medical Museum, designed to help improve medical procedures and conditions during the Civil War. The museum still operates as part of the Armed Forces Institute of Pathology, but its focus has expanded beyond battlefield medicine to include civilian artifacts and exhibitions on timely medical topics. True to its roots, there's still a significant collection of Civil War relics, including the bullet that killed Abraham Lincoln and the probe used in his autopsy. You'll also find a shattered leg bone from Major General Daniel Sickles, who famously murdered Francis Scott Key's son, Philip Barton, in a crime of passion in 1859. Sickles was acquitted of the crime in the first successful application of the "temporary insanity" defense. When war broke out in the aftermath, he joined the Army to clean up his tarnished reputation. He was struck by a cannonball at Gettysburg and donated his mangled leg to the Army Medical Museum. The Major General reportedly visited the specimen every year on the anniversary of the amputation, and some say that his ghost continues to visit today. The museum is open daily except for Christmas from 10:00 AM to 5:30 PM. Admission is free.

Renwick Gallery of Art
17th Street and Pennsylvania Avenue NW
Washington, D.C.
(202) 633-2850
http://americanart.si.edu
Now one of the Smithsonian Institution's repositories of American art, the Renwick Gallery served as a supply depot for Union forces from 1861 through 1864 and as headquarters for

General Montgomery C. Meigs, Army Quartermaster, in 1865. Magnificent paintings and crafts hang where uniforms, tents and other essentials were once meted out to soldiers on their way to fight in Virginia. The gallery is open daily except for December 25 from 10:00 AM to 5:30 PM. Admission is free.

Donald W. Reynolds Center for American Art and Portraiture
8th and F Streets NW
Washington, D.C.
(202) 633-7970
www.reynoldscenter.org
This magnificent Greek Revival building was constructed between 1836 and 1868 to serve as the U.S. Patent Office, developed under the guidance of then-President Andrew Jackson. One of the District's earliest "tourist traps," visitors would flock to the building to view models of new gadgets and gizmos seeking patent protection. The glorious building also played host to Lincoln's second inaugural ball. Today it's an attraction once again, housing two of the Smithsonian Institution's art collections, the National Portrait Gallery and the Smithsonian American Art Museum—both of which hold significant collections of Civil War era art. In the National Portrait Gallery's presidential portraits collection (the only complete collection, outside of White House), there's a photograph of Lincoln taken by Alexander Gardner on a glass negative in February 1865. The negative broke, producing a crack that crosses the crown of Lincoln's head. The crack has since been interpreted as an omen for the impending assassination. The galleries are open daily from 11:30 AM to 7:00 PM. Admission is free.

U.S. Capitol
1st Street between Independence and Constitution Avenues
Washington, DC
(202) 255-6827
www.aoc.gov
During the Civil War, the Capitol was more than just a meeting place for Senators and

Edwin M. Stanton

"The dreadful disaster of last Sunday can scarcely be mentioned," wrote Edwin M. Stanton following the Union defeat at Manassas on July 21, 1861. "The imbecility of this Administration culminated in that catastrophe—an irretrievable misfortune and national disgrace never to be forgotten....the capture of Washington now seems inevitable." The gruff Stanton, an ardent Democrat and, until a few months prior to the battle at Manassas, James Buchanan's Attorney General, was one of Abraham Lincoln's harshest critics in the early days of the Civil War. Six months later he was Lincoln's Secretary of War; with the two eventually becoming warm friends and ironclad partners in the war to end the Rebellion.

A lawyer by trade, the bespectacled and bearded Stanton was not an easy man to like. He preferred to have his own way, suffered opposing opinions with little patience, and was unafraid to make his own feelings clear—as Lincoln was well aware. By January 1862, he was also a close friend of George B. McClellan, the reigning Army of the Potomac commander, who would prove to be more of a thorn in the side of Lincoln than Robert E. Lee. Stanton had earned notoriety in 1859 when he defended Congressman Daniel Sickles (by 1861 a Union officer) in a murder case that rocked the Capital. Entering a plea of "temporary insanity"—a defense never before used successfully in the United States—Stanton won an acquittal for a man who had shot his wife's lover (U.S. Attorney Philip Barton Key, son of Francis Scott Key) in broad daylight in D.C.'s Lafayette Square.

Overriding his personal opinion of Lincoln or politics in general was Stanton's love of the Union. He quickly justified the president's faith in him by straightening out a War Department riddled with corruption and left a shambles by his predecessor, Simon Cameron, whom Lincoln had deftly made Ambassador to Russia. A capable and efficient administrator, Stanton banished undedicated government employees, cancelled wasteful government contracts, and moved the telegraph office into the War Department offices, where he and Lincoln spent endless hours poring over reports from the field.

Between these two former lawyers, a firm partnership formed—one based on a love of law, belief in the Union, appreciation of each other's strengths, and within months, a disdain for George McClellan. Once a member of the Lincoln administration, Stanton quickly saw his old friend for what he really was—a conniving, vacillating, organizer unwilling to or incapable of leading an army. Joining the voices already raised against McClellan, Stanton urged Lincoln to replace the Army of the Potomac commander. Having learned to manage his irascible secretary, the president did—but only when the time was right.

By April 1865, the partnership of Lincoln and Stanton had overseen the final Union victory. The secretary was one of those that visited the wounded president's bedside as he lay dying on April 14 and 15. And when Lincoln passed, it was a heartfelt Stanton who uttered the immortal words: "Now he belongs to the ages."

Congressmen. It was used by Union forces as a barracks for about 4,000 troops, a hospital and even a bakery where bakers made about 16,000 loaves of bread each day. Today, it's better known for its official function as a meeting, working and debating place for members of Congress. All visitors must join a ticketed, guided tour to view the Capitol's interior. Complimentary tickets are distributed at the Capitol Guide Service kiosk (near the intersection of First Street and Independence Avenue SW) beginning at 9:00 AM Monday through Saturday. The building is open for tours Monday through Saturday from 9:00 AM to 4:30 PM. A magnificent new Capitol Visitors Center is currently under construction on the East Front of the building and is expected to open in 2008. Admission is free.

Washington Monument
Constitution Avenue and 15th Street NW
Washington, D.C.
(202) 426-6841
When war broke out between the states, the 555 1/8-foot tall Washington Monument was nearly a third complete, although construction had begun in 1848. Demand for building supplies, funds and able-bodied troops brought construction of the delay-plagued monument to a halt. Construction resumed in 1876 and the monument was completed in 1888, but thanks to the long delays, the marble on the bottom third of the obelisk was taken from a different level in the quarry. As a result, it's a different color. Free tickets are required to ride to the top of the monument; they are distributed beginning at 8:30 AM at the ticket kiosk on 15th Street. The monument is open from 9:00 AM to 5:00 PM daily except Christmas, with the last tour beginning at 4:45 PM. You can also make reservations in advance for a small processing fee by calling 1-877-444-6777 or www.reservations.gov. Admission is free.

The White House
1600 Pennsylvania Avenue NW
Washington, D.C.
(202) 456-7041
www.whitehouse.gov
At the time of the Civil War, the White House looked different than it does today. In fact, it wasn't even officially called the White House. That name was formally bestowed on the presidential residence during the Theodore Roosevelt administration. The mansion was much smaller and quite crowded with the Lincolns and their young family. Conditions were also much less sanitary; sewage emptied onto the Ellipse, fueling diseases like smallpox and typhoid, which claimed the life of Lincoln's son, Willie. The White House Visitors Center, located at 14th Street and Pennsylvania Avenue, NW, sheds some light on the building's history and its role in the Civil War. Touring the building itself requires advance arrangements; contact your Congress member up to six months in advance to inquire about tours, which are available Tuesday through Saturday from 7:30 a.m. to 12:30 p.m. for groups of ten or more. Admission is free.

Statues, Squares and Other Sites of Interest:

Admiral David G. Farragut Memorial
Farragut Square
17th and K Streets NW
Washington, D.C.
Washingtonians know Farragut Square as one of the busiest office districts, home to two bustling Metro lines. The ten-foot statue that sits at the middle of the square honors Rear Admiral David G. Farragut, whose heroics led to the Union's capture of New Orleans and Mobile Bay. Vinnie Ream Hoxie, the creator of the statue, was the first female sculptor to be commissioned by the U.S. government.

Blair House
1651-53 Pennsylvania Avenue NW
Washington, D.C.
Located directly across the street from the White House on the most protected block of

Pennsylvania Avenue, Blair House is best known as the home-away-from-home for foreign heads of state and royalty on official state visits. It's not open to the public, but Civil War buffs may want to stroll past this house for its historic significance. It's here where Robert E. Lee turned down Lincoln advisor Francis P. Blair's offer to command the Union troops, vowing his allegiance to his home state of Virginia instead.

Fort Dupont Park
Minnesota Avenue and Randle Circle SE
Washington, D.C.
(202) 426-7745
www.nps.gov/nace/ftdupont.htm
Fort Dupont was established in 1861 by Union forces as a means of protecting the 11th Street Bridge, an important link between the Southeast neighborhood of Anacostia and capital city itself. No battle was fought here, but the fort gained some notoriety as a safe haven for runaway slaves. Little remains of the fort today, but you can still see its earthworks in the 376-acre Anacostia park that shares its name. The park's Activity Center is open Monday through Friday from 8:00 AM to 4:00 PM; the park is open from sun-up to sun-down.

General George B. McClellan Monument
Connecticut Avenue and California Street NW
Washington, D.C.
Near Washington, D.C.'s Adams Morgan neighborhood, there's a statue of McClellan, the Union commander who faltered during the Peninsula campaign, then emerged victorious at Antietam. Despite his victory, tactical errors caused Lincoln to question his judgment and eventually relieve him of his command. McClellan also had a mixed showing in his political career; he ran unsuccessfully against Lincoln for the presidency in 1864 but served as governor of New Jersey from 1878 to 1881. In his memorial statue, designed by Frederick MacMonnies and dedicated in 1907, he sits atop a horse, overlooking Connecticut Avenue.

General John Alexander Logan Statue
Logan Circle, Vermont Avenue at 13th and P Streets NW
Washington, D.C.
A traffic circle in one of the District's trendiest residential areas is named for General John Alexander Logan. In the center of the circle there's a bronze equestrian statue of Logan, dedicated in 1901. Logan fought with distinction in some of the war's biggest battles: Manassas, Vicksburg and Atlanta, before losing a bid for the vice-presidency in 1884.

General Philip Sheridan Monument
Sheridan Circle
Massachusetts Avenue and 23rd Street NW
Washington, D.C.
Surrounded by some of Washington, D.C.'s finest embassies and diplomatic addresses, this equestrian statue was crafted by Gutzon Borglum, best known for his sculptures at Mount Rushmore. The Union commander led the Cavalry Corps of the Army of the Potomac in the East, pursuing Robert E. Lee and forcing his surrender at Appomattox.

General William Tecumseh Sherman Monument
Sherman Square
15th Street and Pennsylvania Avenue NW
Washington, D.C.
Sherman served valiantly under Grant at the Battle of Vicksburg then took Grant's place as Union commander in the western theater of the war. He led troops to capture Atlanta in September 1864, ensuring Lincoln's re-election. Afterwards, his armies embarked on a devastating march through Georgia and the Carolinas. He's commemorated in a mounted statue in a small park nestled between the White House Ellipse and the Department of the Treasury.

General Winfield Hancock Scott Memorial
Pennsylvania Avenue at 7th Street
Washington, D.C.
Dedicated in 1896, this statue honors General Scott, best known for his triumph over Robert

E. Lee at Gettysburg. Considered one of the most capable commanders of all time, Scott is also credited with developing the Union's Anaconda Plan, which brought down the Confederacy.

Major General George C. Meade Monument
Pennsylvania Avenue and 3rd Street NW
Washington, D.C.
George Meade is credited with orchestrating Lee's defeat at Gettysburg. By positioning his troops for defensive attacks on the left, right and center, he successfully fended off Pickett's Charge. The marble monument, crafted by Charles A. Grafly, was dedicated in 1927.

Major General James B. McPherson Monument
McPherson Square, Vermont Avenue between 15th and K Streets NW
Washington, D.C.
Constructed from a seized cannon by Louis Rebisso, this equestrian statue honors McPherson, Ulysses S. Grant's chief engineer, who commanded the army of Tennessee and faltered near Atlanta. It was dedicated in 1876.

The Peace Monument
Pennsylvania Avenue at 1st Street NW
Washington, D.C.
Built to honor U.S. Navy casualties in the Civil War, this 44-foot marble statue and fountain sits in front of the U.S. Capitol. It was sculpted by Franklin Simmons in 1877. Facing west, toward the National Mall, a female figure representing Grief hides her face on the shoulder of another female figure, representing History. In her hands, History clutches as stylus and tablet reading "They died that their country might live." Below Grief and History, another female figure, Victory, holds a laurel wreath and oak branch, symbolizing strength. Mars and Neptune, representing war and the sea, sit just below. A final female figure, Peace, looks out toward the Capitol.

The Rock Creek Park Forts
Rock Creek Park
3545 Williamsburg Lane NW
Washington, D.C.
(202) 895-6000
www.nps.gov/rocr
Washington, D.C.'s vast urban playground is home to the remains of forts that once protected the capital city. At **Fort Stevens** (13th and Quackenbos Streets, NW), Jubal A. Early's Southern forces took on the Union defenders in 1864 as federal notables, including Abraham Lincoln, looked on. Just north of the fort, Battlefield National Cemetery is the final resting place of the 41 Union soldiers who died defending the fort. There's nothing left at **Fort Reno** (Belt Road and Chesapeake Street NW), but, as the highest point in the city, the grounds do open up to an incredible view. Also nearby: **Ford DeRussey** (Oregon Avenue and Military Road NW) and **Fort Bayard** (Western Avenue and River Road). You can find some parts of the forts still standing at **Fort Slocum Park** (Kansas Avenue, Blair Road and Milmarson Place NE), **Fort Totten** (Fort Totten Drive, south of Riggs Road) and **Battery Kemble Park** (Chain Bridge Road, MacArthur Boulevard, 49th Street and Nebraska Avenue).

Ulysses S. Grant Memorial
Union Square, 1st Street NW
Washington, D.C.
(202) 426-6841
Set against the backdrop of the U.S. Capitol, this striking tribute to Grant was sculpted by Henry Shrady and dedicated in 1922. The statue itself—the largest equestrian statue in the country and the second largest in the world—was modeled after a sketch that Grant drew of a soldier from Massachusetts after the battle at Spotsylvania Court House, surveying the National Mall to the west.

Washington Arsenal Site
4th and P Streets NW
Washington, D.C.
Now home to Fort McNair, the Arsenal was used to ship supplies to battle sites in Vir-

ginia. John Wilkes Booth and his co-conspirators were brought here after Lincoln's assassination, where they were later tried and hanged.

Tours

Cultural Tourism DC (www.culturaltourismdc .org) acts as an umbrella group for many of Washington, D.C.'s small museums and neighborhood heritage sites, many of which are listed in this guide. Walking tours and bus tours of Washington, D.C.'s Civil War heritage sites are occasionally available; you can also download a copy of Cultural Tourism DC's "Civil War to Civil Rights" walking tour route in downtown DC.

Gray Line (www.grayline.com) offers regular day-long tours of Gettysburg departing from downtown Washington, D.C.

Accommodations

Adams Inn
1744 Lanier Place NW
Washington, D.C.
(202) 745-3600
(800) 578-6807
www.adamsinn.com
This cheery, comfortable inn is popular with family travelers, backpackers and even business travelers—and with good reason. The rooms are clean, neatly furnished and very affordable. Fifteen of the inn's 25 guest rooms come with private bath, and all guests enjoy continental breakfast, high-speed Internet and laundry privileges. The surrounding Adams Morgan neighborhood serves up some of the city's best international cuisine, along with fun and festive nightlife.

Chester A. Arthur House Bed and Breakfast at Logan Circle
13th and P Street
Washington, D.C.
(202) 328-3510
(877) 893-3233
www.chesterarthurhouse.com
Civil War buffs will feel right at home at the

Chester Arthur House, which is located on a circle named for Major General John Logan. An equine statue of the man credited as the inspiration behind Memorial Day overlooks the area. One may care little for Logan (who was probably the best of Lincoln's political generals) or Chester A. Arthur (the inn's namesake and the nation's 21st president), but the gracious comfort and beautiful décor of this 1883 townhouse will win anyone over. The inn's location and guest groom rates are excellent. But there are just three rooms, so call well in advance.

The Georgetown Inn
1310 Wisconsin Avenue NW
Washington, D.C.
(202) 333-8900
(800) 424-2979
www.georgetowncollection.com
If you're coming to Washington, D.C. to soak up some history, you may want to stay in Georgetown, a neighborhood that found itself greatly divided during the Civil War. Land-holding gentry with roots in the South sympathized with their slave-holding counterparts even as federal officials struggled to hold the Union together. The 96-room inn sits in the center of Georgetown's dining, shopping and nightlife district. Guests can expect a comfortable stay with complimentary coffee and newspaper, and valet parking.

The Hay-Adams Hotel
16th and H Streets NW
Washington, D.C.
(202) 638-6600
(800) 853-6807
A member of the Leading Hotels of the World, this opulent historic property is named for John Hay, Lincoln's personal assistant and Secretary of State under William McKinley and Theodore Roosevelt, and author Henry Adams, a descendent of the noted political family. In 1884, Hay and Adams bought adjoining lots at 16th and H Streets on the site of the present-day hotel. The homes were later razed and, in 1927-1928, an Italian Ren-

aissance-styled apartment hotel was constructed on the site. Outfitted with posh amenities like kitchens, elevators and an air-conditioned dining room, the Hay-Adams House became the hotel of choice for traveling notables like Charles Lindbergh, Amelia Earhart and Ethel Barrymore. The hotel underwent a massive renovation in 2001-2002 and now offers a full suite of modern amenities.

The Henley Park Hotel
926 Massachusetts Avenue NW
Washington, D.C.
(202) 638-5200
(800) 222-8474
www.henleypark.com
Opened in 1918 as a luxury apartment building, the Henley Park was once home to famous Washingtonians like senators and congressman. Today, this charming Victorian inn is a favorite of European travelers. Rooms are a bit dated, but its location near the Washington Convention Center puts the Henley Park in one of the most desirable locations in town. The on-site restaurant, Coeur de Lion, is also a draw, and the adjacent Blue Bar is a sure bet for mellow live entertainment. Guests enjoy amenities like express check-in, minibars and health club privileges. Because it's located so close to the Washington Convention Center, rates are always higher during big conventions.

Hotel Harrington
11th and E Streets NW
Washington, D.C.
(202) 628-8140
(800) 424-8532
This no-frills, basic hotel is ideally located in the heart of downtown, just a few blocks from the National Mall, the White House and the Penn Quarter arts and entertainment district. Don't expect much in terms of amenities, but parking is a bargain at $10 per day and Harry's, the on-site restaurant, stays open later than most downtown DC eateries.

Hotel Lombardy
2019 Pennsylvania Avenue NW
Washington, D.C.
(202) 828-2600
(800) 424-5486
www.hotellombardy.com
It's nothing fancy, but this inn-like hotel's central location puts it within walking distance of Georgetown, Dupont Circle and the White House, along with a couple of Metro stations. Rooms are equipped with kitchenettes, minibars and other amenities.

Hotel Monaco
700 F Street NW
Washington, D.C.
(202) 628-7177
(800) 649-1202
www.monaco-dc.com
The landmark 1842 Tariff Building that once housed the nation's first General Post Office is now the stunning, 183-room Hotel Monaco. Operated by the Kimpton Hotel Group, the Monaco blends the building's historic character and classic marble elements with chic, stylish and colorful décor. During the Civil War, the hotel's Paris Ballroom is believed to have been used as an operating room for wounded soldiers; guests and event-goers have reported hearing whispered voices that linger to this day. While there's scant evidence to support these claims, there's no doubt that many a distraught bride and mother came here to await news of her loved one's whereabouts. While the building was undergoing renovation between 2001 and 2003, a construction worker reported seeing the figure of a woman in Civil War attire anxiously pacing in the building's courtyard. Like Washington, D.C.'s other Kimpton hotels, the Monaco warmly welcomes pets (and even lets you borrow a goldfish for companionship, if you like) and offers a complimentary wine hour.

Jurys Washington Hotel
1500 New Hampshire Avenue NW
Washington, D.C.
(202) 483-6000

(800) 423-6953
www.jurys.com
You can't beat the Jurys' fantastic Dupont Circle location. There are shops, restaurants, art galleries and coffee houses on every corner, along with glorious Beaux-Arts buildings. The hotel was recently renovated, and rooms are clean, comfortable and outfitted with all of the services you'd expect at a business hotel. It's part of the Irish-owned Jurys Doyle Hotel Group and, as such, it's no surprise to find a lively Irish pub on its ground floor.

Maison Orleans Bed and Breakfast
414 5th Street SE
Washington, D.C.
(202) 544-3694
www.bbonline.com/dc/maisonorleans/
Just six blocks from the Capitol, Library of Congress, and many of the capital's best restaurants and attractions, Maison Orleans is a relaxing and unique oasis in the heart the city. Rates are fair and the ambience is cozy, but there are just three rooms—in addition to furnished one-bedroom and studio apartments.

The Melrose Hotel
2430 Pennsylvania Avenue NW
Washington, D.C.
(202) 955-6400
(800) MELROSE
www.melrosehoteldc.com
It's easy to feel at home here. After all, this West End hotel is another DC hotel fashioned out of a former apartment building. The Melrose's rooms are cheery and spacious, decorated with classic and contemporary touches. There's a Metro station right around the corner, and Georgetown and Dupont Circle are just a few blocks away.

Morrison-Clark Inn
11th Street and Massachusetts Avenue NW
Washington, D.C.
(202) 898-1200
(800) 332-7898
www.morrisonclark.com
Like its sister property, the Henley Park, the

Morrison-Clark is a gracious Victorian property just blocks from the Washington Convention Center. Rooms are charming, if a little tired, and outfitted with modern amenities like free wireless Internet, data ports and complimentary newspapers. The Morrison-Clark Restaurant is a popular choice for romantic dinners, and the hotel's garden room and courtyard are well-suited for weddings.

The Willard InterContinental Washington
1401 Pennsylvania Avenue NW
Washington, D.C.
(202) 628-9100
(800) 327-0200
www.washington.intercontinental.com
There's no hotel in the nation's capital that boasts quite as rich a history as the Willard. In February 1861, representatives from 21 of the 34 states met at the Willard in an effort to avert the pending war. A plaque on the hotel's Pennsylvania Avenue entrance honors these valiant efforts. Amidst countless assassination threats, Lincoln was smuggled into the hotel after his election and prior to his inauguration in March 1861. His folio is on view in the history gallery. During the Civil War, the hotel was a gathering place for both Union and Confederate sympathizers. As a guest at the hotel, Julia Ward Howe wrote the "Battle Hymn of the Republic" as she listened to Union troops march past her window, playing "John Brown's Body." Actor John Wilkes Booth also frequented the Willard, making several visits in the weeks leading up to the Lincoln assassination. Legend has it that Ulysses S. Grant coined the term "lobbyist" here, referring to the favor-seekers who bothered him as he savored cigars and brandy in the hotel lobby. Outfitted with all of the posh amenities you'd expect in a fine luxury hotel, the Willard is located next to the White House and footsteps from the National Mall.

Windsor Park Hotel
2116 Kalorama Road NW
Washington, D.C.
(202) 483-7700
(800) 247-3064
www.windsorparkhotel.com
If the price doesn't attract you to this pleasant, family-friendly inn, the proximity to Washington, D.C.'s eclectic Adams Morgan and
Dupont Circle neighborhoods should. The
hotel's 43 simply-furnished guest rooms come
with small refrigerators, newspaper and complimentary continental breakfast.

Woodley Park Guest House
2647 Woodley Road, NW
Washington, D.C.
(202) 667-0218
(866) 667-0218
www.woodleyparkguesthouse.com
Formerly known as the Connecticut-Woodley
Guest House, this elegant, recently-renovated
district inn blends modern amenities (central
air-conditioning, high-speed Web access, etc.)
with the comfortable look of antiques in its 18
rooms and suites, at reasonable rates for its
location. The owners also do their part to fos-
ter a sense of community; there's always
someone lingering in the kitchen for a chat,
and all of the works of art that adorn the walls
were created by former guests.

Restaurants

Ben's Chili Bowl
1213 U Street NW
Washington, D.C.
(202) 667-0909
www.benschilibowl.com
Ben's Chili Bowl doesn't have any strong Civil
War connections, apart from its proximity to
the African American Civil War Memorial. Nevertheless, no Washington, D.C. dining guide
would be complete without it. Opened in
1958, Ben's has weathered neighborhood
riots and decay and still it manages to attract
throngs of customers for its signature dish:
the chili half-smoke (that's half hot dog, half
sausage, served on a bun and doused in chili,

onions and mustard). Wash it down with a
creamy homemade milkshake. You'll find
urban hipsters, government staffers and longtime neighborhood residents gathered here.
It's open from 11:00 AM to 2:00 AM Monday
through Thursday, through 4:00 AM on Fridays and Saturdays and from noon to 8:00
PM on Sundays.

Bistrot du Coin
1738 Connecticut Avenue NW
Washington, D.C.
(202) 234-6969
www.bistroducoin.com
It's nothing fancy, but locals love this lively
Dupont Circle bistro. It's open every day—
including Thanksgiving and Christmas—and
always seems to draw an eclectic crowd of
young and old, gay and straight diners from
the neighborhood and beyond. Feast on
steamed mussels, decadent tartines, hangar
steaks and other French and Belgian classics.

Blue Duck Tavern
Park Hyatt Washington
1201 24th Street NW
Washington, D.C.
(202) 419-6755
Chef Brian McBride has proven himself to be a
master of regional cuisine at Blue Duck Tavern, which made a splash in the Washington,
D.C. dining scene when it opened in summer
2006. Tasty creations like pork loin with bourbon soaked peaches, rabbit terrine, delectable crab cakes and thick cut fries cooked in
duck fat, and homemade desserts like hand-
churned ice cream and flamed chocolate
bourbon pie have made it a crowd favorite.
While the food is divine, the open kitchen is
enough to make any chef turn green with
envy.

Brasserie Beck
1101 K Street NW
Washington, D.C.
(202) 408-1717
www.beckdc.com
There's a delightful trend in many of Washing-

ton, D.C.'s top new restaurants; notable chefs are serving exquisite food in a comfortable, casual setting at reasonable prices. Brasserie Beck is a prime example. Chef Robert Wiedmaier earned acclaim among fine dining aficionados during a stint at Aquarelle at the Watergate before opening Marcel's, his own restaurant, in the Foggy Bottom neighborhood. His second venture, Brasserie Beck, serves casual French and Belgian fare in a bistro setting. If the cuisine doesn't bowl you over—and the housemade sausages and seasoned steamed mussels likely will—then the beer menu may be your downfall. True to his French-Belgian roots, Wiedmaier has a beer sommelier on staff and serves up an ever-changing line up of more than 50 Belgian beers. The restaurant is open for lunch and dinner Monday through Friday and dinner on Saturday.

Clyde's of Georgetown
3236 M Street NW
Washington, D.C.
202-333-9180
www.clydes.com
Clyde's is a Washington, D.C. area favorite with locations in Georgetown, downtown and in the Maryland and Virginia suburbs. You can count on consistently good American fare made from fresh, local ingredients and served in a casual, distinctly American setting. Burgers, salads, chicken sandwiches and crab cakes are always on the menu, but you can expect lighter salads and berry-laden desserts in the summer months and heartier stews in the colder months. Clyde's is open seven days for dinner (late on Friday and Saturday); Saturday and Sunday for brunch; and weekdays for lunch. There's another DC location in Chinatown at 7th and G Streets NW.

Filomena
1063 Wisconsin Avenue NW
Washington, D.C.
(202) 337-2782
www.filomena.com
When you pass by this quaint Georgetown

eatery, you're apt to see the "pasta mamas" at work in the window preparing fresh noodles and stuffed pastas. It's a hint of what's to come inside the restaurant—fresh Italian creations and a cozy, homelike atmosphere. Bill and Chelsea Clinton were known to dine here during their White House days. In addition to the lavish dinner menu there's a lunch buffet on Fridays, Saturdays and Sundays that features a bounty of Italian creations for $17.95.

Kinkead's
2000 Pennsylvania Avenue NW
Washington, D.C.
(202) 296-7700
www.kinkead.com
If you love seafood and aren't afraid to pay a little more for fine preparation, great ambience and perhaps even some celebrity-spotting, make a reservation at Kinkead's. Though it opened more than a decade ago, Kinkead's still draws crowds. Regional delicacies like soft shell crabs and skate wings are must-tries, and even New Englanders will even appreciate Boston-born chef Robert Kinkead's take on the lobster roll. Kinkead's is open for lunch Monday through Saturday, Sunday brunch and dinner nightly.

Lauriol Plaza
1835 18th Street NW
Washington, D.C.
(202) 387-0035
www.lauriolplaza.com
Lauriol Plaza is a long-time favorite for fresh Mexican cuisine. The zesty grilled fajitas and cheesy enchiladas are consistently good and the margaritas never disappoint, but the real draw here is the huge upstairs patio. Overlooking 18th Street between Dupont Circle and Adams Morgan, it's a popular gathering spot on breezy afternoons and warm evenings for nightlife fun seekers. It's open for lunch and dinner nightly; come prepared to wait for an outdoor table.

Lebanese Taverna
2641 Connecticut Avenue NW
Washington, D.C.
(202) 265-8681
Lebanese Taverna is another Washington, D.C. institution. It started as a single restaurant in Washington, D.C.'s Woodley Park neighborhood but has since expanded to additional locations in Virginia. The family-owned Middle Eastern restaurant is always a sure bet for tasty moussaka, kebabs, shwarma and plenty of vegetarian favorites. It's open for lunch Monday through Saturday and dinner nightly.

Martin's Tavern
1264 Wisconsin Avenue NW
Washington, D.C.
(202) 333-7370
www.martins-tavern.com
History buffs love Billy Martin's Tavern, the oldest establishment of its kind in Georgetown. Opened in 1933, the Martin family is now on its fourth generation of restaurant owners. It's here that John F. Kennedy proposed to Jackie in Booth #3, while Richard Nixon preferred Booth #2. Lyndon Johnson and Alger Hiss were also regulars, and it's not uncommon to see Madeleine Albright there these days. You won't be disappointed by the traditional American dishes nor the lively mix of tourists and neighborhood residents that pack the restaurant most nights of the week. It's open daily for lunch and dinner.

The Monocle
107 D Street NE
Washington, D.C.
(202) 546-4488
www.themonocle.com
A favorite of members of Congress and other Capitol employees, this family-owned, downtown Washington institution was the first white tablecloth restaurant on Capitol Hill. Though new competitors have entered the marketplace, it's still a favorite, serving up traditional American dishes in an elegant dining room or more casual bar. Try the signature roast beef sandwiches; it's easy to see why John F. Kennedy would order them for special delivery to the White House. It is open for lunch and dinner.

The Occidental
1475 Pennsylvania Avenue NW
Washington, D.C.
(202) 783-1475
www.occidentaldc.com
This hundred-year-old restaurant is steeped in history. Next door, there's the Willard Hotel, and the White House sits just beyond. Inside, the restaurant is decorated with black and white photos of the presidents, politicos and celebrities who have dined at The Occidental throughout the century. You'd expect to find fine American fare on the menu, and you won't be disappointed... nor will you be bored. Chef Rodney Scruggs works wonders with natural locally-procured ingredients to make delicious dishes like duck breast served with homemade spaetzle and braised rabbit ragu.

Old Ebbitt Grill
675 15th Street NW
Washington, D.C.
(202) 347-4800
www.ebbitt.com
Established in 1856, Old Ebbitt Grill owns the distinction of being Washington, D.C.'s oldest restaurant. Although it no longer operates out of its original home, its classic furnishings and location just two blocks from the White House give it a historic feel. The restaurant prides itself on offering a fantastic oyster bar, though you also won't go wrong with tasty crab cakes, trout crusted with parmesan cheese and homemade pastas and soups. It's open daily for lunch and dinner and is known as a power breakfast spot during the week.

1789
1226 36th Street NW
Washington, D.C.
(202) 965-1789
www.1789restaurant.com

If your historical tastes run into the Federal period as well, reserve a table at 1789. Fashioned after an elegant country inn, 1789 was named for the year in which nearby Georgetown University was founded. The cozy two-story row house is intimate and romantic; don't be surprised to see a marriage proposal or an anniversary celebration happening at the table next to you. Executive Chef Nathan Beauchamp, voted the metro area's top rising culinary star by the Restaurant Association Metropolitan Washington, crafts masterful American fare from ingredients like pheasant, lobster, lamb and crabs. The restaurant is open for dinner nightly.

Spices Asian Restaurant & Sushi Bar
3333-A Connecticut Avenue NW
Washington, D.C.
(202) 686-3833

If your travels take you to Washington, D.C.'s Cleveland Park neighborhood—and a tour of Civil War forts very well might—treat yourself to a bite at Spices. In true Pan-Asian spirit, the restaurant serves tasty sushi, tempting curries, tasty Pad Thai and classic Chinese dishes, all at affordable prices. It's open for lunch and dinner daily.

The White Tiger
301 Massachusetts Avenue NE
Washington, D.C.
(202) 546-5900

There's a lot to like about this Capitol Hill eatery, which focuses on northern Indian creations. Flavorful biryanis and tandoori dishes are served on gold platters, and, as you'd expect in an Indian restaurant, there are ample vegetarian options. In the summer, dinners flock to the outdoor patio, which twinkles with white lights. One of the most attractive things about this neighborhood favorite: the prices.

Wok 'N Roll
604 H Street NW
Washington, D.C.
(202) 347-4656
www.woknrolldc.com

There's a good reason we're including a quirky Chinatown restaurant with a funny name among our picks. In 1865, Mary Surratt operated a boarding house in the building that now houses Wok 'N Roll. It's here that John Wilkes Booth met Surratt's son, John, and other conspirators in the plot to assassinate the president. Many of the restaurant's patrons don't know the building's significance; they're here for the extensive menu of Chinese and Japanese creations, refreshing bubble teas and $1 sushi during happy hour.

BORDERLAND

NORTHEASTERN VIRGINIA

This tour covers the Arlington, Alexandria, Fairfax, and Falls Church area—Confederate territory occupied by Federal troops following Virginia's secession in May 1861.

In late April 1861, only the murky waters of the Potomac River separated what was left of the old Union from the fledgling Confederate States of America. From the window of his Arlington home, Robert E. Lee could look out at Abraham Lincoln's White House and ponder his own decision to turn his back on the nation he had served so long.

On April 22, Lee left his longtime home forever, and traveled to Richmond to accept command of Virginia's state forces. His wife soon followed, and as Union war preparations continued, Yankee officers turned the historic Arlington House into a headquarters building. In 1864, Quartermaster General Montgomery C. Meigs authorized the burial of fallen Union soldiers on the grounds of Lee's former home—the first of some 20,000 Civil War soldiers to be buried in what became Arlington National Cemetery.

The extension of Washington's fort system into Fairfax County strengthened the Union hold on Northern Virginia territory, which was by September 1861 incorporated into the Union Department of the Potomac. A Confederate Department of Northern Virginia (incorporating the short-lived Department of Alexandria) also existed, although the Union presence south of the Potomac extended its parameters as far south as Manassas and the peninsula.

Alexandria, soon to be the home of Fort Ward, inspired particular anger among Unionists during the Federal occupation of that town on May 24, 1861. After removing a Con-

federate flag from the roof of the Marshall House Hotel, twenty-four-year-old Colonel Elmer Ellsworth was shot to death by the establishment's owner. A close friend of President Lincoln's, Ellsworth was mourned as the Union's first casualty of the war.

Historic Sites

Arlington House, the Robert E. Lee Memorial
Arlington National Cemetery
Arlington, VA
(703) 235-1530
www.nps.gov/arho/

When Robert E. Lee resigned his U.S. Army commission to begin his service to Virginia, he left behind the family home of thirty years. Federal forces soon occupied it. Built between 1802 and 1818 by George Washington Parke Custis (or, more accurately, his slaves) to honor his stepfather, George Washington, Arlington House hosted the wedding of Custis's daughter, Mary Anna Randolph Custis, to Robert E. Lee in 1831.

Arlington House is currently undergoing renovation and will remain empty of furnishings through 2010. The house is open for self-guided tours daily 9:30 a.m. to 4:30 p.m., except for Christmas and New Year's Day; it's best to call ahead during the renovation to ensure that it's open. One floor of Lee's old greenhouse building now houses the Robert E. Lee Museum, a collection of exhibits and artifacts related to the Confederate commander and his family. Hours for the museum are the same as for the house itself. Admission is free.

Arlington Cemetery NATIONAL PARK SERVICE

Arlington National Cemetery
Arlington, VA
(703) 607-8000
www.arlingtoncemetery.org
Replacing the farmland and gardens formerly owned by Robert E. Lee, Arlington National Cemetery was created at the urging of Quartermaster General Montgomery C. Meigs, and dedicated on June 15, 1864. Civil War buffs might look for headstones etched with the word "Civilian" or "Citizen." These are the burial sites of nearly 4,000 former slaves. There's also a section of the cemetery that honors the memory of the United States Colored Troops. Residents of Freedman's Village, a refuge for runaway slaves, are buried nearby.

Arlington National Cemetery is open daily at 8:00 a.m.; it closes at 7:00 p.m. during the summer and at 5:00 p.m. during the winter. Ample parking is available for a small fee. For an overview of the cemetery highlights, we suggest taking Tourmobile, a narrated sightseeing vehicle that conveys you to the most popular points of interest in the cemetery, including the Kennedy gravestone, Arlington House, and the Tomb of the Unknowns. Tourmobile tickets are $7.00 for adults and $3.50 for children.

Chantilly Battlefield
West Ox Road and Monument Drive
Chantilly, VA
(703) 324-8700
The only major battle to take place in Fairfax County, the Battle of Chantilly took place on September 1, 1862, following the second battle of Manassas. Stonewall Jackson fought, and two Union generals, Philip Kearny and Isaac Stevens, both lost their lives. In the small park that marks the battle site, you can visit a monument to the two fallen generals.

Fort Ward Museum and Historic Site
4301 West Braddock Road
Alexandria, VA
(703) 838-4848
http://oha.alexandriava.gov/fortward/

Fort Ward explores the history of the ring of defensive forts that encircled Washington, D.C. during the Civil War. The museum offers permanent and rotating exhibits, a research library, educational programs and artifacts that offer a snapshot of Civil War life. There's even an 1862 topographical map outlining the capital city's defenses and one of three Hale rocket launchers that are still known to exist. A full tour of the fort's trenches, bombproofs, and gun emplacements is a unique experience that Civil War buffs should not miss.

Other Points of Interest

Lee-Fendall House
614 Oronoco Street
Alexandria, VA
(703) 548-1789
www.leefendallhouse.org
Robert E. Lee's Virginia roots are evident throughout northern Virginia, especially in Alexandria. The Lee-Fendall House was home to thirty-seven members of the Lee family, passed down through the generations from 1785–1903. The furnishings on display show the house as it looked during the antebellum period and during the war itself. It's open Tuesday through Saturday 10:00 a.m. to 4:00 p.m. and Sunday 1:00 to 4:00 p.m. Tours are offered every hour on the hour. It's best to call ahead to confirm that the house is open; it's frequently rented for weddings and other private events.

The Lyceum: Alexandria's History Museum
201 South Washington Street
Alexandria, VA
(703) 838-4997
http://oha.alexandriava.gov/lyceum/
A trip to Old Town Alexandria is a step back in time, and there's no better place to learn about the history of this charming port town than the Lyceum. Founded in 1839, the Lyceum serves as a library, lecture room, exhibition hall, and gathering place for residents and visitors to Alexandria. The building was used as a hospital during the Civil War and,

more than a century later in 1985, it was designated Alexandria's History Museum. It's open Monday through Saturday 10:00 a.m. to 5:00 p.m. and Sunday 1:00 to 5:00 p.m. Admission is free.

Fairfax Museum and Visitor Center
10209 Main Street
Fairfax, VA
(703) 385-8414
www.fairfaxva.gov/MuseumVC/Exhibitions.asp
The City of Fairfax and its role in the Civil War fall into focus at this small-town museum. A permanent town history exhibition—which also includes information on the Battle of Chantilly, which was fought nearby—is staged in the museum's Hammill Gallery, while other galleries house timely and topical temporary exhibitions. The museum doubles as a visitor center, providing information on popular regional attractions. The museum is open daily 9:00 a.m. to 5:00 p.m. Admission is free.

Fairfax Station
11200 Fairfax Station Road
Fairfax Station, VA
(703) 425-9225
www.fairfax-station.org
Both sides battled for control over this critical stop on the Orange and Alexandria Railroad. Whichever side controlled it would have access to the quickest and most direct way to ferry soldiers and supplies between Alexandria and Richmond. The former train depot is now home to the Fairfax Station Railroad Museum, a quaint community museum that pays a fair amount of attention to the town's role in the Civil War. The museum is open Sunday 1:00 to 4:00 p.m. Admission is $2 for adults and $1 for children 4–10.

St. Mary's Church
Fairfax Station Road at Route 123
Fairfax Station, VA
(703) 978-4141
www.stmaryofsorrows.org

Arlington House, the Robert E. Lee Memorial NATIONAL PARK SERVICE

When war broke out, Confederate forces controlled the area surrounding St. Mary's Church and the railroad west to Manassas, but the Union's domain followed the railroad east to Burke, putting the newly constructed Catholic church in the middle of the crossfire. After the First Battle of Manassas, St. Mary's was used as a field hospital. Wounded soldiers were laid out and treated on pews taken from the church, and many that succumbed were buried on the church grounds. Clara Barton was among the volunteer nurses who traveled to St. Mary's to treat the injured soldiers. Inspired by her experience at Fairfax Station, she established a civilian society that would later become the American Red Cross. The church is still open for Sunday Mass and is one of the region's most sought-after wedding venues.

Sully Plantation
3601 Sully Road
Chantilly, VA
(703) 437-1794
www.fairfaxcounty.gov/parks/sully/
Constructed at the end of the eighteenth century, Sully was established by Richard Bland Lee, Northern Virginia's first congressman and Robert E. Lee's uncle. Both sides stopped at this Georgian-style manor during the war, though the Union-sympathizing gentlemen owners were known to flee to Alexandria during the war, leaving the women in charge. The estate's slave quarters have also been

Robert E. Lee

Few military commanders have ever inspired the kind of loyalty, even worship, that Army of Northern Virginia soldiers felt for their beloved "Marse Robert." The son of Revolutionary War hero Henry "Light Horse Harry" Lee, Robert E. Lee was born in Westmoreland County, Virginia, in 1807, grew up in Alexandria, and entered West Point in 1825. After a series of stops at U.S. Army posts, Lee got the chance (along with dozens of former classmates and future enemies) to prove his mettle on the rugged battlefields of Mexico.

While General Winfield Scott further cemented his American-hero status with his 1847 Mexico City Campaign, Lee established himself as perhaps Scott's finest junior officer with his daring and smarts. Lee learned much from his superior, but as he returned to drudgery of peace-time army life, did not figure to use those lessons anytime soon. After a

LIBRARY OF CONGRESS

three-year stint as superintendent of West Point, Lee received a bump up to lieutenant colonel and command of the 2nd U.S. Cavalry in Texas. His direction of the U.S. Marines capture of John Brown in 1859 (Lee happened to be in the nation's capital at the time) interrupted his otherwise mostly uninteresting stint on the frontier.

With civil war approaching, Lee remained in U.S. Army blue; he even accepted a promotion in March 1861 to command of the 1st U.S. Cavalry. But while Lee opposed secession, he could not bring himself to lead an army against his home state; if Virginia was for the South, then so was Lee. On April 18, he declined Scott's offer of command of Union armies; on the 20th he resigned his commission.

The man whose name would soon echo across the continent began his Confederate service on a relatively low rung, as commander of Virginia's state forces. He was serving as a military advisor to Confederate President Jefferson Davis in June 1862, when Union General George McClellan drove his Army of the Potomac to within a dozen miles of Richmond. Lee's rise to legend status began after Davis sent him into the field to replace Joseph E. Johnston following the Battle of Seven Pines.

restored, offering a realistic snapshot of slave life in Northern Virginia. The plantation is open every day except Tuesday 11:00 a.m. to 4:00 p.m. Guided tours of the house are given every hour on the hour. The cost is $6 adults, $5 students, and $4 seniors and children. Tours of the slave quarters and outbuildings are available for an additional $2.

Northern Virginia Forts

Several earthworks forts were constructed in Northern Virginia by Union forces to bolster the defense of the Federal capital. Fort Ward boasts the most extensive remains, artifacts, and interpretation, but many of the other forts have evolved into popular parks for picnics and outdoor recreation.

Fort C. F. Smith
2411 North Twenty-Fourth Street
Arlington, VA

Fort Ethan Allen
3829 North Stafford Street
Arlington, VA

Fort Marcy
671 Chain Bridge Road
McLean, VA

Accommodations

Almost Heaven Bed and Breakfast
6339 Brocketts Crossing
Alexandria, VA
(703) 921-9043
(877) 418-8256
www.bbhost.com/almostheavenbb
Any place that claims to be "almost heaven" isn't afraid of setting its guests' expectations fairly high, and this Alexandria B&B doesn't disappoint. The beautiful private home is furnished with antiques, hardwood floors, and even an in-ground pool and Jacuzzi. Families traveling with children can take advantage of kid-friendly amenities like a pool table, darts, electronic basketball, and even an air-hockey table. On the weekends, guests enjoy home-

made, fruit-filled waffles and cooked-to-order omelets for breakfast. It's just a few minutes away from Metrorail and Old Town Alexandria. $139-$150

Arlington-Alexandria Bed &
Breakfast Network
(888) 549-3415
(703) 549-3415
www.aabbn.com
Arlington and Alexandria are brimming with national hotel chains, but bed-and-breakfasts are somewhat of a rarity. This network connects you with several of the region's private homes that offer short-term accommodations and extended stay leases.

Bailiwick Inn
4023 Chain Bridge Road
Fairfax, VA
(703) 691-2266
If you're looking for a place to stay in Fairfax with a little bit of history and charm, you can't beat the Bailiwick Inn, a lovely, Federal-style town house that boasts an inn, bakery, and fine-dining restaurant all in the same space. Even Confederate Colonel John Singleton Mosby understands the appeal; he once raided it! There are fourteen guest rooms, all named for famous Virginians, decorated with antiques and reproductions. Some guest rooms are also outfitted with fireplaces and whirlpool tubs, and room rates include afternoon tea and breakfast. $230

The Captain McGuire House
Prince Street
Alexandria, VA
(703) 549-3415
Although Alexandria's charming cobblestone streets practically scream "bed-and-breakfast country," there are surprisingly few in town, thanks in part to strict real estate codes and sky-high property values. The circa 1816 Captain McGuire House is a fine exception, nestled between historic row houses a block from the shops and restaurants on King Street. There are only two rooms, one outfit-

ted with a queen-size bed, decorative fireplace, and private bath. A third-floor bedroom has two twin beds and a private bath with a shower. Rooms start at $140-$145.

Hotel Monaco
480 King Street
Alexandria, VA
(703) 549-6080
www.hotel-ot.com
Alexandria's other Kimpton hotel tells a different story than the stately Morrison House. For years, the property operated as a Holiday Inn Select. After a $22 million renovation that brought the 241-room hotel up to four-star standards, it reopened as the sleek, stylish Hotel Monaco in fall 2007. Although it's loaded with twenty-first-century amenities, the Monaco's location in the heart of the Old Town Historic District is one of its top selling points. You can walk down to the waterfront for open-air dining or walk to Metro to access Washington, D.C.'s most celebrated sites. $175-$300

Inns of Virginia—Falls Church
421 West Broad Street
Falls Church, VA
(703) 533-1100
www.innsofvirginia.com
There's nothing fancy about this no-frills Falls Church hotel, but you can't beat the value. It's clean, safe, and well-located near Metrorail, shops, and restaurants. Rooms were recently renovated and now boast 27-inch flat-screen TVs, free wireless Internet, free parking, and complimentary continental breakfast. $110-$115

Morrison House
116 South Alfred Street
Alexandria, VA
(703) 838-8000
www.morrisonhouse.com
While most other hotels managed by San Francisco–based Kimpton are known for their bold décor and funky furnishings, the Morrison House is decidedly demure, complementing its Old Town Alexandria location with

antiques, reproductions, and other classic touches. In the boutique hotel's forty-five guest rooms, you'll find two- and four-poster beds, even decorative fireplaces, crystal chandeliers, and round-the-clock butler service. It's not all about the past, however. Guest rooms are also outfitted with wireless Internet capabilities, multiline phones with free local calls, and yoga and pilates equipment available to borrow. Rates start at $150 but can pass $400 during peak season.

Stafford House
3746 Chain Bridge Road
Fairfax, VA
(703) 385-9024
www.staffordhouse.net
Don't let the Stafford House's "married couples only" policy prevent you from enjoying a stay at this luxurious B&B. It's perfect for a romantic getaway or a relaxing respite after a day of intense sightseeing. Guests enjoy access to an enormous, private whirlpool bath and dry sauna and enjoy room-service breakfast. Single travelers are also welcomed, and unmarried couples are referred to other nearby B&Bs.

Restaurants

Argia's
124 North Washington Street
Falls Church, VA 22046
(703) 534-1033
www.argias.com
If you're staying in Falls Church, and you're hungry for Italian, this neighborhood eatery should be at the top of your list. Argia's takes recipes handed down from chef and co-owner Adam Scott's grandmother (note the family photographs on the wall) and adds in a few modern variations. The eggplant al formaggio is a delectable take on eggplant parmesan, grilled and layered with goat cheese and tomatoes. Calamari comes lightly dusted in parmesan and flavored with a dusting of fresh basil. Dishes are served as single portions or family style, designed for sharing. Average dinner entrée price: $15-$20.

Artie's
3260 Old Lee Highway
Fairfax, VA
(703) 273-7600
www.greatamericanrestaurants.com
This family-friendly favorite serves classic American creations like crab cakes, baby back ribs, and succulent pork tenderloin glazed with a citrus-chipotle sauce and paired with parmesan potatoes. Artie's boasts one of the region's best brunches as well. Brioche French toast is decadent and sweet, and you can't miss with the egg dishes and the fresh-baked bread. It's open daily for lunch and dinner. Average dinner entrée price: $20-$25.

Bazin's on Church
111 Church Street, NW
Vienna, VA
(703) 255-7212
www.bazinsonchurch.com
The Town of Vienna's historic district is peppered with a few Civil War sites, along with a few eateries. Among them is Bazin's, a new venture for chef Patrick Bazin, who earned acclaim at the Occidental, one of D.C.'s leading historic restaurants. Inventive surf-and-turf creations abound on the menu: Mushroom-crusted rockfish is served with parmesan orzo, and filet mignon comes paired with a wild mushroom and baby spinach enchilada. It's open for lunch and dinner Tuesday through Friday, dinner Saturday, and Sunday brunch. Average dinner entrée price: $20-$25.

Del Merei Grille
3106 Mount Vernon Avenue
Alexandria, VA
(703) 739-4335
www.delmereigrille.com
Alexandria, Virginia's up-and-coming Del Rey neighborhood has emerged on the dining and nightlife map in recent years, and with good cause, thanks to places like Del Merei Grille. It's a friendly gathering place for locals and visitors who are beginning to discover that there's more to Alexandria than its eighteenth-century cobblestone streets. Start with an order of fried pickles—a Southern specialty—or beer-battered mozzarella served with spicy tomato sauce, and then choose something from the grill like filet mignon, shrimp, or scallops and jazz it up with the sauce of your choice: peppercorn brandy cream, blue cheese, dill cream, or barbecue sauce. If you don't want to create your own meal, there are also plenty of things to choose from. Shrimp is sautéed with mushrooms and andouille sausage and served over creamy cheese garlic grits with a Cajun cream sauce. Braised barbecue ribs are paired with collard greens and home-baked macaroni and cheese. It's open for lunch Monday through Friday and for dinner nightly. Average dinner entrée price: $20-$25.

Farrah Olivia
600 Franklin Street
Alexandria, VA
(703) 778-2233
www.farraholiviarestaurant.com
If you plan to spend some time in Alexandria, you'll no doubt hear buzz about the city's thriving restaurant scene. Taking credit for the city's culinary reputation are chefs like Morou Ouattara. Named for his three year-old daughter, Farrah Olivia serves modern American cuisine with global accents that hint at the chef's native Africa. The menu doesn't pretend to be traditional. Start with something exotic: plantain fritters served with refried coconut and dusted with peanut butter powder or diver scallops with bacon powder and melon seed milk. For the main course, it's on to lemongrass duck breast, complemented by steamed cabbage, dried apricot and sweet potato, or the slow-roasted lamb, marinated in cardamom, coriander, cilantro, and cumin and paired with a plantain loaf and red palm jus. If you've saved room for dessert, you're in for a treat: baked palm Alaska served with a blistered pineapple and guava jus or yellow beet pineapple cake with yogurt foam are just a couple of the options available. Average dinner entrée price: $10-$15.

Five Guys
107 North Fayette Street
Alexandria, VA
(703) 549-7991
www.fiveguys.com
In the Washington, D.C., metropolitan area, Five Guys is synonymous with hamburgers. It's just what you want in a burger joint: juicy burgers, available in regular and "little" sizes that are large enough to satisfy most appetites. Pay a little extra to top it with bacon and cheese, then make it your own with free toppings like fried onions, sautéed mushrooms, and jalapeno peppers. Not in the mood for a burger? There are also hot dogs, veggie burgers, and gooey grilled cheese sandwiches. Split a heaping order of hand-cut fries, cooked in peanut oil and served boardwalk style or doused in Cajun spice. While this is the local chain's flagship location, you'll find other locations in Arlington, Chantilly, D.C., and elsewhere in the mid-Atlantic. Average dinner entrée price: under $10.

Idylwood Grill and Wine Bar
2190 Pimmit Drive
Falls Church, VA
(703) 992-0915
www.idylwoodgrill.com
It's easy to drive right past this Falls Church eatery. It's tucked into a suburban strip mall located near busy Leesburg Pike. The two-level restaurant is developing a regional reputation as a fine choice for savory Mediterranean fare. Sit down and feast on fresh flat bread, perfectly paired with fruity olive oil. While you'll likely recognize the names of many dishes on the menu, you'll be amazed by the preparations. Calamari are doused in a beurre blanc sauce, flavored with herbs and shallots. You can't go wrong with lamb dishes or hearty pastas, topped with tasty pesto and tomato-based sauces. Average dinner entrée price: $20-$25.

Ray's the Steaks
1725 Wilson Boulevard
Arlington, VA
(703) 841-7297
Ask any steak lover in the region for a dinner recommendation, and they're likely to point you to Ray's. It's located in an unassuming Arlington shopping center, but it's not uncommon to find a throng of hungry customers waiting to get in. The steaks are delicious, hand-procured, butchered, and aged by proprietor Michael Landrum. While the tender meats get top billing here, it's easy to fall in love with side dishes like creamy spinach and buttery mashed potatoes. It's also easy to find an affordable bottle of wine to pair with the choice cuts of meat. It's open for dinner Tuesday through Sunday. Average dinner entrée price: $15-$20.

Restaurant Eve
110 South Pitt Street
Alexandria, VA
(703) 706-0450
www.restauranteve.com
Fine dining hit its stride in Old Town Alexandria when Restaurant Eve appeared on the scene. Cathal Armstrong, voted chef of the year by the Restaurant Association Metropolitan Washington and one of the country's best new chefs by *Food + Wine*, has earned acclaim for this cozy American bistro. Sign up for the five- or nine-course tasting menu in the Chef's Tasting Room or craft your own menu in the comfortable bistro. Specialties include veal sweetbreads with porcinis, new potatoes and garlic, and soft-shell crabs with tomatoes and avocado emulsion. Desserts are decadent and divine. One of the best sellers: a mini-birthday cake covered in pink frosting and sprinkles. It's open for lunch Monday through Friday and dinner on Saturday. Average dinner entrée price: $25-$30.

Southside 815
815 South Washington Street
Alexandria, VA
(703) 836-6222
www.southside815.com
If you book a table at Southside 815, there's not much chance that you'll leave hungry. The Old Town Alexandria restaurant is known for its generous servings of Southern classics served at affordable prices. Start your meal with a basket of fresh-baked buttermilk and sweet potato biscuits or an order of fried pickles, then move on to main courses like grilled pork chops smothered in apple chutney, drunken pot roast, or baby back ribs. For dessert, dive into the luscious peach pound cake topped with vanilla ice cream and warm caramel sauce. Southside serves lunch and dinner daily. Average dinner entrée price: $15-$20.

Sunflower Vegetarian Restaurant
2531 Chain Bridge Road
Vienna, VA
(703) 319-3888
www.crystalsunflower.com
Metropolitan Washington, D.C.'s vegetarian community has fallen for the Sunflower, and with good cause. The food is delicious enough to trick carnivores into enjoying it, and the service is warm and inviting. Start your meal off with an order of edamame, seasoned with a tasty bouquet of spices and salts. Main dishes come with a serving of healthy brown rice. Some of our favorites include "Sweet and Sour Sensation," a vegetarian interpretation of sweet-and-sour pork made with soy protein, "Songbird," an interesting take on kung pao chicken, and "General Tso's Surprise," a delectable interpretation of General Tso's chicken. Wash it down with a glass of homemade lemonade, sweetened with honey. Don't understand all of the healthy ingredients on the menu? There's a glossary that sheds some light on some of the trickier terms. The Sunflower is open daily for lunch and dinner. Average dinner entrée price: $10-$15.

Tallula
2761 Washington Boulevard
Arlington, VA
(703) 778-5051
tallularestaurant.com
Arlington's Clarendon neighborhood is earning a reputation among the culinary minded, thanks to dining hot spots like Tallula. Wine plays a key role in the menu here, served in tumblers to show their colors and characteristics in the best possible light. And because many of the bottles are reasonably priced, it's a good excuse to try out New World vintages that are uncommon in other D.C. restaurants. Some of the starters are designed to be shared or relished in two-bite servings and bargain-priced at $3 and less. Among the main courses, the diver scallops with braised pork belly and sweet corn puree and bison short ribs are interesting choices. If you're not a fan of meat, check out the enticing vegetarian menu. Average dinner entrée price: $20-$25.

BEFORE RICHMOND

FREDERICKSBURG/ SPOTSYLVANIA

This tour focuses on the battlefields west and southwest of Fredericksburg, and the towns of Fredericksburg and Spotsylvania. If in separate campaigns, each battle waged here—Fredericksburg, Chancellorsville, the Wilderness, and Spotsylvania—featured Robert E. Lee's Army of Northern Virginia defending against Union commanders trying to force their way to Richmond with the Army of the Potomac.

THE BATTLE OF FREDERICKSBURG

Only "Pickett's Charge" on the third day at Gettysburg compares with the horrible bloodletting that took place before Marye's Heights, above Fredericksburg, Virginia, on December 13, 1862. The Confederate shredding of one wave of blue-coated Yankees after another topped off the failure of yet another Army of the Potomac commander, this time heavy-whiskered Major General Ambrose Burnside.

The fourth commander (including two stints by George B. McClellan) of the Union's mightiest army, Ambrose Burnside inherited command from his old friend McClellan on November 7, after the latter general's mediocre performance during and after the Battle of Antietam. Hoping to strike General Robert E. Lee's Confederate army again before the arrival of winter, the burly Rhode Islander marched his massive, 130,000-man force south to Falmouth, Virginia—lost three weeks waiting for pontoon boats to arrive—then continued toward Fredericksburg, where Lee's army was encamped. Union engineers

spent December 11 stretching their pontoon bridges across the Rappahannock River (which ran northwest to southeast), while Yankee cannon lobbed shells over them and into the city, on the opposite shore. The following day, while Burnside reconnoitered and discussed with his senior commanders his plan of attack, thousands of his restless foot soldiers marched into Fredericksburg and looted it.

With his army stretched roughly north to south beyond the fields west of Fredericksburg, Robert E. Lee had a number of advantages: supportable interior lines, high ground, and for the men in his center, a an almost unassailable position behind a 400-foot stone wall along the crest of Marye's Heights, above the town. Having lost the initiative and any hope of surprise, Burnside would have to count on sheer numbers: he had a 2-1 edge in man power. For the Federals on December 13, there would be no elaborate feints; no flanking movements or surprise cavalry assaults—only power.

But as at Antietam and other battlefields, the Union commander nullified his advantage through inefficient—and eventually, suicidal—deployment. Hoping to nail down Lee's right while he hammered the Virginian's left-center, Burnside ordered left-wing commander Major General William Franklin to launch an attack. But Franklin's small-scale, early afternoon assault petered out in the face of a vigorous Confederate response.

For the shivering, blue-garbed infantrymen of Major General Edwin Sumner's right wing, meanwhile, a hideous nightmare had begun. All afternoon, regiment after regiment filed through the streets of Fredericksburg, formed up, and trudged up the slowly ascending, half mile of ground toward Marye's

Heights. Confederate cannon blazed away. By the hundreds, astonished Confederate infantrymen lay their rifles across the stone wall and pulled triggers. It was a perfect shooting gallery. Only Brigadier General Thomas Meagher's vaunted Irish Brigade managed to stagger within shouting range of the Confederate lines. Remembering the scene years later, one Union officer, Josiah Favill, wrote "there was no romance, no glorious pomp, nothing but disgust for the genius who planned so frightful a slaughter."[1]

Night fell. On into December 14—as thousands of bleeding and freezing Yankee soldiers lay on the hilly turf below Marye's Heights—a heartsick Burnside pondered another attack, this time with himself at its head. Finally talked out of it, he arranged for a belated truce to bury the dead and collect the wounded, and then ordered a withdrawal back across the river.

For the stunned Army of the Potomac, the headaches were not quite over. Resolving to make up for the devastating setback by surprising Lee from the rear, Burnside ordered a looping march around Lee's left across the Rappahannock. Campaigning at this time of year was hard enough with the onset of rain and snow that now swamped Burnside's army, freezing soldiers and halting the endless Union wagon trains in feet of frosty mud. Still, soldiers retained their sense of humor, even coming up with a poem about their plight:

Now I lay me down to sleep
In mud that's many fathoms deep;
If I'm not here when you awake,
Just hunt me up with an oyster rake.

Unsympathetic witnesses derided the Union columns as they struggled, shivering, down icy roads. With his doomed movement already being laughed off as the "Mud March," Burnside called it off on January 25. For his used up troops, the long, 1862 cam-

paigning season was at a merciful end. Two days later, so was Ambrose Burnside's reign as Army of the Potomac commander.

THE BATTLE OF CHANCELLORSVILLE

Having deposed the unfortunate Burnside, Abraham Lincoln turned to Major General Joseph Hooker, a capable, hard-fighting and hard-drinking forty-eight-year-old veteran of corps command who had served under his predecessor at Fredericksburg. Hooker immediately replaced Burnside's unwieldy Grand Division army structure with the more traditional corps setup, and reorganized the long-neglected Union cavalry into a single command under Major General George Stoneman. (Major General Alfred Pleasanton would replace Stoneman in June.)

Rested after a winter in camp, Hooker's Army of the Potomac opened the 1863 campaign season in stunning fashion. Sending Major General John Sedgwick and 30,000 Federals to keep Lee busy at Fredericksburg, and Stoneman's cavalry raiding to the south, Hooker crossed the Rappahannock with 65,000 men and swung around behind Lee. The surprised and shorthanded Lee (elements of James Longstreet's corps had been detached and sent south to Richmond) found himself trapped between the two halves of Hooker's massive army. On April 30, Hooker's staff confidently announced to the army:

It is with heartfelt satisfaction the commanding general announces to the army that the operations of the last three days have determined that our enemy must either ingloriously fly, or come out from behind his defenses and give us battle on our own ground, where certain destruction awaits him.

Lee was certainly not about to fly anywhere. Never afraid to try the unconventional, he divided his 53,000-man army, leaving just 10,000 to watch Sedgwick while he turned

[1] Josiah Favill, *The Diary of a Young Army Officer* (Army of the Potomac; Baltimore: Butternut & Blue, 2000).

Fredericksburg and Spotsylvania County Battlefields Memorial NATIONAL PARK SERVICE

and marched 10 miles west to confront his latest Union opponent. He found Hooker's army in line 2 miles east of the forbidding Wilderness—a tangled mess of undergrowth, trees, and briars through which a man could scarcely walk. Hooker made the first move on May 1, sending elements of three corps attacking east down local roads. Lee counterattacked, and as the fighting raged just west of the village of Chancellorsville, Hooker stunningly called a halt to his assault. Ignoring the protests of his corps commanders, Hooker pulled his flanks back and centered his new position at Chancellorsville. With his army dug in behind stiff fortifications, his position was formidable. His reasons for giving up his momentum and the initiative to Lee—the clear underdog in this contest—have never been made clear. The normally aggressive army commander apparently told one subor-

dinate that he had lost confidence in Hooker.Whatever the reason for his decision, it opened the door for the most famous flank attack of the war. After discussing it with Lee, Stonewall Jackson and 26,000 Confederates set out early on May 2 to spring a surprise attack on Hooker's right flank, which scouting Rebel cavalry had found unprotected. The absence of most of Stoneman's Yankee cavalry—still missing to the south—was a blessing. Still, it was a risky plan; should Hooker change his colors and attack, Lee, with just 17,000 men, would be hard-pressed to escape Hooker's blue-coated hordes.

Aside from some skirmishing with a portion of Jackson's flanking party, Hooker did not attack. Neither he nor 11th Corps commander, Major General Oliver Otis Howard, seemed to be aware of what was brewing on their right. Howard found out at about 5:30

p.m., when the piercing Rebel yell filled the ears of his shocked 11th Corps men as they cooked up their rations. Bullets screamed by, followed by Jackson's divisions. Dropping their food, Yankees bolted from their camp at top speed, their pursuers hard on their heels. The fighting on the Union right continued past dusk, as Yankee reinforcements fought to stem the slowing Confederate tide.

For the Confederate Army, the good news of the day was tempered by a horrifying report that Jackson had been seriously wounded. Reconnoitering under the moonlight, the corps commander had been mistakenly shot three times by his own soldiers. He was out of the fight; cavalryman J. E. B. Stuart took command of his corps. Informed of Jackson's injuries by a junior officer, a troubled Lee replied: "Ah, Captain, any victory is dearly bought that deprives us of the services of General Jackson even for a short time."

May 3 saw Hooker's army tightening into a loop-shape with its flanks extended toward the Rapidan and Rappahannock Rivers. Hooker—knocked senseless by the concussion of an exploding shell—had little to do with the day's fighting, during which Lee, Stuart, and dominating Confederate artillery compressed the Union lines. Only the news of John Sedgwick's approach from the east stalled Lee, who detached a force to deal with the oncoming Yankees. Sedgwick, who had overrun Jubal Early's Marye's Heights defenders and chased him south, was himself now repulsed at Salem Church.

The following day, Lee led some 20,000 men east to dispose of Sedgwick, who retreated carefully north over the Rappahannock. The recovered Hooker—whose man power advantage in the absence of Lee offered an opportunity to wipe out Stuart— did little but prepare to retreat. By noon on May 6, his army was back north of Rapidan, and the Chancellorsville Campaign was over, with Lee's Confederates—again—the clear winner. Each side had lost more than 1,600 men killed. The loss of Jackson, who after losing an arm to amputation would succumb to

pneumonia on May 10, particularly stunned the South. Jackson's loss would be hard to overcome. But with conditions otherwise favorable for something audacious, Lee began to prepare for an invasion of the North.

GRANT'S 1864 OVERLAND (RICHMOND) CAMPAIGN

The Battle of the Wilderness

Hailed by some as the Union's savior, Ulysses S. Grant returned to the east during the spring of 1864 to take command of all Union armies. His victories out west had helped secure the Mississippi River for the Union; now he had been charged with bringing Confederate General Robert E. Lee to heel. Eastern veterans grown skeptical by the repeated failure of much-ballyhooed new commanders accepted the Western hero with hope. "If he succeeds, the war is over," a Massachusetts captain wrote. "For I do assure you that in the hands of a General who gave them success, there is no force on earth which would resist this army."[2]

Grant's plan, basically, was to attack on all fronts. From Tennessee, Major General William T. Sherman would slash through Georgia, destroying Confederate supplies, communications, and transportation. In the east, Major General Benjamin Butler would march up the James River to pressure Richmond from the east. And while Franz Sigel (or his eventual successor Philip Sheridan) took control of the Shenandoah Valley, George Gordon Meade's beleaguered Army of the Potomac would deal with Lee. Now a lieutenant general, Grant would travel with Meade's army.

Launching his Overland Campaign on May 4, Meade marched his 120,000 Yankees across the Rapidan River toward Lee's 60,000 Confederates. Grant hoped to advance through the infamous Wilderness—a hellish

[2] Gregory Jaynes, *The Killing Ground: Wilderness to Cold Harbor* (Alexandria, VA: Time-Life Books, 1986).

tangle of woods and underbrush—and strike Lee on open ground before Lee could respond. The next day, however, elements of Meade's right and Lee's left collided on the worst possible terrain for fighting. The smoke of musketry saturated the area, blotting out the sky in the middle of the day. With cavalry and artillery of little use, infantry struggled to maintain any kind of formation—even to distinguish friend from foe just a few yards away. It was, one survivor testified, a "battle of invisibles against invisibles." Another veteran remembered the "puffs of smoke, the 'ping' of the bullets, and the yell of the enemy. It was a blind and bloody hunt to the death, in bewildering thickets, rather than a battle."[3]

The bloody, terrifying fighting in the woods continued on May 6. Lee sent Lieutenant General Richard Ewell's corps up the Orange Turnpike against Meade's right, while Major General Winfield Scott Hancock and James Longstreet dueled back and forth on the Federals' left. With no room for elaborate maneuver, the two armies slugged it out to exhaustion. Separated from their units by entangling thickets, enemy soldiers fought hand to hand with rifles and bayonets. "There wasn't a tree…but what was all cut to pieces with balls," one Yankee remembered, "and the dead and wounded was lying thick. It was an awful sight."[4] Badly wounded soldiers cut off from their units could only die alone. Others suffered a worse fate after darkness fell, perishing in fires set by heavy musketry.

Aside from costing the two armies a combined 28,000 casualties, the two-day fight settled nothing.

The Battles of Spotsylvania Court House

After two days of killing in the Wilderness, George Gordon Meade—putting into practice Grant's relentless strategy—kept up the pres-

sure on Robert E. Lee's Confederates by sliding southeast toward Spotsylvania Court House. But units of Lee's army beat him to the crossroads town and proceeded to fashion a mule-shoe-shaped line of virtually impregnable fortifications of logs, earth, and sharpened stakes that covered three sides of the town and protected the Confederates' flanks. It was the sort of defense that less determined Union generals would have done their best to avoid.

Near dusk on May 10, 5,000 Federals charged and carried a northern section of the Rebel works, before being forced to withdraw with heavy casualties. Encouraged, Grant sent a larger force—some 15,000 infantrymen with bayonets fixed—charging into the Rebel fortifications at 4:30 a.m. on May 12. The Confederates counterattacked from within their own lines, kicking off nearly a full day of back-and-forth struggle in a section of Lee's lines that became known as the "Bloody Angle." Under darkened skies and drenching rains, soldiers fought at close quarters: "Skulls were crushed with clubbed muskets," one of Grant's aides wrote, "and men stabbed to death with swords and bayonets thrust between the logs in the parapet which separated the combatants."

Exhausted following the nightmarish slaughter of May 12–13, the two armies continued to probe and skirmish for another week until Grant and Meade—with Lee following—stepped off to the east, then the south, again, moving inexorably toward Richmond. In two weeks, Grant had incurred some 18,000 casualties (killed, wounded, or missing) compared to Lee's 12,000, proving to some that he cared little for his soldiers and to others that he would fight until victory was won.

Cold Harbor

Grant and Meade continued moving south along the railroad, occasionally testing Lee's sliding lines with little success. After several clashes along the North Anna River, Meade and Lee met at another crossroads called Cold Harbor, 10 miles northeast of Richmond.

[3] Warren Lee Goss, *Recollections of a Private: A Story of the Army of the Potomac*. (Alexandria, VA: Time-Life Books, 1984).

[4] Gordon C. Rhea, *The Battle Of The Wilderness, May 5-6, 1864*, (Baton Rouge, LA: Louisiana State University Press, 2004), 397.

Fredericksburg and Spotsylvania County Battlefields Memorial NATIONAL PARK SERVICE

After a day of skirmishing on June 1, Grant prepared a massive frontal assault designed to exploit any weakness in Lee's lines. Nearly a month of bloody stalemate had Grant chomping at the bit and determined to smash through the armies of his nemesis.

On June 3, three Union corps attacked Lee's army, again barricaded behind impressive earthworks. The badly coordinated assault resulted in one of the war's bloodiest (alongside Fredericksburg and Gettysburg) repulses, and 7,000 Yankee casualties in less than an hour. Grant's month-long campaign resembled, to some, a horrific waste of life and expense. Once the Union's best hope, Grant was now decried as a "Butcher." "I do think there has been too much assaulting, this campaign!" one frustrated Federal declared. Major General Gouverneur K. Warren—a hero of Gettysburg who would later be relieved of his command—complained: "For thirty days

now, it has been one funeral procession, past me; and it is too much!" Nearly four days passed as Lee and Grant haggled over the details of a truce for burial detail. Meanwhile, hundreds of suffering, wounded soldiers died on the battlefield.

Grant had learned his lesson. His next move—a lightning crossing of the James River to ensnare Petersburg—would leave both Lee and his detractors stunned.

Historic Sites

Chatham
120 Chatham Lane
Falmouth, VA
(540) 654-5121
www.nps.gov/frsp/chatham.htm
When you visit the Fredericksburg battlefields, be sure to make time to see Chatham, a Georgian-style mansion that served as the Union headquarters during the Battle of Fred-

ericksburg. It's also one of only three houses in the United States to have been visited by George Washington, Thomas Jefferson, and Abraham Lincoln. When war broke out, the house was owned by James Horace Lacy, a slave holder and Southern sympathizer who left his wife and children on the estate and joined the Confederate army. Union forces took over the house in 1862, using it as a hospital to treat some of the 12,600 casualties from the disastrous defeat at Fredericksburg. Clara Barton and Walt Whitman were among the medical attendants. There's a replica pontoon boat inside, fashioned after the ones used by the troops to cross the Rappahannock River. You can also catch a free movie, which illustrates the effects of the war on residents of the area. Chatham is open daily 9:00 a.m. to 4:30 p.m.

Civil War Life: The Soldier's Museum
4712 Southpoint Parkway
Fredericksburg
(540) 834-1859
www.civilwar-life.com
This small, private museum is dedicated to the story of the Civil War fighting man. It offers a number of fine exhibits, most of which explore how soldiers lived, trained, and fought. The museum's latest exhibit—"Civil War Life in 3-D"—revolves around stereograph cards; examples can be seen at the museum's Web site. The Soldier's Museum hours of operation are: Winter hours September through December 20, February through April, 10 a.m. to 5 p.m. Closed December 20 through February 1 except for weekends in January. Summer hours May through August, 9 a.m. to 5 p.m. Admission is $5.00 for adults and $2.50 for children. The 3-D Theater is $3.00 per person over 6.

Cold Harbor Battlefield and Visitor Center
Route 156 (5 miles SE of Mechanicsville)
(804) 226-1981
www.nps.gov/rich
Although Cold Harbor is closer to Richmond and is part of Richmond National Battlefield

Park, we've included it in this section due to its relationship to the other locations in the campaign. Cold Harbor has a visitor center that boasts an electric map program and exhibits depicting the 1862 Battle of Gaines' Mill and the 1864 Battle of Cold Harbor. The battlefield itself features original entrenchments, which can be examined from numerous interpretive walking trails. The Cold Harbor visitor center is open 9:00 a.m. to 5:00 p.m. daily.

Cold Harbor National Cemetery
6038 Cold Harbor Rd.
Mechanicsville
Also a part of the battlefield (but administered by the Veterans Administration) is Cold Harbor National Cemetery, where more than 2,000 victims of area battles lay. On the cemetery grounds, there's a masonry lodge designed by Quartermaster Montgomery Meigs and monuments donated by the states of Pennsylvania and New York to honor their fallen soldiers. The Tomb of the Unknown Soldier, erected in 1877, honors the 889 unknown Union soldiers who were killed and buried in trenches in and around Cold Harbor.

Ellwood
36380 Constitution Highway
Locust Grove
(540) 786-2880
http://www.nps.gov/frsp/ellwood.htm
Like Chatham, Ellwood was owned by the Lacy family at the start of the war and is now part of the battlefield park. While it lacks the grandeur of Chatham, it's not without its historic significance. During the Battle of Chancellorsville, many of the wounded were treated here, including Confederate General Stonewall Jackson. His amputated arm is famously buried in the Lacy family cemetery on the house's grounds. Union troops used Ellwood as a headquarters a year later during the Battle of the Wilderness. It's open 11:00 a.m. to 5:00 p.m. Saturday, Sunday, and holidays May through October; as well as Friday from mid-June through mid-August.

Fredericksburg and Spotsylvania National Military Park
120 Chatham Lane
Fredericksburg
(540) 373-6122
www.nps.gov/frsp
Second only to Chickamauga and Chattanooga in terms of size, this military park is one of the most significant: It includes four important battlefields (including the Wilderness and Chancellorsville), two visitor centers (Fredericksburg and Chancellorsville), and four historic buildings. One of these structures is now the Stonewall Jackson Shrine, the small Chandler Plantation building in which Stonewall Jackson died on May 10, 1863. In addition to numerous walking trails and driving tours (with audiotape), the park often provides guided tours. Its two visitor centers offer twenty-two-minute films for a $2 fee (it is free for most students and just $1 for seniors).

A number of recent changes to the park have brought its battlefields closer than ever to their original appearance. During the summer of 2006, the National Park Service (NPS) set about restoring the "Sunken Road" and stone wall along Marye's Heights. Along this battered old road (and behind this wall), Lee's Confederates stood as they mowed down Ambrose Burnside's Federals during the Battle of Fredericksburg. The park has also managed to acquire the land over which Stonewall Jackson launched his crushing flank attack on Joseph Hooker's army at Chancellorsville, along with the site of James Longstreet's flank attack in the Wilderness.

The park is open free of admission from dawn to dusk daily, but closed on Thanksgiving, Christmas, and New Year's Day. The visitor centers are open Monday through Friday 9:00 a.m. to 5:00 p.m., and on weekends (and holidays) 9:00 a.m. to 6:00 p.m. from late March through October 28. From October 29 through late March, they are open daily 9:00 a.m. to 5:00 p.m. (Ask about the popular Kenmore and Washington Street Tour.) Rather than visitor centers, the Wilderness and Spotsylvania Court House Battlefields feature interpretive shelters where historians are often available (during warmer months) to answer questions.

Fredericksburg Area Museum and Cultural Center
907 Princess Anne Street
Fredericksburg
(540) 371-3037
www.famcc.org
This community museum located in Fredericksburg's 1816 Town Hall/ Market Square building reaches beyond the Civil War to showcase the town's colonial history, its ties to the railroad, and other themes. Artifacts like Confederate currency and officers' uniforms and weapons help relate the town's role before, during, and after the war. It's open Monday through Saturday 10:00 a.m. to 5:00 p.m. and 1:00 to 5:00 p.m. Sunday (till 4:00 p.m. December through February). Admission is $7 adults, $2 children 7 and up, with discounts for AAA and AARP members.

Massaponax Baptist Church
5101 Massaponax Church Road
Fredericksburg
(540) 898-0021
www.massaponaxbaptist.org
Massaponax Baptist Church was just four years old when Union Lieutenant General Ulysses S. Grant, Major General George Meade, and their staffs stopped there on May 21, 1864, following the Battle of Spotsylvania Court House. Grant had a number of the church pews carried outside, where he and his subordinates rested and plotted their next moves. Timothy O'Sullivan, one of the war's most prolific photographers, subsequently captured the gathering in one of the war's best-known sequence of images.

Often used as officers' headquarters or as temporary shelter for passing soldiers, the church still bears visible signs (scrawled names and messages) of the soldiers' presence. It is also still open for regular services, so call ahead before stopping in.

Lieutenant General Richard S. Ewell LIBRARY OF CONGRESS

Spotsylvania County Museum
8956 Courthouse Road
Spotsylvania
(540) 582-7167
The Old Berea Church, constructed in 1856, now houses the Spotsylvania County Museum. While the small collection of local artifacts and genealogical records will be of most interest to local history buffs, the church bears the marks of shots and shells from the Battle of Spotsylvania Court House, which raged nearby. The museum is open Monday through Saturday 10:00 a.m. to 5:00 p.m. Admission is free.

Spotsylvania Court House
9104 Courthouse Road
Spotsylvania
(540) 891-8687
Established in 1839, Spotsylvania Court House witnessed one of the bloodiest battles of the Civil War, which marked the beginning of the fall of the Confederacy. The Court House stood at the intersection of Routes 613 and 208, guarding the shortest route to Richmond. The building sustained significant damage during the Civil War and was reconstructed in 1900, using the Doric columns of the original building.

White Oak Museum
985 White Oak Road
Falmouth, VA
(540) 371-4234
Housed in a one-room schoolhouse, the White Oak Museum's collection includes a mix of Union and Confederate artifacts like reconstructed huts, bullets, belt plates, and buttons gathered from area battle sites. The museum is located on the original site of the White Oak School, which was burned and rebuilt in 1912. The museum is open Wednesday through Sunday from 10:00 a.m. to 5:00 p.m. Admission is $4.00 for adults, $2.00 for seniors and students, and free for children under 7.

Tours

Ghosts of Fredericksburg Tours
623 Caroline Street
Fredericksburg
(540) 654-5414
www.ghostsoffredericksburg.com
Offered Friday and Saturday evenings in season, author Mark Nesbitt's eerie tours trace the macabre past of a town considered the most haunted in America. The eighty-minute tours are led by costumed guides who relate stories from Fredericksburg's colonial and Civil War past. Reservations are strongly recommended. $10

Trolley Tours of Fredericksburg
(540) 898-0737
www.fredericksburgtrolley.com
If you've got a short time to explore, leave your car at the hotel and climb on board the trolley. In an hour and fifteen minutes, you'll get a nice overview of downtown's rich history and the nearby Civil War battlefields. The tour is $15 and departs from the visitors center at 10:30 a.m., noon, 1:30 p.m., and 3:30 p.m. June through October, and at 11:00 a.m. and 1:30 p.m. November through May. Evening tours are also offered June through September.

Accommodations

Kenmore Inn
1200 Princess Anne Street
Fredericksburg
(540) 371-7622
www.kenmoreinn.com
A charming Old Town Fredericksburg inn, the Kenmore has nine rooms, all with private baths, and four with working fireplaces. The building itself dates to 1793 and claims members of George Washington's family as its former owners. Despite the historic location, the rooms are outfitted with modern amenities like wireless Internet and flat-screen TVs. Guests enjoy a tasty cooked-to-order breakfast, featuring farm-fresh eggs, pancakes, and other classics. The inn's fine-dining restaurant

serves delectable American cuisine prepared by Chef Josh Oleson on Thursday, Friday, and Saturday nights. $123-$168

La Vista Plantation Bed & Breakfast
4420 Guinea Station Road
Fredericksburg
(540) 898-8444
(800) 829-2823
www.lavistaplantation.com
Located just 2 miles from the Massaponax Baptist Church (where photographer Timothy O'Sullivan photographed Union Generals Grant, Meade, and a host of others in May 1864), Ed and Michele Schiesser's La Vista Plantation sits in the heart of Spotsylvania Campaign ground. Follow a long driveway to the 1838 farmhouse, whose spacious rooms and common areas are meticulously and tastefully furnished with antiques. Guests enjoy gracious hospitality and a tasty breakfast made with fresh brown eggs from one of the resident hens, along with amenities like central air, satellite TV, and VCRs, working fireplaces, big canopy beds, and even refrigerators. Those guests that simply can't get enough of the Civil War can help themselves to books in the inn's library. Rooms are rented by reservation only, so call ahead. $145-$185

The Little White House Bed and Breakfast
1107 Princess Anne Street
Fredericksburg
(540) 538-5196
www.thelittlewhitehousebnb.com
True history lovers will relish a stay at The Little White House B&B. The house in which it's located is Fredericksburg's oldest residence, constructed in 1740 and known as the Charles Dick House. The Dick family lived across the Rappahannock River from their friends, the Washingtons. Rooms are airy and cheerful, furnished with glorious four-poster beds and antiques. In addition to a hearty gourmet breakfast, the innkeepers will also tempt you with complimentary desserts, like a decadent bread pudding made with fresh-picked blueberries and drizzled with rum cream sauce. $105-$195

On Keegan Pond Bed & Breakfast
11315 Gordon Road
Fredericksburg
(888) 785-4662
www.bedandbreakfast.com/virginia-fredericksburg-onkeeganpondbedbreakfast.html
This cozy B&B is a good choice for Civil War travelers who prefer more of a bucolic setting. Artifacts found on its five-acre grounds indicate that Union scouts were on the grounds during the opening sequences of the Battle of Chancellorsville. The inn's two rooms are clean and comfortable, furnished with antiques and equipped with central air, heat, and private baths. $85-$150

The Richard Johnston Inn Bed & Breakfast
711 Caroline Street
Fredericksburg
(540) 899-7606
(877) 557-0770
www.therichardjohnstoninn.com
If you're looking for a historic place to stay in the heart of Old Town Fredericksburg, check into the Richard Johnston Inn. The inn's seven rooms and two suites are charming and comfortable, furnished with antiques and big, comfortable beds. The top selling point, however, is the inn's central location, with shopping, dining, and sightseeing options on its doorstep—and the visitor center just across the street. $125-$210

Schooler House Bed & Breakfast
1303 Caroline Street
Fredericksburg
(540) 374-5258
www.schoolerhouse.com
If you want to mix in a little romance and elegance with your history, you can't beat the Schooler House. Built in Victorian Italianate style in the town's historic district, the house itself dates to the late nineteenth century. Period antiques and art decorate its two bedrooms, both of which come with private baths—and you might even happen upon a claw-foot bathtub. Period antiques are also found throughout the inn. Innkeeper Andi

Major General Ambrose Everett Burnside LIBRARY OF CONGRESS

Grimsley, an expert on local history, treats her guests to a healthy, generous breakfast spread, served on antique dishes and silver. On the grounds, you'll also find a tranquil garden with a goldfish pond and waterfall that's perfect for relaxing after a day of sightseeing. $125-$175

Wingate Inn
20 Sanford Drive
Fredericksburg
(540) 368-8000
www.wingateinns.com
We usually don't include chain hotels in *Insiders' Guides,* but the Fredericksburg location of this growing chain (a division of Wyndham Hotels) warrants a visit for its value and convenience to the interstate. This 129-room hotel serves up a host of amenities for business travelers like a twenty-four-hour business center and high-speed Internet, but leisure travelers will also enjoy the free local calls, indoor pool, and ample breakfast service. It's clean and comfortable, an excellent home base for exploring the battlefields in and around Fredericksburg. $80-$120

WyteStone Suites
4615 Southpoint Parkway
Fredericksburg
(540) 891-1112
(800) 794-5005
www.wytestone.com
The eighty-five-room WyteStone Suites is another example of a business hotel that provides a great value for tourists as well. Traveling families will especially benefit from the all-suite layout, indoor swimming pool, in-room refrigerator and microwave, and complimentary hot breakfast. There are also six wheelchair-accessible suites. It's easy to spot from Interstate 95, and there's no shortage of quick service restaurants and shopping options nearby. $100-$150

Restaurants

Allman's BBQ
1299 Jefferson Davis Highway
Fredericksburg
(540) 373-9881
allmansbarbecue.com
Allman's unassuming exterior belies its reputation as Fredericksburg's longtime king of Carolina-style barbecue. Its vintage 1954 interior sports the look of a classic diner; but it's the food that fills barstools, and Mary "Mom" Brown's ribs and coleslaw have been doing just that for nearly fifty years. Allman's is open 11:00 a.m. to 8:30 p.m. Monday through Saturday. There's a second drive-through location at 2022 Plank Road. Average dinner entrée price: $10-$15.

Augustine's at Fredericksburg Square
525 Caroline Street
Fredericksburg
(540) 310-0063
www.augustinesrest.com
When Augustine's opened its doors in 2001, it sought to prove that elegant dining could find an audience in Fredericksburg. One of the town's top eateries, it's a lovely place to relax over a sumptuous meal with a bottle of wine after a busy day of sightseeing. Choose from prix fixe menu selections that change every six weeks or order a la carte. The building itself is not without its own history; the oldest part of the restaurant dates to 1838. It was home to the town's first mayor, then housed a post office, a soup kitchen, and an Elks Lodge. Augustine's is open for dinner Tuesday through Saturday, beginning at 5:00 p.m., with the last reservations taken at 9:00 p.m. during the week and at 10:00 p.m. on weekends. Average dinner entrée price: $25-$30.

Major General Joseph Hooker LIBRARY OF CONGRESS

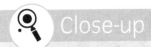

Union Personality: Ulysses S. Grant

Other American presidents have risen from obscure beginnings to reach the nation's highest office. None, however, had to bounce back from personal misfortunes quite as often or as late in life as did Grant, whose Missouri farm was appropriately named "Hardscrabble."

Born in Point Pleasant, Ohio, in 1822, Hiram Ulysses Grant seemed to have escaped a life as a farmer or tanner (his father's occupation) when he received a nomination to West Point in 1839. Like many other officers whose academic records at West Point offered little hint of their battlefield potential, Grant stood out in horsemanship, and little else. He graduated in 1843, and accepted his second lieutenant's commission in the infantry.

The Mexican War offered Grant (and scores of other officers destined for Civil War fame) opportunities for adventure and advancement; the Ohioan earned two brevets for gallantry, and served as quartermaster for the 4th Infantry. Groomed for command in Mexico, Grant soon found himself back in the highly competitive officer corps of the small, stagnant, peacetime army—no place for a man of exceptional ability or ambition. Bored, separated from his wife, and desperately lonely, Grant struggled on the frontier. He occasionally drank too much and feuded with his superior officer. By July 1854, he had had enough of army life; he resigned his commission and returned home to be with his family.

But civilian life proved equally challenging. After struggling as a farmer, Grant moved from Missouri to Galena, Illinois, where he clerked in his father's leathergoods shop. The Civil War saved Grant from frustration and obscurity. Given command of the 21st Illinois, Grant was bumped up to brigadier general before a near-disaster in the November 7, 1861, Battle of Belmont, Missouri.

Bistro Bethem
309 William Street
Fredericksburg
(540) 371-9999
www.bistrobethem.com
Blake and Aby Bethem's chic, casual bistro offers an enticing seasonal menu, featuring fresh fish, wild game, and other tasty creations prepared with a Southern accent. Macaroni and cheese is prepared with gruyere, fontina, and white cheddar and a hint of shallots. You can also nibble on house-made charcuterie plates and antipasto selections and treat yourself to heavenly desserts. It's open

Tuesday through Sunday for lunch (11:30 a.m. to 2:30 p.m.) and dinner (5:00 to 10:00 p.m.). Average dinner entrée price: $25-$30.

Brock's Riverside Grill
503 Sophia Street
Fredericksburg
(540) 370-1820
www.brocksgrill.com
You can't beat the ambiance at Brock's Riverside Grill. The comfortable, casual eatery is perched on the banks of the Rappahannock River. On the menu you'll find delectable seafood and hand-cut steaks, along with an

Subsequent victories at Forts Henry and Donelson, and, later, Chattanooga and Vicksburg, convinced President Abraham Lincoln to give him control of all Union armies in March 1864. Combat command brought out the best in Grant. Simply put, Southern diarist Mary Chesnut wrote, Grant had "the disagreeable habit of not retreating before irresistible veterans."

Four other Yankee soldiers (all from Ohio) went on to become president of the United States: Rutherford B. Hayes (1877–1881) was brevetted to major general, and was wounded four times; James Garfield (mortally wounded by assassin three months after March 1881 inauguration) reached the rank of major general; Benjamin Harrison (1889–1893) was brevetted to brigadier general; and William McKinley (1897–September 1901 (assassinated)) served in the 23rd Ohio with Hayes, and was brevetted to major.

LIBRARY OF CONGRESS

assortment of pastas, sandwiches, and salads. If you're in the mood for dancing, stop by on a Thursday, Friday, or Saturday evening. It's open daily for lunch and dinner. Average dinner entrée price: $20-$25.

Carl's Frozen Custard
2200 Princess Anne Street
Fredericksburg
Ice cream lovers—and especially frozen custard lovers—won't want to miss a stop at Carl's, a local favorite since 1947. While there's no food service here, you can easily make a meal of the chocolate, vanilla, and

strawberry frozen concoctions churned in a 1940s-era Electro-Freeze ice-cream machine. It's open daily from mid-February to mid-November. Under $5

Claiborne's Restaurant
200 Lafayette Boulevard
Fredericksburg
(540) 371-7080
www.claibornesrestaurant.com
Claiborne's is located next to the Fredericksburg train station, and there's a railroad theme that permeates its décor and design. The menu is fresh and flavorful, peppered

with low Southern favorites like shrimp and grits and crispy catfish served with collard greens, along with local seafood. For dessert, there's chocolate pecan pie, strawberry shortcake, and a host of other temptations. It's open for dinner Tuesday through Saturday and for prime rib brunch on Sunday. Average dinner entrée price: $25-$30.

Eileen's Bakery and Cafe
623 Caroline Street
Fredericksburg
(540) 372-4030
www.eileensinc.com
If you're staying in Old Town Fredericksburg, stop by Eileen's for a cup of coffee and breakfast sandwich or warm mushroom popover on your way to see the sights. Or, pick up one of Eileen's gourmet sandwiches or salads for a picnic lunch. In addition to classic turkey and ham creations, you'll also find some inventive vegetarian options like a grilled asparagus sandwich served with roasted tomato mayo and curried mushrooms. It's open daily except Tuesday for breakfast and lunch. Average lunch entrée price: under $10.

Goolrick's Pharmacy
901 Caroline Street
Fredericksburg
(540) 373-3411
www.goolricks.com
For another retro dining experience, stop in to Goolrick's pharmacy in downtown, home to the oldest operating soda fountain in the country. If you're looking for a little nostalgia, you'll find it in a thick, creamy milkshake, fresh-squeezed lemonade, or grilled cheese sandwich served in the back of this independent drug store. Average lunch entrée price: under $10.

J. Brian's Tap Room
200 Hanover Street
Fredericksburg
(540) 373-0738
Charles Dickens once stayed and dined in the historic hotel building that now houses J.

Brian's Tap Room. With its tall ceilings and hardwood floors, the restaurant blends in well with its historic location. Fare here is simple and satisfying: think burgers, steaks, and pizzas, perfectly paired with a beer or glass of wine. It's open for lunch and dinner Tuesday through Sunday and for dinner on Monday. Average dinner entrée price: $15-$20.

Olde Towne Steak and Seafood
1612 Caroline Street
Fredericksburg
(540) 371-8020
www.oldetownesteakandseafood.com
Established in 1981, Olde Towne Steak and Seafood is a Fredericksburg classic, consistently ranked among Fredericksburg's top eateries. The name says it all: generous platters of lobster, shrimp, and other seafood creations, along with juicy steaks, tender chicken, and "surf and turf" selections. All entrées are served with a garden salad, potatoes, and fresh-baked sourdough bread. The restaurant is open Tuesday through Saturday 4:00 p.m. to 10:00 p.m. and until 9:00 p.m. Sunday. Average dinner entrée price: $20-$25.

Ristorante Renato
422 William Street
Fredericksburg
(540) 371-8228
www.ristoranterenato.com
For delicious northern Italian cuisine, pull up a chair at Ristorante Renato, where you'll find a tasty selection of homemade pastas and Mediterranean classics like gnocchi doused in veal ragu and eggplant parmesan. Finish it off with a delicious bite of tiramisu, spumoni, or cannoli. The 260-seat restaurant is ideal for parties and festive occasions, just footsteps from Fredericksburg's historic core. It's open for lunch Monday through Friday and for dinner nightly. Average dinner entrée price: $20-$25.

Sammy T's
801 Caroline Street
Fredericksburg
(540) 371-2008
www.sammyts.com
If you're looking for a light and healthy dining choice, grab a table at Sammy T's. The menu is packed with creative vegan and vegetarian creations like black bean cakes, apple and cheddar sandwiches, and a to-die-for bean

and grain burger topped with sautéed mushrooms, peppers, tomatoes, and onions and smothered in cheese. The building itself dates to 1804; after the Civil War, Brigadier General Darrel Ruggles (CSA) lived here as he developed new innovations for the railroad. It's open for lunch and dinner daily 11:00 a.m. to 9:00 p.m. during the week, till 10:00 p.m. Friday and Saturday. Average dinner entrée price: $10-$15.

ON TO RICHMOND!

THE PENINSULA

This tour concentrates on the ground covered by George McClellan in his 1862 Peninsula Campaign—including the Seven Days' Battle before Richmond—from the tip of the Virginia Peninsula west to the gates of the Confederate capital.

"Our neighbors are in a very strong position," Major General George McClellan wrote of his Confederate opponents at Yorktown, Virginia, in April 1862. "I cannot turn Yorktown without a battle, in which I must use heavy artillery & go through the preliminary operations of siege."[1] It was a letter that would have drawn angry catcalls from McClellan's opponents in Washington and hails of laughter from the few Rebels in the works opposite his own. With more than 100,000 well-trained and well-supplied Federals under his command, the wary McClellan had halted his drive for Richmond in the face of perhaps 20,000 Confederates. Instead of unleashing his considerable power, he pent it up behind massive earthen fortifications and laid siege to the town. For a month his coiled army waited, while Major General John Magruder vacated the town under his nose.

And so began McClellan's promising Peninsula Campaign, a drive that—had it been under the control of a more aggressive officer—might have ended the war in 1862. Rather than approaching the Confederate capital from the north, McClellan convinced Abraham Lincoln to accept a more elaborate strategy (with minor modifications): He would transport his huge army south by water, and then march it up the Virginia Peninsula to threaten Richmond from the east. McClellan put his 105,000 men and equipment ashore at Fort Monroe, and in April marched north.

After his "grand victory" at Yorktown, McClellan pushed his massive and sharp-looking Army of the Potomac up the Peninsula. Lead elements of his army engaged in a sharp fight with Johnston's retreating Confederates at Williamsburg on May 5. The advance continued northeast, until McClellan was just six miles from Richmond. When heavy rains stranded two of McClellan's corps north of the swollen Chickahominy River, Johnston lashed out at the Federals at Seven Pines. The two sides fought to a bloody draw, but—of more importance—Johnston fell with a bullet in his shoulder. The next day, President Jefferson Davis gave Johnston's command to Robert E. Lee, who had no intention of allowing the army to remain on its heels.

Lee assigned the two corps of his Army of Northern Virginia to Major Generals Thomas Jackson and James Longstreet. Then, assured by his dashing cavalry commander, Major General J. E. B. Stuart, that McClellan's right flank was open, Lee left a defending force at Richmond and marched east with some 45,000 Rebels. After a brief clash at Oak Grove on June 25, Lee attacked the now-withdrawing Federals at Mechanicsville on June 26, Gaines' Mill on the 27th, then at Garnett's Farm, Savage's Station, Glendale, and Malvern Hill in succession. In this last clash, devastating Yankee artillery fire shredded waves of Confederate attackers, spurring futile requests from McClellan's subordinates to counterattack. But the commanding general, who had long since abandoned a campaign while on the brink of complete victory, was too intent on "saving" his army. After leading his army back to Harrison's Landing, McClellan was relieved of it altogether, in favor of (briefly) John Pope.

---

[1] Eric Ethier, "George Sears Greene: Gettysburg's Other Second Day Hero," *Rhode Island History 53*, no. 2, (May 1995).

Historic Sites

Battle of Dam No. 1
13650 Jefferson Avenue
Newport News, VA
The entrance to this battlefield park sits just behind the Newport News Visitor Center. If you're up for a good hike, it's interesting to follow the April 16, 1862, battle, where McClellan's only real attempt to break Magruder's lines was handily rebuffed by Confederate forces. The Confederate fortifications in this park are very well preserved, and a well-marked trail describes the battle action in detail. The park is open daily; a small museum on-site is open seasonally.

Berkeley Plantation
12602 Harrison Landing Road
Charles City, VA
(804) 829-6018
(888) 466-6018
www.berkeleyplantation.com
Although this historic plantation isn't quite on the peninsula, situated between Williamsburg and Richmond, we've included it in this chapter because it was McClellan's final stop, the supply headquarters where the troops gathered to assess the damages and triumphs of the campaign. The military bugle call "Taps" was composed here during this time. Beyond its Civil War significance, Berkeley Plantation is a must-see for any American history enthusiast. Built in the 1600s, the plantation was the site of the first Thanksgiving celebration and was the birthplace of President William Henry Harrison. It's open 9:00 a.m. to 5:00 p.m. daily; admission is $11.00 for adults, $6.00 for children, and $7.50 for students.

Casemate Museum
Fort Monroe, VA
(757) 788-3391
www.tradoc.army.mil/museum
The largest moat-encircled masonry fort in the United States, Fort Monroe was built between 1819 and 1834 to protect the entrance to Hampton Roads and the port

cities located nearby. If you're exploring the Peninsula Campaign, the Casemate Museum is a great starting point. In May 1861, mere weeks after the first shots were fired on Fort Sumter, three slaves escaped from the peninsula fortifications, to which they were assigned, to this Union fortification. Union Major General Benjamin F. Butler refused to return the slaves to their owner, suggesting that the Fugitive Slave Act did not apply in a foreign country, which Virginia was claiming to be. Prior to the war, Robert E. Lee was assigned here as the post engineer. The fort was never taken by the South during the war. As part of the Fort Monroe tour, you can also take a boat over to Fort Wool (in season), an island fort was used by Union forces against the Confederate forts at Norfolk during the campaign. The Casemate Museum outlines the history of the fort, highlighting the area where ex-Confederate President Jefferson Davis was imprisoned after the war. It is open daily 10:30 a.m. to 4:30 p.m. Admission is free.

Congress and Cumberland Overlook, Christopher Newport Park
2500 West Avenue
Newport News, VA
(757) 247-8523
The first major naval battle in Hampton Roads took place March 8, 1862, when the thirty-gun, wooden USS Cumberland and its likewise wooden sister vessel, the fifty-gun USS Congress clashed with the CSS Virginia. The Virginia was formerly known as the USS Merrimack, a steam frigate whose hull was cut down to the waterline and covered with four inches of iron plate. The ship was also fitted with a 6-foot, 1,500-pound iron ram. The Virginia rammed the Cumberland, quickly sinking the ship and the 121 sailors aboard. Watching its cannon shot merely bounce off the ironclad ship, the Congress surrendered, handing the Confederate navy a fantastic victory. Interpretive plaques offer more insights into the day's events.

Endview Plantation
362 Yorktown Road
Newport News, VA
(757) 887-1862
www.endview.org
Endview was used first by the Confederacy
and later by the Union as a hospital, but even
prior to the Peninsula Campaign, it had
already witnessed a fair amount of military
action in the Revolutionary War and during
the War of 1812. Nevertheless, the circa-1769
house was reconstructed to its appearance
during the Civil War era, which remains the
focus of many of its interpretive programs
and living history activities. It is open for tours
January through March from Thursday
through Monday; it's open Wednesday
through Monday from April through December. Admission is $6 for adults, $5 for seniors,
and $4 for children.

Fort Norfolk
810 Front Street
Norfolk, VA
(757) 640-1720
www.norfolkhistorical.org/fort/index.html
The last of nineteen harbor-front forts commissioned by George Washington, Fort Norfolk helped protect the port city during the
War of 1812. In the Civil War, the fort was
occupied by both sides. Confederates used its
magazines to arm the *Virginia* prior to its battle with the *Monitor*. Union forces claimed the
fort back later the same year and used it as a
prison. The fort is open to the public daily
10:00 a.m. to 4:00 p.m.; tours are free.

Hampton History Museum
120 Old Hampton Lane
Hampton, VA
(757) 727-1610
www.hampton.va.us/history_museum
Opened in 2003, the Hampton History
Museum traces more than four centuries of
local history through ten fascinating galleries,
including one with a special emphasis on the
Civil War era. Visitors explore the importance

of Fort Monroe and the nearby Battle of Big
Bethel through displays and artifacts. The
port of Hampton sustained considerable damage during the Civil War, burned by Confederate loyalists on August 7, 1861, to prevent it
from falling into Union hands. Near the
museum, St. John's Church, built in 1728, is
the only building to partially survive the fire.
The museum is open Monday through Saturday 10:00 a.m. to 5:00 p.m. and Sunday 1:00
to 5:00 p.m. Admission is $5 for adults and $4
for seniors, children, and active-duty military.

Lee Hall Mansion
163 Yorktown Road
Newport News, VA
(757) 888-3371
www.leehall.org
Confederate commanders Johnston and
Magruder used this elegant 1850s mansion as
their headquarters at the height of the action.
The last large plantation house of its era in
the region, today Lee Hall is home to a
museum that interprets the actions and activities of the Peninsula Campaign. Many of the
house's public rooms—including a formal dining room, music room, ladies' parlor, and two
bedrooms—have been carefully restored to
their antebellum glory. In the English base-
ment, you'll find exhibits related to the campaign, such as a tablecloth recovered from
the *Monitor* and artifacts recovered from
nearby battlefields. The museum also serves
as a starting point for bus tours of local Civil
War sites; check the Web site for more information. It's open Thursday through Monday
from January through March and daily April
through December. Admission is $6 for
adults.

Lee's Mill Battlefield Park
180 River's Ridge Circle
Newport News, VA
(757) 247-8523
Lee's Mill was the site of the first notable
exchange during the Peninsula Campaign.
General George McClellan and his Union

General George Brinton McClellan LIBRARY OF CONGRESS

forces left nearby Young's Mill on April 5, 1862, and were met with more than 1,800 Confederate soldiers and massive earthen fortifications at Lee's Mill, prompting McClellan to lay siege to the Confederates' Yorktown-Warwick defense line. Trails and interpretive signs in the park outline each side's positions during the brief skirmish.

The Mariners' Museum &
USS *Monitor* Center
100 Museum Drive
Newport News, VA
(757) 596-2222
www.mariner.org
www.monitorcenter.org
Long one of the nation's top maritime outfits,

the Mariners' Museum recently opened the new USS *Monitor* Center just in time to mark the 145th anniversary of the ironclad's epic battle with the CSS *Virginia*. The *Monitor*, which foundered and sank off Cape Hatteras on December 31, 1962, was discovered in 1973. While the bulk of the vessel remains on the ocean floor—protected by her status as a National Marine Sanctuary—the *Monitor*'s massive Dahlgren guns and gun carriages, turret, steam engine, propeller, anchor, and hundreds of other artifacts have been raised from the deep in recent years.

Conservation of these historic pieces continues in the massive new, $30 million, 40,000-square-foot *Monitor* Center, certainly a facility without peer in the country. The centerpiece of the museum is the fantastic new, full-size replica of the ironclad, which was christened in July 2006. The museum also offers a battle theater and state-of-the-art exhibits designed to tell the story of the *Monitor* from her birth through her discovery, recovery, and conservation. Already a must-see for history buffs, the Mariners' Museum has added a unique jewel that any Civil War buff will want to see and experience.

The Mariners' Museum is open daily Monday through Saturday 10:00 a.m. to 5:00 p.m. and Sunday from noon to 5:00 p.m. It is closed on Thanksgiving and Christmas. Admission is $12.50 for adults, $7.25 for children 6–17, and free for kids 5 and under. The museum is wheelchair accessible.

Monitor-Merrimack Overlook
Anderson Park
Sixteenth Street and Oak Avenue
Newport News, VA
(757) 247-8523

Anderson Park, located on the tip of the peninsula, offers a perfect view of the site where the two legendary ironclads clashed on March 9, 1862, forever changing naval warfare. The USS *Monitor* charged into the waters surrounding Newport News in the aftermath of the sinking of the USS *Cumberland* and the

surrender of the USS *Congress*. The two ironclads fired shells at each other for hours, yet neither managed to cause much damage on the other.

Nauticus and Hampton Roads Naval Museum
One Waterside Drive
Norfolk, VA
(757) 664-1000
www.nauticus.org

Hampton Roads's maritime history comes to life in this 120,000-square-foot science center. The Civil War is just one of the topics explored at this maritime center, whose focus ranges from sharks and aquatic life to meteorology to naval warfare. The Hampton Roads Naval History Museum, located on the second floor of the museum complex, pays careful attention to the battle of the *Monitor* and the *Virginia*, along with other Civil War exchanges. The museum is also responsible for the operations of the Battleship *Wisconsin*, docked in the harbor and considered part of the center. Admission to the Naval History Museum and the *Wisconsin* is free; for the Nauticus, expect to pay $10.95. It's open daily 10:00 a.m. to 5:00 p.m. in the summertime; from September through May, it's open Tuesday through Saturday 10:00 a.m. to 5:00 p.m. and Sunday from noon to 5:00 p.m.

Portsmouth Naval Shipyard Museum
2 High Street
Portsmouth, VA
(757) 393-8591
www.portsnavalmuseums.com

Portsmouth is home to the oldest naval shipyard in the United States, the Gosport Navy Yard. Confederates took command of the yard on April 21, 1861, and used it to convert the USS *Merrimac* into the ironclad CSS *Virginia*. In later years, Gosport would also see the construction of the *Texas*, the country's first battleship, and the *Langley*, the world's first aircraft carrier. A new permanent exhibition at the museum focuses on the history of

Portsmouth and the Gosport Navy Yard, focusing on the country's pivotal early years, 1785–1840. The museum is open Tuesday through Saturday 10:00 a.m. to 5:00 p.m. and 1:00 to 5:00 p.m. Sunday. Admission is $3 and includes entry to the Lightship *Portsmouth*.

Seven Days' Battle Sites
(See Richmond National Battlefield Park in the Confederate Capital chapter)
The Seven Days' Battle refers to offensive action by Robert E. Lee, which forced Union troops to retreat back to the James River in June–July 1862. Many of the places that saw action, including Drewry's Bluff, Beaver Dam Creek, Gaines' Mill, Savage's Station, Glendale, and Malvern Hill, are considered part of the Richmond National Battlefield Park, due to their location between the Peninsula and the Confederate capital.

Virginia War Museum
9285 Warwick Boulevard
Newport News, VA
(757) 247-8523
www.warmuseum.org
This local museum displays more than 50,000 artifacts from wars fought on Virginia soil from 1775 to the present. With so many Civil War battles waged in Virginia, it's no surprise to find a sizeable part of the exhibit space and artifacts dedicated to the war, plus the antebellum era and the aftermath. It's also a good place to check for living history programs and Civil War sites tours. The museum is open Monday through Saturday 9:00 a.m. to 5:00 p.m. and Sunday 1:00 to 5:00 p.m. Admission is $6 for adults, $5 for senior citizens, or $4 for children.

Tours
Miss Hampton II
710 Settlers Landing Road
Hampton, VA
(757) 722-9102
www.misshamptoncruises.com
To truly appreciate the history that transpired in these tidewater ports, your best bet may

be to see the sights from the water. From Hampton, hop on board the *Miss Hampton II*, which offers daily (twice daily during the summer) tours of Hampton Roads. The two-and-a-half hour tour shows off the historic Chesapeake Bay and even includes a stop at Fort Wool, opposite Fort Monroe, in season (weather permitting). Tours are $22 for adults, $20 for seniors and active duty military, and $11 for children.

Accommodations
Aldrich House Bed and Breakfast
505 Capitol Court
Williamsburg, VA
(757) 229-5422
(877) 745-0887
www.aldrichhouse.com
While most of the Civil War attractions listed in this section are located to the east of Williamsburg, we've included some lodging and dining options in the area. By stationing yourself in Williamsburg for a few days, you'll be within a short drive of not only the peninsula, but also Richmond and Petersburg. You'll also have access to some of southern Virginia's top accommodations, restaurants, and other historical attractions. Located just a few blocks from Colonial Williamsburg, Tom and Sue Patton's Aldrich House is a great choice for family travelers who prefer the intimacy of a B&B. There are three spacious, elegantly appointed rooms, one with its own fireplace and one with a whirlpool tub. Cat lovers (and those with allergies) should be aware that KC, the resident cat, has free rein throughout the house. Breakfast is delightful, featuring fresh fare like eggs, pancakes, and fruit salad. $125-$140

Boxwood Inn
10 Elmhurst Street
Historic Lee Hall Village
Newport News, VA
(757) 888-8854
www.boxwood-inn.com
This small and charming, 1896 bed-and-breakfast in the heart of Virginia's Historic Tri-

angle offers friendly service, queen-size beds, private baths, and antique furnishings at bargain prices. Military history buffs may want to stay in the room that once played host to General John J. Pershing and other military officers stationed at nearby Fort Eustis during World War I and II. Lee Hall Mansion, used by John Magruder and Joseph E. Johnston as headquarters during the Peninsula Campaign, is just a half-mile away. The inn offers not only a continental breakfast, but an "early bird" to-go basket if you want to get an early start to a busy day of sightseeing or a "sleepy head" breakfast for late risers. If you don't spend the night here, consider coming by for dinner. The Boxwood Inn produces a regular lineup of themed dinner shows: a plantation dinner featuring the South's finest, a 1940s-themed buffet of victory garden classics, murder mysteries, Dickensian Christmas celebrations, and more; most priced at $35 per adult. $95-$125

Cedars Bed and Breakfast
616 Jamestown Road
Williamsburg, VA
(800) 296-3591
www.cedarsofwilliamsburg.com
With ten rooms and suites, Cedars is not only the biggest B&B in Williamsburg, but also one of the best in the South. The Georgian-style mansion was built in the 1930s using bricks collected by schoolchildren from the demolition of a century-old building on the nearby campus of the College of William & Mary. History buffs will love the location, a mere seven-minute walk to Colonial Williamsburg. A bountiful breakfast is served each morning, featuring entrées like eggs Florentine, blueberry French toast, and peach cobbler, and the refrigerator and common areas are stocked with snacks for midday noshing. Amenities range from central air, fireplaces, and mini-refrigerators to private baths and wireless Internet access. Elegantly appointed, room/suite rates range from $150 to $350, with a cozy, two-bedroom, two-bathroom cottage priced at $400.

Glencoe Inn
222 North Street
Portsmouth, VA
(757) 397-8128
www.glencoeinn.com
Further down the peninsula, the charming town of Portsmouth puts you in easy driving distance of Hampton and Newport News, but also within 30 miles of the inviting sandy coastline of Virginia Beach. Portsmouth's Glencoe Inn is historic and romantic, situated alongside the Elizabeth River in the heart of the Portsmouth historic district. The innkeeper, Ann McGowan McGlynn, carries a Scottish theme throughout the four-bedroom Victorian-style property. Rooms are affordably priced, outfitted with comfortable beds, private baths, and postcard-perfect views of the surrounding harbor and gardens. Some even feature kitchenettes and Jacuzzis. $119-$149

Lady Neptune Bed & Breakfast
507 North First Street
Hampton, VA
(757) 848-5877
http://ladyneptuneinn.com
This 1930s-era house was narrowly spared from demolition in 1988 when development pressures threatened the land on which it was located. Too attached to their home to watch it come down, the owners elected to have the house lifted off its foundation, placed on a large barge and carried across the Chesapeake to its new home in Hampton. There are four clean and comfortable guest rooms, each appointed with a four-poster, queen-size bed. For breakfast, you can expect a generous buffet loaded with Southern classics like fried catfish, Chesapeake crab eggs benedict, shrimp, grits, and eggs. The inn also puts together special packages with pampering treats for romantic getaways or theme park and attractions tickets for family vacations. $135-$175

Magnolia House Bed & Breakfast
232 South Armistead Avenue
Hampton, VA
(757) 722-2888
www.maghousehampton.com
This impeccably furnished bed-and-breakfast offers a delightful stay in historic Hampton and provides easy access to the other towns and attractions on and around the peninsula. Hosts Joyce and Lankford Blair are warm and hospitable, eager to help you with sightseeing suggestions, information, and, of course, a delicious breakfast each morning. Rooms are beautifully decorated with art and accents that match the historic character of the house, plus luxurious linens, terry robes and slippers, wireless Internet, and other amenities. $160-$215

The Pequod Inn of Port Warwick
145 Herman Melville Avenue
Newport News, VA
(757) 596-1023
www.thepequod.com
Port Warwick is a symbol of Newport News's urban revitalization, a mixed-use development of eclectic retailers and trendy restaurants, plus residential development and a sprawling public green. Located within the Port Warwick development, The Pequod Inn immerses travelers in this vibrant quarter of a historic region. Named for the boat featured in *Moby Dick*, the inn keeps up the literary theme in each of the guest rooms, named for authors John Steinbeck, Maya Angelou, and Mark Twain. Each of the rooms is light and airy, furnished with DVD players and flat-screen TVs, wireless Internet capabilities, private bath, and a complimentary newspaper. Guests also enjoy a delicious, healthy breakfast prepared with locally procured ingredients. $140

Williamsburg Inn
136 East Francis Street
Williamsburg, VA
(757) 229-1000
www.colonialwilliamsburg.com
If you want to treat yourself to luxurious accommodations as you explore the peninsula—and you're prepared to pay prices that match—book a room at the legendary Williamsburg Inn. It's here that Queen Elizabeth II stayed during her 2007 visit to commemorate the 400th anniversary of the founding of Jamestown (and, incidentally, it's where she stayed during her 1957 visit for the 350th anniversary as well). Renovated in 2001, the sixty-two guest rooms in the main hotel are large and tastefully decorated, featuring bathrooms with granite sinks, marble floors, and wonderful soaking tubs, plus free wireless Internet and other posh amenities. Perhaps the inn's best selling point, however, is its location in the heart of Colonial Williamsburg, and golfers will find its surrounding course to be both beautiful and challenging. If an overnight stay here isn't in your budget, however, it's also a great choice for afternoon tea service. $209-$630

A Williamsburg White House
Bed and Breakfast Inn
718 Jamestown Road
Williamsburg, VA
(757) 229-8580
(866) 229-8580
www.awilliamsburgwhitehouse.com
Billing itself as the "Williamsburg White House," this historic B&B takes its name quite literally. Each room—even the dining room and the library—bears the name of a former commander-in-chief. Civil War travelers may opt for the Lincoln Suite, which features his-and-hers private baths and a king-size four-poster bed (but be wary of the adjacent Ford's Theatre sitting room). Slightly smaller rooms are named and decorated in honor of Washington, Jefferson, and Theodore Roosevelt. You're also given executive privilege to linger in the Diplomatic Reception Room, the Reagan Dining Room, or the Kennedy Library as you enjoy complimentary drinks and hors d'oeuvres in the afternoon. For breakfast, you'll enjoy decadent pastries, quiches, frittatas, and other tasty creations. Colonial Williamsburg is a quick walk away, and the

peninsula Civil War sites are easily reachable with an hour's drive. $140-$205

Restaurants

Barclay's
943 J. Clyde Morris Boulevard
Newport News, VA
(757) 952-1122
www.barclays.bz
Discerning foodies might normally take a pass on a hotel restaurant—particularly one that's located in a Holiday Inn. Barclay's, however, is worth a visit. The dining room is decorated with works by local artist Barclay Sheeks (whose art is also on display in the fine-dining favorite, The Trellis). The menu is peppered with surprising fare like quail, lamb, and duck, even ostrich. Instead of a regular baked potato, steaks come served with caramelized sweet potato wedges. While the fare is often on the fancy side, the dining room itself is simple and welcoming, with wood paneling, wood floors, and even a fireplace. It's open daily for lunch and dinner. Average dinner entrée price: $20-$25.

Bill's Seafood House
10900 Warwick Boulevard
Newport News, VA
(757) 595-4320
You won't find any seafood restaurant gimmicks here—not even a waterside location. But if you're curious where locals go to taste fresh catches from the surrounding bay, this is it. Feast on generous portions of fried flounder, homemade hush puppies, delicious crab cakes, and other fresh and flavorful classics. There's no need to dress up to dine at this comfortable family-friendly eatery, located near the Mariner's Museum. It's open daily for lunch and dinner. Average dinner entrée price: under $10.

Create Bistro
10417 Warwick Boulevard
Newport News, VA
(757) 240-2776
This stylish eatery made a splash on the New-

port News dining scene when it opened in October 2006. Create serves up the kind of fashionable, flavorful cuisine that diners have come to expect in better-known culinary destinations. Begin your meal with "mouth amusements" like coconut-crusted calamari with tomato escabeche or tiger prawns. For the main event, tender buffalo meatloaf is a top seller, served with caramelized onions and cheese, but you'll also do well with seafood dishes like succulent crab cakes and blackberry-glazed king salmon. The wine list is diverse and interesting, with plenty of good options priced under $50. If you have a sweet tooth, you'll want to sample decadent finishing touches like the upside-down bananas foster cheesecake or baked Alaska key lime pie. The restaurant is small and cozy, housed in the former site of a greasy spoon diner; you'll want to make a reservation in advance. It's open Tuesday through Saturday for dinner. Average dinner entrée price: $20-$25.

Fat Canary
410 Duke of Gloucester Street
Williamsburg, VA
(757) 229-3333
Fat Canary consistently earns rave reviews as one of Colonial Williamsburg's top culinary attractions—and for that reason, you may wish to make a reservation in advance. The menu is constantly changing to reflect what's fresh and in season, and given Chef Thomas Power's diverse culinary experience, you never know what to expect. Try something unique like sea scallops in coconut curry or soft shell crabs. The Fat Canary shares its location with The Cheese Shop, a great place to pick up a sandwich or snack to go. It's open for dinner nightly. Average dinner entrée price: $25-$30.

Second St.
140 Second Street
Williamsburg, VA
(757) 220-2286
www.secondst.com
An "American Bistro" and a Williamsburg

mainstay for more than twenty years, Second St. sports the look of a converted foundry or a community brew pub—but with much better food, including a burger voted Williamsburg's best. Beyond the burgers, you'll find a menu stocked with all sorts of American classics: meatloaf, shrimp and grits, and a hearty pile of jumbo lump crab meat served with au gratin potatoes and garlic spinach. The price is right, too; burgers and sandwiches are a bargain at $8, while dinners (country fried steak, ribs and chicken combos, etc.) run from $11 to $22. Desserts like carrot cake and sticky bun bread pudding are designed to be shared. It's open daily for dinner. Average dinner entrée price: $15-$20.

Shields Tavern
422 East Duke of Gloucester Street
Williamsburg, VA
(757) 229-2141
One of four taverns operated by the Colonial Williamsburg Foundation, Shields Tavern is a combination coffee house/tavern. During the day, it's a great place for a pick-me-up cappuccino or a light bite like egg custard or Smithfield honey ham biscuits. During the evening, the tavern side becomes more prominent as diners enjoy Welsh rarebit, Yorkshire beef patties, and other period classics. Hours change seasonally; it's best to call in advance. Average dinner entrée price: $15-$20.

Smokin' Joe's BBQ
1312 Pembroke Avenue
Hampton, VA
(757) 723-1444
This family-owned barbecue joint operates five locations in and around the peninsula, and many locals swear it's the best around. The meat is slow cooked with hickory and seasoned with spices, so flavorful and succulent that the sauces are optional. Nevertheless, Joe's offers seven varieties of sauces to please most palates, along with a whole suite of tempting side dishes. For most barbecue lovers, the baby back ribs are the prime attraction. It's open Tuesday through Saturday

for lunch and dinner. Average dinner entrée price: $10-$15.

Surf Rider Restaurant
1 Marina Road
Hampton, VA
(757) 723-9366
Although it's not easy to locate, this out-of-the-way eatery serves up some of the region's finest seafood, including delectable lump crab cakes, fried shrimp, and scallops, oysters, and soft shell crabs in season. It's often packed with locals, which should always be a good sign that you've successfully stepped beyond the tourist scene. While the seafood is bound to please, you also shouldn't pass on their signature vegetable, a gigantic broccoli stalk, perfectly cooked and paired with hollandaise sauce. There's plenty for two or more to share. An added bonus: You can take in the glorious view of the marina through the floor-to-ceiling windows. It's open for lunch and dinner daily. Average dinner entrée price: $15-$20.

The Trellis
403 Duke of Gloucester Street
Williamsburg, VA
(757) 229-8610
www.thetrellis.com
A longtime favorite restaurant for special occasions, The Trellis serves regional fare that changes regularly to make the most of what's in season. Look for light and flavorful salads in summer and hearty soups and roasted vegetables in winter. When it comes to main courses, you won't go wrong with a fresh seafood selection or succulent cuts of meat, best when paired with healthy side dishes like bourbon-braised peaches or saffron-infused rice. For chocolate lovers, dessert is a must; The Trellis is famous for its "Death by Chocolate" cake. It's open daily for lunch and dinner. Average dinner entrée price: $20-$25.

CONFEDERATE CAPITAL

RICHMOND

This tour focuses on the major sites related to the Confederate defense of Richmond, the Confederate capital.

For a few months during the spring of 1861, Montgomery, Alabama, was the capital of the Confederacy. Had it remained there, the war likely would have been fought much differently. For reasons of military and political expedience, however, the Confederate government relocated to Richmond in July. From then on, the Rebel defense of that city—and Federal attempts to capture it—came to represent the Confederacy's struggle for survival. Entire Union campaigns revolved around its capture until 1864, when Ulysses S. Grant's siege of Petersburg made its fall inevitable.

One of the South's top manufacturing cities prior to 1861, war-time Richmond housed one of the nation's top makers of ammunition and railroad steel (Tredegar Iron Works) along with multiple hospital facilities (such as the massive Chimborazo Hospital) within its protective line of earthen fortifications. Its citizens suffered increasingly as the war ground on, as prices multiplied and food grew scarce. Fiercely protected for four years, Richmond fell within hours of Petersburg's capture on April 3, 1865. Shortly after, a massive fire scalded the city, leaving much of downtown an ashen skeleton of its former self. And while Washingtonians greeted news of the city's fall with wild celebrations, weary Richmond residents cringed. "The saddest moment of my life," one Virginian said, "was when I saw that Southern Cross dragged down and the Stars and Stripes run up above the capitol."

Historic Sites

American Civil War Center at Historic Tredegar
500 Tredegar Street
(804) 780-1865
www.tredegar.org
Opened in 2006, the American Civil War Center is a great starting point for a Civil War odyssey. It's the only facility of its kind to tell the story of the war from three perspectives: Northern, Southern and African-American. Each side's contributions, principles, battles, and leaders are woven together in the flagship permanent exhibition, In the Cause of Liberty, housed in the 1861 Tredegar Iron-works Gun Foundry. Start your visit with an introductory film, "What Caused the Civil War?" to brush up on the historical basics. The Richmond Civil War Visitors Center (see listing in this section) is located on the site as well. The center is open daily 9:00 a.m. to 5:00 p.m. Admission is $8 for adults, $6 for students and seniors, $2 for children 7–12, and free for children under 6.

Confederate War Memorial Chapel
2900 Grove Avenue
(804) 740-4479
Constructed in 1887 by Confederate veterans, this chapel honors fallen soldiers who fought for the Southern cause. It's now operated by the Sons of Confederate Veterans. The chapel's unusual mosaic stained glass windows make it worth a visit for art and architecture lovers. It's open Wednesday through Sunday 11:00 a.m. to 3:00 p.m.

Hollywood Cemetery
412 South Cherry Street
(804) 648-8501
www.hollywoodcemetery.org

The burial site of Presidents James Monroe and John Tyler, beautiful Hollywood Cemetery is better known to Civil War folk as the resting place of George Pickett, (and a number of Gettysburg victims), J. E. B. Stuart, Fitzhugh Lee, and Confederate President Jefferson Davis. The cemetery is open 8:00 a.m. to 5:00 p.m. daily.

Monument Avenue
Harrison Street to Horsepen Road
Monument Avenue is the only street in the United States that's also a National Historic Landmark. Development of the avenue began in 1890, following the dedication of a monument to Robert E. Lee. Other Confederate notables honored with statues along the 5-mile street include Jefferson Davis, J. E. B. Stuart, Stonewall Jackson, and Matthew Fontaine Maury. Between the monuments, you'll also find beautiful, elaborate homes in a variety of architectural styles.

Museum and White House of the Confederacy
1201 East Clay Street
(804) 649-1861
www.moc.org
For more than one hundred years this museum has been the place to go to learn about all things Confederate, from the brief history of the Confederate nation through the fabled idea of the Lost Cause. Today the museum boasts three floors of exhibits, an unmatched collection of Confederacy-related artifacts (including the original Confederate White House located next door), a research library, and a museum store. Among the objects on permanent display here are the original oil painting, "The Last Meeting of Lee and Jackson," and the first-ever Army of Northern Virginia battle flag.

The Museum of the Confederacy is open Monday through Saturday (except Wednesday) 10:00 a.m. to 5:00 p.m. and noon to 5:00 p.m. on Sunday from Labor Day through Memorial Day. Summer hours are the same, but the museum is also open on Wednesdays.

It is wheelchair accessible. Admission to the museum is $8 for adults, $7 for seniors, and $4 for students. Admission to the White House is the same. Combination tickets to both sites are available at a discount.

Richmond National Battlefield Park
3215 East Broad Street
(804) 226-1981, ext. 23
www.nps.gov/rich/
There is plenty to see around Richmond, and much of it is packed into Richmond National Battlefield Park. Divided into thirteen separate areas, this massive park incorporates a number of battlefield sites that could easily stand as parks on their own. Visitors should plan to spend a couple of days in the area, as the park boasts dozens of miles of original (and elaborate) field fortifications, self-guided trails, and several museums and visitor centers.

The first stop on a visit here should be at the Richmond Civil War Visitor Center at Tredegar Iron Works (490 Tredegar Street), a fantastic, three-floor collection of exhibits, artifacts, interactive displays, and machinery used by Tredegar to produce much of the South's artillery and ammunition. The center also offers maps, a cassette for a Seven Days' Battle driving tour, and a park orientation film, which only the most learned Civil War students should consider passing up.

A second major highlight of the park is the Chimborazo Medical Museum (3215 East Broad Street), a facility dedicated to the history of the hospital and Civil War medicine. A collection of original surgical instruments, exhibits, and a short film are offered at this facility, where more than 75,000 Confederate soldiers received treatment during the war.

Most of the park, of course, is comprised of battlefields and other sites, including Chickahominy Bluff, Beaver Dam Creek, Gaines' Mill, Cold Harbor Battlefield and Visitor Center (5515 Anderson-Wright Drive), the Garthright House, Glendale Battlefield and Visitor Center (8301 Willis Church Road), Malvern Hill Battlefield, Fort Harrison (visitor center located at 8621 Battlefield Park Road), Drewry's Bluff,

Jefferson Davis

LIBRARY OF CONGRESS

A senator from Mississippi and a former secretary of war (under President Franklin Pierce), Jefferson Davis was also a Mexican War veteran, and he longed for a field command in the new Confederate Army. Instead, he was selected as the Confederacy's first president.

During four years of civil war, both the Union and Confederate governments suffered from internal political squabbling—the kind of infighting that affected military policy and, ultimately, success on the battlefield. Forced to handle ambitious politicians such as William Seward and Simon Cameron, Abraham Lincoln proved to have an amazingly deft political touch. Jefferson Davis had it at least as bad in Richmond, dealing with a recalcitrant Congress and cabinet while mediating constant and legendary feuds among his generals, and often between officers (such as Joseph E. Johnston) and himself. (Davis went through six secretaries of war in four years.) Cold and impersonal with anyone outside of his family, Davis lacked both the off-putting charm and management skills of his Washington counterpart. "He did not know the arts of the politician," his wife Varina wrote of him, "and would not practice them if understood."

The fall of Richmond left the Confederate government on the run. Davis was eventually captured and shipped off to prison at Fortress Monroe, where he languished for two years. He was never charged with anything, however, and eventually resettled in Mississippi, where he died in 1889. Davis was buried in Richmond's Hollywood Cemetery.

and Parker's Battery. Several of these sites have been included in other tours due to their relation to other campaigns, such as the Peninsula Campaign.

The park battlefields are open free of charge from sunrise to sunset. Visitor centers at Tredegar Iron Works, Chimborazo, and Cold Harbor are open daily 9:00 a.m. to 5:00 p.m. The Glendale and Fort Harrison visitor centers maintain the same hours, from June through August. The park is closed on Thanksgiving, Christmas Day, and New Year's Day.

Other Sites of Interest

Valentine Richmond History Center
1015 East Clay Street
(804) 649-0711
www.richmondhistorycenter.com
If you want to learn more about the history of the Richmond region, plan a stop at this museum. The centerpiece is the 1812 Wickham House, which offers a glimpse of Richmond life in the early nineteenth century. Other permanent exhibits explore the sculptures of museum namesake Edward Viginius Valentine and offer a glimpse of the residents who have called Richmond home since its settlement days. The History Center also organizes regularly scheduled bus tours and walking tours that showcase Richmond history. Admission is $10 for adults, $7 for children over 4, seniors, and students and includes entrance to the History Center, Wickham House, Monumental Church, and the John Marshall House, home to the former Supreme Court chief justice. The museums and houses are open Tuesday through Saturday 10:00 a.m. to 5:00 p.m. and Sunday noon to 5:00 p.m. The church is open Saturday and Sunday from May through October, noon to 5:00 p.m.

Virginia Historical Society
428 North Boulevard
(804) 358-4901
www.vahistorical.org
There's no place in the Commonwealth that boasts a collection of Virginia artifacts quite

like this one, housed in a building that was once known as "Battle Abbey." Long-term exhibits focus on Virginia history, residential life, and archaeology, but temporary exhibits occasionally focus on Civil War themes. Admission is $5 for adults, $4 for seniors, $3 for students, and free for children under 18. It's open Monday through Saturday 10:00 a.m. to 5:00 p.m. and Sunday 1:00 to 5:00 p.m.

Virginia State Capitol and Executive Mansion
Capitol Square at Ninth and Grace Streets
(804) 698-1788
www.virginiacapitol.gov
Thomas Jefferson designed the seat of Virginia's government, now home to America's oldest continuous representative assembly. During the Civil War, the Confederate legislature convened in the neoclassical building. The Capitol recently completed a major renovation—its first since 1906—just in time for the Jamestown 400th anniversary celebration and Queen Elizabeth II's 2007 visit. It is open Monday through Saturday 8:30 a.m. to 5:00 p.m. and Sunday 1:00 to 5:00 p.m. Admission is free.

Accommodations

The Berkeley Hotel
1200 East Cary Street
(804) 780-1300
www.berkeleyhotel.com
Follow a lamp-lit cobblestone road to this charming boutique hotel in the Shockoe Slip neighborhood, one of Richmond's most popular destinations for eclectic dining, shopping, and nightlife. While the hotel does its part to blend in with the surrounding historic neighborhood through design and decor, it was actually constructed in 1988. Its fifty-six rooms are quite spacious and outfitted with amenities like wireless Internet and in-room coffee makers, along with service befitting its AAA four-diamond rating. If you haven't gotten enough exercise walking the battlefields, you can also take advantage of gym privileges at a nearby YMCA. $175-$225

Richmond National Battlefield Park NATIONAL PARK SERVICE

Grace Manor Inn
1853 West Grace Street
(804) 353-4334
www.thegracemanorinn.com
The Grace Manor Inn takes the B&B experience to new heights. "Let us pamper you" is
the motto around here, and innkeepers Dawn
and Albert Schick (and their three pet Yorkies)
do their part to live up to the promise. Their
1910 Victorian house, located in the Fan District, is a delightful retreat after a long day of
sightseeing. They've thought of everything—
even bubble bath in the bathroom. You'll be
treated to a sampler of cheeses and a complimentary bottle of wine, perfect for savoring
on the second-floor balcony overlooking picturesque gardens. Of course, a gourmet
breakfast awaits you in the morning and
fresh-baked cookies are on hand for an afternoon snack. $175-$215

Jefferson Hotel
101 West Franklin Street
(804) 788-8000
www.jeffersonhotel.com
A National Historic Landmark, Jefferson is a
grand place, boasting nearly 300 rooms, a
five-diamond restaurant, and top-of-the-line
service. It's the best hotel in the region, hands
down, and a great choice for an on-the-road
splurge. The Jefferson was built in 1895 at the
whopping cost of nearly $10 million by Lewis
Ginter, who served in the Confederate army
then later made a fortune in the tobacco
industry. The luxurious hotel narrowly survived a fire at the turn of the century and,
after a few fashionable decades, eventually
fell into disrepair in the 1950s and 1960s,
closing in 1980. It reopened in 1983 following
a $34 million renovation. Rooms are large and
elegantly furnished to match the circa-1895

character of the hotel. Step into the lobby, and you'll be greeted by a life-size marble sculpture of Mr. Jefferson himself, carved by Richmond sculptor Edward Valentine prior to the hotel's opening. For many guests, however, the dramatic, thirty-six-step spiral staircase is the prime attraction, reminiscent of *Gone with the Wind*. The hotel's on-site fine-dining restaurant, Lemaire, serves outstanding American cuisine, or guests can take advantage of the Jefferson's complimentary shuttle service for more nearby dining options. $250-$500

Linden Row Inn
100 East Franklin Street
(804) 783-7000
www.lindenrowinn.com
Located in historic downtown Richmond within walking distance of the state capitol, the circa-1840 Linden Row Inn reflects European styling while offering Southern hospitality. The inn keeps true to its historic setting with architectural features like high ceilings, fireplaces, and elegant Victorian décor. At the same time, its seventy spacious rooms (and seven suites) feature modern conveniences such as high-speed Internet service, newly remodeled bathrooms, complimentary continental breakfast, and premium TV channels at very reasonable prices. $90-$120

West-Bocock House
1107 Grove Avenue
(804) 358-6174
The circa-1871 West-Bocock House blends the charms of the country with the conveniences of the city. You'll fall asleep on luxurious French linens in an antique four-poster bed and wake up to a plantation-style breakfast in the morning. At the same time, you're just footsteps away from Richmond's dynamic restaurant and nightlife scene. Innkeeper Billie Rees West goes out of her way to show her guests the true meaning of Southern hospitality. Rooms are comfortable and reasonably priced. $85

William Catlin House
2304 East Broad Street
(804) 780-3746
Built in 1845, this B&B lacks the frills of some of the other properties listed in this guide, but it's clean, quiet, and comfortable, located in the Church Hill neighborhood. There are seven guest rooms, including a couple of two-bedroom suites, all furnished with antiques to match the historic setting. The Shockhoe Slip neighborhood is just a few minutes away, lending to great shopping, dining, and nightlife options. $100

The William Miller House
1129 Floyd Avenue
(804) 254-2928
www.ourfanhomes.com
This cozy B&B is a fantastic find, nestled among lovely Victorian homes in the historic Fan District. Named for its first owner, the Greek-Revival-style home was built just after the Civil War. Both guest bedrooms are colorfully furnished—one with a king-size bed and one with a queen-size bed—and outfitted with a full private bathroom. Co-owner (and accomplished chef) Mike Rohde prepares sumptuous breakfast creations like orange-poppyseed waffles with blueberry sauce or scrambled eggs with Boursin cheese. $155-$190

Restaurants

Bank and Vault
1005 Main Street
(804) 648-3070
www.bankandvault.com
What was once a turn-of-the-century Richmond bank is now home to one of the city's hottest dining destinations. The space itself—"Bank" refers to the dining section and "Vault" to the bar—is chic and stylish, with high ceilings and walls decorated with bright fabric paintings. On the menu, you'll find New American cuisine, including some new takes on Southern classics. Fried green tomatoes are served with pepper maple boursin-style cheese and pancetta. Grilled flat-iron steak is

topped with cabrales cheese and paired with piquant patatas bravas. For a satisfying main dish, try the grilled double pork chop, served atop white cheddar grits with greens on the side. The wine list focuses on value, serving interesting varietals from Spain, Italy, Australia, and California. It's open Monday through Friday for lunch and dinner and Saturday for dinner. Average dinner entrée price: $20-$25.

Caliente
2922 Park Avenue
(804) 340-2920
www.calienterichmond.com
If you're a fan of spicy food—be it Mexican, Cajun, or Thai—book a table at this fun, roadhouse-style Richmond eatery. Caliente lives up to its name, specializing in anything and everything that's hot and spicy. Even the décor is red, decorated with peppers and bottled hot sauces for diners in need of an extra kick. Start with a jerk chicken quesadilla or buffalo gator bites, made with fried alligator tail. Move on to main dishes like a chorizo and black bean sub, jambalaya, or coconut-crusted chicken with orange chipotle vinaigrette. Finish it off with a dessert that's cool and refreshing, like the decadent piña colada bread pudding. Whatever you choose, you can count on it being flavorful and reasonably priced, and the outdoors patio seating is an added plus in mild weather. Caliente is open Monday through Friday for lunch and dinner and Saturday for dinner. Average dinner entrée price: $15-$20.

Comfort
200 West Broad Street
(804) 780-0004
www.comfortrestaurant.com
You might not expect a hot new restaurant to have a simple name like Comfort, but you'll be sorry if you pass on this one. Comfort's menu, much like its light, airy décor, is simple and basic. At lunch, you'll find BLTs and fried catfish sandwiches, while dinner entrées include heartier servings of meatloaf, pulled pork, rabbit, and grilled trout. For many diners,

however, the side dishes are the main attractions; macaroni and cheese, baked squash casserole, black-eyed peas, and cheddar cheese grits are delectable and perfect for sharing. It's open for lunch Monday through Friday and dinner Monday through Saturday. Average dinner entrée price: $15-$20.

Extra Billy's BBQ
5205 West Broad Street
(804) 282-3949
www.extrabillys.com
A Richmond tradition for more than twenty years, Extra Billy's is named for William Smith—the sixty-something Virginia politician who led a brigade in Stonewall Jackson's corps before becoming governor in 1864. He would be proud of his namesake restaurant, whose ribs have been rated the area's best. A mouth-watering "Billy Burger," plate of honey-glazed ribs, or sizzling spit-roasted half-chicken will more than satisfy Civil War buffs fresh from the battlefields of Richmond. Extra Billy's is open for lunch and dinner. Average dinner entrée price: $15-$20.

The Hard Shell
1411 East Cary Street
(804) 643-2333
www.thehardshell.com
Perhaps the top seafood restaurant in all of Richmond, The Hard Shell offers a luscious selection of the freshest oysters, clams, lobster, clams, and more. But there are plenty of delicious items on the menu for nonseafood eaters, such as filet mignon, ribs, and even vegetarian dishes. A nice wine list complements the dinner menu, and a wedge of the restaurant's key lime pie tops off any meal. Its location in Shockhoe Slip makes it a good starting point for a night on the town. The Hard Shell is open Monday through Friday for lunch and dinner, Saturday for dinner, and for brunch and dinner on Sunday. Average dinner entrée price: $20-$25.

Richmond National Battlefield Park NATIONAL PARK SERVICE

La Grotta
1218 East Cary Street
(804) 644-2466
www.lagrottaristorante.com
If you're a fan of Italian cuisine, you won't want to miss a meal at the intimate La Grotta, a below-ground restaurant located in Shockhoe Slip. A popular "special occasion" choice for locals, don't be surprised to find diners celebrating prom night, birthdays, anniversaries, or even engagements. Nevertheless, you won't feel out of place if you didn't pack a jacket and tie. The menu is loaded with Italian favorites like gnocchi, veal scallopine, and osso bucco, served with lovely focaccia and hard-crusted Italian bread. For dessert, you can't go wrong with profiteroles or ricotta cheesecake. It's open Monday through Friday for lunch and daily for dinner. Average dinner entrée price: $20-$25.

Legend Brewing Company
321 West Seventh Street
(804) 332-2446
www.legendbrewing.com
Beer lovers should pay a visit to Legend Brewing Company, the oldest and largest microbrewery in central Virginia. The brewery makes nine varieties of beer, including the Legend Brown Ale, the most popular variety, flavored with caramel and malt. While the handcrafted beers are the draw for beer lovers, Legend is also a good choice for a light meal. Beer-friendly appetizers range from basics like soft pretzels and bratwursts to complex pairings like barbecue strawberry duck crepes with mushroom ceviche. Choose from main dishes like ribs, burgers, crab cakes, and bratwurst paired with German potato salad, plus a full selection of classic desserts. The brewery serves lunch and dinner daily. Average dinner entrée price: $10-$15.

Millie's
2603 East Main Street
(804) 643-5512
www.milliesdiner.com

Opened in 1989, Millie's is one of Richmond's best-loved eateries, fashioned after a 1950s-style diner but known for its innovative, upscale cuisine prepared in an open kitchen. The restaurant is housed in the former turn-of-the-century building that used to serve the workers who toiled in Richmond's tobacco fields. Menus change regularly, but you can count on fresh, seasonal fare. Summertime selections might include pan-seared rockfish with zucchini gratin or spicy Thai shrimp with asparagus, shiitake, lime, and red cabbage, while heartier fare reigns supreme in the winter. Millie's is open for lunch and dinner Tuesday through Sunday. Average dinner entrée price: $20-$25.

Sidewalk Café
2101 West Main Street
(804) 358-0645

Ask a Richmond local for a restaurant pick, and they're likely to name this popular eatery in the Fan District. It's packed most nights of the week with diners savoring the Mediterranean, American, and Italian favorites. Share an order of hot fries, hummus and pita, or nachos to start, then choose from main courses like souvlaki, pasta, or scallops baked with feta which are nicely complemented by selections from the simple, affordable wine list. It's open daily for lunch and dinner; come early, or be prepared to wait for a table. Average dinner entrée price: $15-$20.

The Tobacco Company Restaurant and Club
1201 East Cary Street
(804) 782-9555
www.thetobaccocompany.com

For more than three decades, The Tobacco Company has been delighting Richmond diners with casual dining in a pleasant Victorian setting. You can expect extensive brunch, lunch, and dinner menus featuring flavorful regional fare. Sample tasty selections like zesty crab croquettes, velvety she-crab soup, crab-stuffed flounder, and prime rib. The three-story restaurant is also a popular choice for late-night entertainment, with live music every Tuesday through Saturday night in its first level. Dinner reservations are required. The Tobacco Company is open Monday through Saturday for lunch and dinner and Sunday for brunch and dinner. Average dinner entrée price: $20-$25.

Zeus Gallery
201 North Belmont Avenue
(804) 359-3219

The small and cozy Zeus Gallery has drawn crowds of food-loving locals and visitors to its home in the Fan District for more than a dozen years. The menu, spelled out on a chalkboard, is fresh, funky, and ever-changing, peppered with Mediterranean flavors. Look for starters like wild mushroom and Sonoma goat cheese or shrimp and chevre-stuffed wontons and main dishes like spicy dry-rubbed pork medallions with dried cherries and apricots or porcini-dusted pan-seared salmon. There are only twelve tables, however, so you'd be wise to make a reservation. Dine here nightly for dinner, or try the Sunday brunch. Average dinner entrée price: $20-$25.

SIEGE WARFARE

PETERSBURG

This tour focuses on the city of Petersburg, whose collapse after a ten-month siege led to the war's brief, final campaign, in April 1865.

Located 25 miles south of Richmond, Petersburg was a massive conduit through which railroads connected the Confederate capital with Virginia's southern and western neighbors. With Petersburg in his pocket, a well-supplied and supported Union general could isolate and gradually squeeze the life out of Richmond's defenders.

That is precisely what happened. After a month of vicious combat capped by the stunning June 3 reverse at Cold Harbor, Lieutenant General Ulysses S. Grant suddenly drove south and over the James River in mid-June, putting the Army of the Potomac in place to grab sparsely defended Petersburg and isolate Richmond.

Between June 15 and 20, Major General P. G. T. Beauregard's stalwart Rebel defenders—helped after the 17th by Robert E. Lee's shifting army—repelled a series of Union attacks on the extensive Petersburg fortifications. Resigning himself to a siege, Grant continued to probe and dig toward Lee's lines, attacking Lee's communications and transportation while stretching the Confederate trenches west. In July, Jubal Early's raid up the Shenandoah Valley forced a reluctant Grant to detach elements of two corps to Washington, but it made little difference.

Grant's grip on their city tightened, and Petersburg residents struggled to find the bare necessities of life. Weary infantrymen dug in around Petersburg ducked shells and skirmished. Most were still trying to sleep on the morning of July 30 when Yankees lit a fuse beneath their trenches. Minutes later, the sizzling combustible ignited four tons of gunpowder, catapulting tons of earth, sandbags, logs, and lifeless soldiers toward the sky and ripping a gap in the Rebel lines southeast of town.

While Union batteries delivered a follow-up barrage of shells, shocked Confederate officers recovered from their surprise to shift troops into the hole in their lines, which Union regiments were rushing to expand. Botched orders and shoddy leadership turned this opportunity into disaster. Federals charged straight into the huge ditch created by the explosion, and they were quickly pinned in by howling Confederates. Reinforcements of the United States Colored Troops (USCT) fought bravely, as vicious hand-to-hand fighting turned into a near massacre. Federals fell by the score.

Blame for the disastrous "Battle of the Crater" fell on Ninth Corps commander Major General Ambrose Burnside, who had developed a nasty penchant for wasting the lives of his soldiers. Meanwhile, the siege continued. Booming Union artillery drove thousands of people into the hills, where they struggled to avoid shells and find enough food to survive in makeshift bunkers. On the inland side of the city, Confederate soldiers pinned down in miles of trenches fought their own battle to survive—enemy soldiers as well as hunger. Beyond the Rebel trenches were even more extensive Union pits, into which more men in blue seemed to pour each week.

Although Lee managed to keep Grant at bay throughout the fall of 1864, his army withered away during the winter. On March 25, 1865, Lee sent Major General John Gordon after a Union outpost to the east. Gordon briefly overran Fort Stedman, but could not hold it, and lost more than 3,000 men in the process.

By April 3, 1865, Petersburg, Virginia, was a dusty ghost town, pinned against the Appomattox River by hideously scarred landscape and Major General George Gordon Meade's Union Army of the Potomac (now more often identified with General-in-Chief Ulysses S. Grant, who had made it his headquarters). Nearly ten months of dirty, dusty siege had sealed the city's fate.

On April 1, Union infantry and cavalry overwhelmed Confederate defenders west of the city at a crossroads called Five Forks. With his right flank turned, Robert E. Lee could do little when Grant attacked his lines a day later. Finally convinced of success, Grant attacked Lee's thinly manned trenches west of the city late on April 2. Lee evacuated the remnants of his army and headed west, while Federals occupied Petersburg and, a day later, the Confederate capital. The war was all but over.

Historic Sites

Blandford Church
111 Rochelle Lane
Petersburg, VA
(804) 733-2396
www.petersburg-va.org/tourism/
blandford.htm

This historic church was built in 1735, but abandoned in 1806 as the congregation drifted to a new downtown location. It regained prominence in 1901 when the Ladies Memorial Association of Petersburg began to rebuild the church as a Confederate Memorial. The association turned to each former Confederate state and solicited funds to create and install a Tiffany commemorative window to honor the fallen soldiers from that state. The adjacent cemetery was the site of the first Memorial Day celebration, held in June 1866 in honor of the 30,000 Confederate soldiers buried on the hillside. The church is open daily 10:00 a.m. to 5:00 p.m. Admission is $5 for adults, or you can buy a combination ticket for the church, Siege Museum (below), and the Centre Hill Museum, a community history museum, for $11.

Pamplin Historical Park and the National Museum of the Civil War Soldier
6125 Boydton Plank Road
Petersburg, VA
(804) 861-2408
(877) PAMPLIN
www.pamplinpark.org

Pamplin Park is an absolute must-see. Since opening in 1994, this combination museum/battlefield has ranked among the nation's most visited historical sites. Continuous expansion (now 422 acres) coupled with state-of-the-art exhibits and educational programs have since made it the top Civil War attraction in the country.

The park is named for its benefactors—Robert B. Pamplin Sr. and Dr. Robert B. Pamplin Jr.—who in 1991 purchased a parcel of land that bore remnants of the Confederate earthworks overrun by Ulysses S. Grant's Union soldiers on April 2, 1865. A second purchase, of the adjacent Tudor plantation, was made in 1994; restoration of this home (once used as a headquarters by Confederate General Samuel McGowan) was completed two years later. In 1999, Pamplin Park's title grew a little longer with the opening of the National Museum of the Civil War Soldier, a fantastic, 25,000-square-foot facility that beautifully countered the park's natural features with state-of-the-art exhibits and visitor services. Even more recently, the park has opened reconstructed slave quarters on the Tudor Hall Plantation, hiking trails, the Banks House (Grant's headquarters), and a new Education Center.

Strengths of the park include its superb staff and the opportunities for visitors to learn about the Civil War in several different ways, including hands-on outdoor exhibits; living history demonstrations; interpretive, audio-aided museum exhibits; and classes designed for all age groups. Excellent permanent exhibits include "Duty Called Me Here," "A Land Worth Fighting For," "The Battle of the Breakthrough," and "Slavery in America." Visitors with children, meanwhile, will want to

Petersburg National Battlefield NATIONAL PARK SERVICE

consider contacting the park about its new Adventure Camp, a fun but educational introduction to soldier life for folks of all ages.

Pamplin Park really must be seen to be appreciated. It is open daily 9:00 a.m. to 5:00 p.m., and closed on Thanksgiving, Christmas, and New Year's Day. Admission is $15.00 for adults, $13.50 for seniors (62+), and $9.00 for children 6–12.

Petersburg National Battlefield
1539 Hickory Hill Drive
Petersburg, VA
(804) 732-3531, ext. 200
www.nps.gov/pete/
The ugly, daily struggle at Petersburg was unlike the fighting on any other battlefield, insuring that its earthen remnants would found a park like no other. Stretching more than 30 miles from the Union supply depot at

City Point to the Five Forks Battlefield west of the city, this remarkable park includes three visitor centers along its thirteen-stop driving tour. The foremost of these, the Eastern Front Visitor Center, is a minimuseum, using exhibits and interactive displays to tell the military and civilian story of the nine-and-a-half month siege.

Highlights of the park include the City Point headquarters cabin used by Grant during the siege; a massive, 13-inch seacoast mortar (like the terrifying "Dictator" used here by Federals); outstanding examples of fieldworks; the Elliott's salient entrance to the Petersburg mine shaft; the original crater site; and endless earthworks.

Petersburg National Battlefield is open daily 9:00 a.m. to 5:00 p.m. It is closed on Thanksgiving, Christmas, and New Year's Day. Admission is free.

Close-up

A. P. Hill

Born in Culpeper, Virginia, in 1825, Ambrose Powell Hill graduated from West Point in 1847. After stints in Mexico and on various frontier posts, Hill, in March 1861, traded his U.S. Army commission for the colonelcy of a Confederate army regiment, the 13th Virginia. Promoted rapidly up to major general, Hill established himself as one of the South's great fighting generals, with a knack for saving the day. At Antietam in September 1862, the timely arrival of Hill's division on the battlefield south of Sharpsburg prevented a disaster brewing for the Confederates. After taking command of Robert E. Lee's III Corps following the death of Stonewall Jackson, Hill fought at Gettysburg, the Wilderness, and Spotsylvania—proving to be better suited to a smaller command. In the predawn darkness of April 2, 1865, just a week before Lee's surrender at Appomattox, a Union bullet killed Hill outside the trenches west of Petersburg.

LIBRARY OF CONGRESS

The Siege Museum
15 West Bank Street
Petersburg, VA
(804) 733-2404
www.petersburg-va.org/tourism/siege.htm
The Siege Museum takes a closer look at civilian life in the town of Petersburg before, during, and in the aftermath of the Civil War. Much of the collection focuses on how the town suffered and persevered during the ten-month siege, the longest of its kind in American military history. As you tour the museum,

you can also catch an eighteen-minute film outlining the town's involvement in the Civil War, narrated by Joseph Cotton. It's open daily 10:00 a.m. to 5:00 p.m. Admission is $5 for adults, or you can buy a combination ticket for the church, Siege Museum, and Centre Hill Museum, a community history museum, for $11.

Accommodations

High Street Inn
405 High Street
Petersburg, VA
(804) 702-0800
The Queen Anne–inspired High Street Inn was built just before the dawn of the twenty-first century and has enjoyed quite a colorful past. Built as a residence, it was later used as a funeral home and a Veterans of Foreign War outpost before becoming a B&B more than twenty years ago. Check in to one of the six spacious guest rooms, each of which bears the name of a historic street or character in Petersburg history. You'll be treated to hospitable touches like lemonade and cookies delivered to your room and generous breakfast service. $85-$125

Mayfield Inn Bed and Breakfast
3348 West Washington Street
Petersburg, VA
(804) 861-6775
www.mayfieldinn.com
Built in 1750, this quiet and picturesque inn rests on property defended by Confederate troops during the last day of the Petersburg siege. A bed-and-breakfast since 1986, Mayfield is charming and perfectly relaxing. Its rooms feature hardwood floors and oriental carpets, antiques, and private baths. Four acres of fabulous landscape surround the building with lovely gardens, a gazebo, and an in-ground pool. Rates are very fair.

Ragland Mansion Guesthouse
205 South Sycamore Street
Petersburg, VA
(800) 861-8898
www.ragland-mansion.com
Italianate in design, the grand Ragland Mansion stands out in the historic Poplar Lawn district. The antebellum mansion survived the siege and was expanded on by railroad tycoon Alexander Hamilton. Its seven rooms (plus a suite) all feature air-conditioning, private baths, queen- or king-size beds, and TV, at very reasonable prices. $75-$135

Walker House Bed & Breakfast
3280 South Crater Road
Petersburg, VA
(804) 861-5822
www.walker-house.com
This circa-1815 mansion boasts four bedrooms named for the four seasons, each of which is equipped with cable TV, wireless Internet, and private bath. Each room is decorated to reflect its namesake season. Even if the inn is full, however, you'd never know that you were sharing it with four other parties. Help yourself to snacks and beverages, available 'round the clock in a second-floor kitchenette. Wake up to a breakfast of fresh waffles, sausages, and other tasty creations. The house itself is not without its own Civil War connections; it was used for the inquiry after the Battle of the Crater featured in the movie *Cold Mountain*. $98-$120

Restaurants

Alexander's
101 West Bank Street
Petersburg, VA
(804) 733-7134
Located in historic Old Towne Petersburg, this charming and friendly little restaurant offers Italian and Greek cuisine, including gourmet sandwiches and salads and flavorful specialties like souvlaki, roasted leg of lamb, lasagna, and manicotti. Closed on Sunday and Monday, it is open Tuesday 11:00 a.m. to 3:00 p.m. and Wednesday through Saturday 11:00 a.m. to 3:00 p.m. and 5:00 to 9:00 p.m. Average dinner entrée prices: $10-$15.

Andrade's International Restaurant
7 Bollingbrook Street
Petersburg, VA
(804) 733-1515
Recommended by local innkeepers, Andrade's is known for serving Peruvian and Spanish fare like delicious garlic shrimp and seasoned steaks. On a pleasant afternoon, you can also sit outside and enjoy dining al fresco. It's open Monday through Thursday 11:00 a.m. to 10:00 p.m., and Friday and

James Longstreet

Four years of war took their toll on James Longstreet, who was severely wounded in 1864 and widely blamed for the crucial Confederate defeat at Gettysburg in July 1863. For Robert E. Lee's longest-serving corps commander, it only got worse at war's end.

Born in South Carolina in 1820 and raised in Georgia, James Longstreet graduated from the U.S. Military Academy at West Point in 1842. There he lived and studied with a number of future Civil War generals and began a lifelong friendship with Ulysses S. Grant. After service in the Mexican War and several years of frontier duty, Major Longstreet resigned from the army in May 1861. He subsequently accepted a commission as a lieutenant colonel in the Confederate States Army.

Between the June 25, 1862, clash at Oak Grove and the May 3, 1863, Battle of Chancellorsville, Longstreet and Thomas J. Jackson commanded the two corps of Robert E. Lee's seemingly invincible Army of Northern Virginia. Without Jackson, who was mortally wounded at Chancellorsville, Lee was finally beaten at Gettysburg in July 1863. The stinging defeat ended his invasion of the North and spurred charges of insubordination against Longstreet, who had disagreed with Lee on tactics. The following May in Virginia's tangled Wilderness, a Yankee bullet knocked Longstreet from the saddle, leaving Lee without his two best subordinates in his ongoing duel with Longstreet's old friend, and now Union general-in-chief, Ulysses S. Grant.

By the time Longstreet returned to action in October 1864, Grant had Lee's army in a stranglehold that could only end in submission. Near Appomattox Court House, Virginia, on April 9, 1865, Union Major General George Custer approached Longstreet under a flag of truce and demanded—in the name of Major General Philip Sheridan—the Confederate army's surrender. "I am not the commander of this army," an irritated Longstreet replied, "and if I were, I would not surrender it to General Sheridan." Later that day, Lee surrendered the army to Grant.

After the war, Longstreet's acceptance of federal Reconstruction legislation, his willingness to accept Federal employment (including an appointment by President Grant as surveyor of customs for New Orleans, and a later stint as U.S. minister to Turkey), and, especially, his defection to Grant's Republican Party, made him a prime target for ex-Confederates looking to cast blame. Longstreet's slowness, they claimed, had cost Lee time and again—especially at Gettysburg, where the corps commander had waited too long to attack the Union left on July 2.

Longstreet defended his Civil War service in his memoirs; a few friends also came to his defense. In recent years, historians have restored to a large degree the general's tarnished reputation, returning him to his place in Civil War memory as Lee's "old war-horse."

Saturday 11:00 a.m. to 11:00 p.m.. Average dinner entrée price: $15-$20.

Jimmy's Grill
16 Goodrich Drive
Petersburg, VA
(804) 733-3181
This local favorite is tucked away from the main strip, but the rewards are worth it if you seek it out. Feast on lavish breakfasts like omelets and pancakes or lunch and dinner entrées like barbecue pork sandwiches or classics like meatloaf and fried chicken featured in the daily special. Average dinner entrée price: $10-$15.

King's Barbeque
3221 West Washington Street
Petersburg, VA
(804) 732-5861
www.kingsfamousbarbecue.com
A Petersburg institution, opened in 1946, locals and visitors know King's for its leg-endary barbecue, with pork, beef, ribs, and chicken constantly smoking in an open pit in the pine-paneled restaurant dining room. The meat is flavorful when served straight from the pit or seasoned with King's vinegar-flavored sauce. That's not the only thing on the menu, though; there's also southern-fried chicken, ham steak, and fresh seafood. It's open Wednesday through Sunday 11:00 a.m. to 8:30 p.m. Average dinner entrée price: $10-$15.

Nanny's
11900 South Crater Road
Petersburg, VA
(804) 733-6619
Bring your appetite to Nanny's, where you'll find one of the most generous, ample buffet spreads in town. The menu varies every day, but you can count on fried chicken, barbecue beef, pulled pork, fried fish, and other Southern classics. Average dinner entrée price: $10-$15.

THE END

APPOMATTOX

This tour focuses on the brief Appomattox Campaign, which ended with Robert E. Lee's surrender of the Army of Northern Virginia on April 9, 1865.

Though his beloved, dwindling Army of Northern Virginia had been forced from its Petersburg and Richmond trenches on April 2–3, General Robert E. Lee was not quite ready to give up the fight. If his hungry army could obtain provisions and elude Union pursuit long enough to link up with General Joseph E. Johnston's army in North Carolina, the combined Confederate force could, in turn (hopefully), confront Grant's hordes and those of Major General William T. Sherman, whose three-wing army had by now scorched its way through Georgia and on through the Carolinas.

Lee had limited options and Grant had the resources to account for each. Marching west to Amelia Court House, Lee found ammunition rather than the rations he had ordered. Losing a day to foraging, he next found his path blocked by Philip Sheridan's Union cavalry. Lee skirted the trouble and continued west, hoping to find rations and transportation south at Farmville. On April 6, however, elements of Grant's army caught up with Lee's divided rear guard near Sailor's Creek, smashed in its center, and forced the surrender of some 8,000 Confederates—including Union nemesis Lieutenant General Richard Ewell.

Seventy-two hours later it was over. Leading his last 30,000 men west in a bid for the rail head at Lynchburg, Lee found Federal cavalry awaiting him at the village of Appomattox

Court House. Early on April 9, Lee half-heartedly ordered a probe of Grant's encircling lines, and realized that the inevitable had finally occurred. After exchanging notes with his Yankee antagonist, Lee agreed to meet with Grant to discuss surrender terms. A comfortable meeting place was found in the home of Wilmer McLean, whom Lee and an aide encountered early in the afternoon.

Dressed in a typically dusty and informal uniform, Grant entered the McLean home at about 1:30 p.m. and shook Lee's hand. The worn-out Confederate commander looked resplendent in his best dress grays. During the afternoon, the two old West Pointers ironed out an agreement that allowed Lee's officers to retain their side arms, and his soldiers to return home with their horses, requiring only that they agree not to take up arms again. Grant then arranged for the delivery of rations to Lee's disheartened soldiers. "I felt anything other than rejoicing at the downfall of a foe who had fought so long and valiantly," Grant recalled later, "and had suffered so much for a cause."

By late afternoon, it was all over. Although Joseph E. Johnston's small army and other Confederate units were still active, they would not remain so for long. Lee's surrender was the South's death knell. After shaking hands with Union officers, many of whom he knew well from the pre-war army, Lee walked slowly outside and mounted up. Grant emerged behind, and his subordinates joined him in doffing their hats as Lee rode off, returning the salute.

Appomattox Court House National Park NATIONAL PARK SERVICE

Historic Sites

Appomattox Court House National
Historical Park
VA Route 24 (2 miles northeast of the town
of Appomattox)
Appomattox, VA 24522
(434) 352-8987
www.nps.gov/apco
The site of Robert E. Lee's surrender to
Ulysses S. Grant on April 9, 1865, the tiny
town of Appomattox is now a historical village
of twenty-seven buildings spread across
1,700 acres. The gem of the park is, of
course, the Wilmer McLean House, which
stands near the park visitor center. The park
offers tours and audiovisual programs, and
also features a seventy-seat theater in which
two slide shows are presented daily. Admission is $3 during the summer season and $4

during the winter. The park visitor center is
open daily 8:30 a.m. to 5:00 p.m.; it is closed
on Thanksgiving, Christmas, and New Year's
Day.

Sailor's Creek Battlefield Historical
State Park
788 Twin Lakes Road
Green Bay, VA 23942
(434) 392-3435
Lee's army began to lose steam at Sailor's
Creek, and a handful of the sites that witnessed the action and the decline are open to
the public. At Hillsman House, the centerpiece of the state park, Union troops plotted
their attack on the Confederates stationed
across the creek. Drive through the park and
listen to radio interpretations of the events of
April 6, 1865. Admission is free.

Tours

Lee's Retreat Driving Tour
www.varetreat.com
Radio messages and interpretive signs at
more than twenty-five points of interest follow
the movement of Lee and his troops during
the last days of action, April 2–9, 1865. As
you drive through the area and spot Civil War
Trails signs, tune your radio to 1600 or 1620
AM to hear commentary at sites like
Namozine Church, which witnessed some
action on April 3 and later served as a hospital; Amelia Springs, the site of a skirmish on
April 6; and Rice's Depot, which served as
Lee's headquarters in the final days. The Web
site varetreat.com outlines the points of interest along the way.

Accommodations

Babcock House Bed and Breakfast Inn
250 Oakleigh Avenue
Appomattox, VA 24522
(800) 689-6208
www.babcockhouse.com
Located just minutes from the site of Robert E.
Lee's surrender of his army to Ulysses S. Grant,
Babcock House is at the center of all there is to
see in this historic town. Built in 1884, Babcock
House retains its nineteenth-century looks,
while offering all the modern amenities.
Innkeepers Jerry and Sheila Palamar pride
themselves on offering "gracious hospitality
and elegant dining in a friendly and informal
atmosphere." Room rates are quite reasonable, especially considering the location. If
you're staying elsewhere, make the Babcock
House your stop for dinner. $100-$140

Ivy Creek Farm B&B
2812 Link Road
Lynchburg, VA 24503
(434) 384-3802
www.ivycreekfarm.com
While Appomattox is the real attraction for
Civil War buffs who visit the region, the small
town is limited in its lodging and dining
options. Fortunately, Lynchburg is a short

thirty-minute drive away, and it presents additional options for travelers looking for a place
to relax after a day of sightseeing. This popular eight-acre country estate-turned-B&B
located just outside of Lynchburg features
three roomy guest suites furnished with
period décor. Guests are treated to a full
gourmet breakfast featuring decadent treats
like brioche stuffed with eggs and fresh mushrooms, pumpkin–chocolate chip muffins and
caramel-glazed biscuits. There's also an
indoor pool on the property, and rooms are
outfitted with wireless Internet, flat-screen
TVs, and Bose sound systems. $129-$189

Longacre
107 South Street
Appomattox, VA 24522
(434) 352-9251
www.longacreva.com
Just three miles from the court house, this
Tudor-style country retreat rambles across
two acres with gardens, a fish pond, and
spectacular forests. Guests can take advantage of common amenities like an indoor lap
pool, a cozy tea room, a screened-in porch
that's perfect for nature watching, plus ham-
mocks for lazy afternoons. The breakfast
spread is loaded with homemade goodies like
pancakes, quiche, and home-baked breads,
plus cereals and fruits. Rooms range from
$90-$160, or you can check into the Carriage
House, which also boasts a private pool and
full kitchen, for $300.

Rockcliffe Farm Retreat & Lodge
816 Walkers Ford Road
Concord, VA 24538
(434) 933-4371
www.rockcliffefarm.com
This woodsy retreat is perfect for Civil War
buffs who love the great outdoors and for
touring groups. The three-bedroom lodge can
accommodate up to sixteen guests. You'll
have run of the house, including its full
kitchen, library, and sunroom. Despite its rustic setting, you'll find the farm equipped with
modern must-haves like wireless Internet and

satellite TV. For a true outdoors adventure, ask about bicycle, canoe, and kayak rentals. Rates start at $200 for up to four guests.

Spring Grove Farm Bed and Breakfast
3440 Spring Grove Road
Appomattox, VA 24522
(434) 352-7429
(877) 409-1865
www.springgrovefarm.com
For a combination of indoor and outdoor relaxation (and the opportunity to really get away), it would be hard to top Spring Grove Farm Bed and Breakfast—a beautifully restored, eleven-room (or suite), sixteen-fire-place, house on 200 acres of lush Virginia farmland. After wandering around the grounds or enjoying its gardens, guests can relax inside by enjoying a movie in the inn's stylish media room, playing one of its two grand pianos, or spending some quiet time with a book on a porch or walking the prop-erty with one of the property's seven dogs. Rates, which depend on the room booked, are a bit pricey, but no one could argue with the surroundings. $125-$225

Restaurants

Granny Bee's Restaurant
Corner of Main and Lee Streets
Appomattox, VA 24522
(434) 352-2259
www.appomattox.com/html/grannybees.html
If you only eat one meal in Appomattox, there's a good chance it'll be at Granny Bee's. It's the best place in town for "Yummy Home Style Cooking," plain and simple. Breakfast and lunch specials can be had for just $4, and the dinner menu features country staples like baked ham and hamburger steak in addition to excellent steak and prime rib dinners. Its downtown location is convenient, but visitors should keep its hours in mind: Granny Bee's closes at 8:00 p.m. during the week and at 9:00 p.m. on Friday and Saturday. It's open 7:00 a.m. to 4:00 p.m. Sunday. Average dinner entrée price: under $10.

The Huddle House
Route 460 and Court Street
Appomattox, VA 24522
(434) 352-9104
www.huddlehouse.com
Although Insiders' rarely recommends national chains, Georgia-based Huddle House gets our nod in Appomattox due to its "open twenty-four hours" status—a plus for Civil War buffs who arrive in town late after a long day of sightseeing and driving. Tourists can relax in Huddle House's classic diner atmos-phere while plotting the next day's itinerary over a "Big House Platter," steak, or omelet (breakfast is served all day), all at reasonable prices. Average dinner entrée price: $10-$15.

Isabella's Italian Trattoria
3225 Old Forest Road, Unit 2
Lynchburg, VA 24501
(434) 385-1660
www.isabellasitalian.com
If it's Italian fare you're craving, drive to Lynch-burg and plan a stop at Isabella's. It's not your traditional Italian fare, however; you might start with a light and refreshing Italian mojito, made with limoncello, rum, club soda, and fresh basil. You'll find inventive spins on Italian classics; a Caprese salad is prepared with grilled tomatoes, and chicken parmesan comes crusted in parmesan cheese and pep-per, doused in mozzarella cream and served atop a bed of linguini with tomato and basil sauce. Garden-fresh salads come dressed up with Mediterranean accents like port wine–soaked figs or toasted hazelnuts. It's open for lunch Monday through Friday and dinner Monday through Saturday.

Meriwether's Market
4925 Boonsboro Road
Lynchburg, VA 24503
(434) 384-3311
www.meriwethers.com
Another standout among Lynchburg restau-rants is Meriwether's Market, a casual gour-met bistro that serves flavorful American dishes, many of them with Southern accents.

Wilmer McLean

Following the July 21, 1861, Battle of Bull Run, forty-seven-year-old, Manassas, Virginia, native Wilmer McLean moved his family out of town to protect them from the violence sure to come. Prior to the battle, Confederate Brigadier General P. G. T. Beauregard had commandeered McLean's farmhouse as a headquarters; shortly after, a Union shell smashed through his kitchen. McLean sent his family south, and eventually purchased a home for them in the picturesque central Virginia village of Appomattox Court House.

On April 9, 1865, McLean encountered Confederate Colonel Charles Marshall, an aide to Lee, who asked him to recommend a suitable meeting place for the opposing commanding generals. After some discussion, the bewildered McLean offered to open his own home to the generals. By early afternoon, Ulysses S. Grant and Robert E. Lee were sitting at small tables in McLean's front parlor.

In the wake of the historic meeting, McLean found his parlor looted—rooted through for souvenirs by excited Yankee officers (some of which, at least, they paid for). The table at which Lee signed the surrender document eventually wound up in the hands of Mrs. George Armstrong Custer, a gift from Major General Philip Sheridan, who reportedly bought it from its owner. (The Smithsonian Institution now owns it.) It has since been said that the Civil War began in Wilmer McLean's kitchen and ended in his parlor.

McClean House NATIONAL PARK SERVICE

Another plus: The restaurant divides its menu selections into three categories: small plates, medium plates, and large plates, so that you can easily design a meal to share or pace yourself if you're watching your waistline. Nibble on light bites like cornmeal-crusted oysters or grilled shrimp with bourbon barbecue sauce; savor medium-size dishes like crawfish etouffee or shrimp and grits, or indulge in larger items like pecan-crusted rainbow trout or a grilled filet with sautéed shrimp, crab meat, and béarnaise sauce. It's open Monday through Saturday for lunch and dinner; a lighter menu is served between 2:30 and 5:30 p.m.

INDEX